*The Duchess of Angoulême
and the Two Restorations*

Marie Therese Charlotte

THE

DUCHESS OF ANGOULÊME

AND THE

TWO RESTORATIONS

BY

IMBERT DE SAINT-AMAND

TRANSLATED BY
JAMES DAVIS

WITH PORTRAIT

WILDSIDE PRESS

COPYRIGHT, 1892, BY
CHARLES SCRIBNER'S SONS.

MANHATTAN PRESS
474 W. BROADWAY
NEW YORK

CONTENTS

PART FIRST

THE FIRST RESTORATION

CHAPTER		PAGE
I.	CALAIS	1
II.	COMPIÈGNE	8
III.	SAINT-OUEN	22
IV.	THE ENTRY INTO PARIS	31
V.	THE ALLIES	41
VI.	THE COURT	51
VII.	THE CITY	64
VIII.	THE KING	76
IX.	MONSIEUR	93
X.	THE DUKES OF ANGOULÊME AND OF BERRY	99
XI.	MADAME	108
XII.	THE ORLEANS FAMILY	129
XIII.	THE FAMILY OF CONDÉ	141
XIV.	THE FÊTE AT THE HÔTEL DE VILLE	151
XV.	THE DISTRIBUTION OF FLAGS	161
XVI.	SAINT-DENIS	167
XVII.	THE BEGINNING OF 1815	179
XVIII.	THE RETURN OF NAPOLEON	188
XIX.	THE ROYAL ASSEMBLAGE	202

CHAPTER	PAGE
XX. The King's Departure	208
XXI. Bordeaux	224
XXII. London	245
XXIII. Ghent	254

PART SECOND

THE SECOND RESTORATION

I.	Louis XVIII.'s Return	262
II.	The Return of the Duchess	275
III.	General de Labédoyère	281
IV.	Fouché	296
V.	Marshal Ney	310
VI.	The Death of Marshal Ney	325
VII.	Count de Lavalette	338
VIII.	Madame de Lavalette	352
IX.	The Beginning of 1816	372
X.	The Ashes of Louis XVII.	384
	Conclusion	392

THE DUCHESS OF ANGOULÊME AND THE TWO RESTORATIONS

PART FIRST

THE FIRST RESTORATION

I

CALAIS

FROM the return of Louis XVIII. to France until the arrival of the Duchess of Berry, the Duchess of Angoulême is the only woman who can be described as a woman of the Tuileries. It is she who attracts all eyes; she who represents the legend of the Temple; she who may be called the living poetry of the Restoration. As soon as the Duchess of Berry touches French soil, people turn more especially toward the young Neapolitan Princess. But from 1814 to 1816, the most important position at court belonged to the daughter of Louis XVI. We shall try to show her as she really was during these two years, and, in reviving her image, to animate also the scenes in which she lived, and the principal events in which she took a part.

This history begins at Calais on the 24th of April, 1814, at the moment when the Duchess of Angoulême had just landed with Louis XVIII., the Prince of Condé, and the Duke of Bourbon. Between France and royalty a sort of "Lamourette kiss" had been exchanged. Credulous persons fancied that the iron age had gone, never to return; that the golden age had come, and would be eternal. The sky is blue. A superb spring day makes all things radiant. Not a breath of air ruffles the glassy surface of the sea. No one thinks about present disasters, the mourning country, or the strangers who tread its sacred soil. To enthusiastic royalists, the Republic and the Empire are only an evil dream that vanishes at dawn. *Émigrés* and purchasers of national property experience the same exaltation. No one suspects the profound hatred which, at the end of three months, will divide minds that now seem to be in perfect accord. It is a sort of truce of God in the midst of social and political success. It is the eclogue, the idyl which precedes the tragedy.

When, to the sound of bells and salvos of artillery, Louis XVIII. disembarks from the English ship, the *Royal Sovereign*, and is seen leaning on the arm of the orphan of the Temple, as once before on the frozen plains of Lithuania, unanimous cheers break out, and there are tears in every eye. Sixteen of the inhabitants of Calais, elegantly dressed, come forward to draw the royal carriage with their own hands. The clergy appear led by a curé who had long been expatriated for having refused the constitutional oath. "Curé," says the King, "after more than twenty years of absence, Heaven gives my children back to me, Heaven gives me back to my children; come, let us thank God in His temple." The procession advances between a double row of national guards and troops of the line, and goes up the quays. All the vessels have their flags out, all the streets are sanded and strown with foliage, all the houses tapestried with verdure, and adorned with white banners, all the women wear white frocks, wave their handkerchiefs, and scatter flowers. On reaching the church, the King, who walks under a canopy, seats himself in the centre of the choir. The *Te Deum* is intoned. The daughter of Louis XVI. unites her voice in the canticle of thanksgiving; she is astonished that tears of joy can flow from her eyes. But she has seen her country once more!

After leaving the church, Louis XVIII. receives the civil and military authorities. He says to the mayor: "The people of Calais have never, since the time of Philip of Valois, ceased to give proofs of love and fidelity to their sovereigns; I count on their attachment, as they may count on my protection." To the Christian Brothers he says: "Make good Christians, and you will have made good Frenchmen." The Duchess of Angoulême listens to this speech gladly, for it is her whole political programme. The inhabitants of Calais decide that on the very spot where the King descended from his ship, they will place a bronze plaque, on which shall be traced the imprint of his royal foot. Beside it they will raise a monument bearing the date, the 24th of April, 1814, made memorable in the annals of Calais by the arrival of the brother and the daughter of Louis XVI.

The sight of the orphan of the Temple inspires general emotion of compassion. The words of Chateaubriand, published on the 30th of March, in his pamphlet, *Buonaparte et les Bourbons*, were recalled: " This young princess whom we have persecuted, whom we have made an orphan, longs every day, in foreign palaces, for the prisons of France. She might have received the hand of a powerful and glorious prince, but she preferred to unite her destiny with that of her cousin, a poor exile, proscribed because he was French, being unwilling to separate herself from the misfortunes of her family. All the world admires her virtues; people from all parts of Europe follow her whenever she appears in public, and crown her with blessings; we alone can forget her! When she left the country where she had been so unhappy, she turned back to look at it, and wept. The constant object of her love and her prayers, we hardly know that she exists. Ah! may she at least find some consolation in promoting the welfare of her guilty country! This land bears lilies spontaneously; they will grow again more beautiful than ever, since they have been sprinkled with the blood of the Martyr-King."

Such is the theme repeated even to satiety at the

beginning of the reign of Louis XVIII. Accompanied by the Duchess of Angoulême, the Prince of Condé, and the Duke of Bourbon, Louis XVIII. leaves Calais on the 26th of April, and passes that night at Boulogne-sur-Mer. There he finds Marshal Moncey, Duke of Conegliano, that valiant warrior who, less than a month before, on the 30th of March, had defended the barrier of Clichy against the foreigners, and who now comes to meet and congratulate the head of the House of Bourbon. The King effusively embraces the marshal who had heroically defended Paris against the Allies, without whose aid royalty could not have been re-established. This is what is painful in the situation of the Bourbons. The defeat of the foreigner would have been their ruin; his victory has been their salvation. Had not Chateaubriand, sometimes so patriotic, just written: "Like Athens, Paris has seen aliens enter her walls who have respected her, in remembrance of her glory and her great men. Eighty thousand conquering soldiers have slept beside our fellow-citizens without disturbing their slumbers, offering them the least violence, or even singing a triumphant hymn. These are liberators, not conquerors. Immortal honor to the sovereigns who have been able to give the world such an example of moderation in victory! How many injuries they had to revenge! But they have not confounded France with the tyrant who oppressed them. Hence they have already reaped the fruit of their magnanimity. They have been received by the inhabitants of Paris as if they were our real monarchs, like French princes, like the Bourbons. We shall see them soon, the descendants of Henri IV.; Alexander has promised it; he remembers that the marriage contract between the Duke and the Duchess of Angoulême is deposited in the Russian archives. He has faithfully guarded for us the last public act of our legitimate government; he has brought it back to our own archives, where, in our turn, we will preserve the account of his entry into Paris as one of the greatest and most glorious moments of history."

It must be confessed that although such language may be adroit, it is utterly undignified. Chateaubriand himself must have been sadly surprised, when, later on, he read once more these lines which he had written: "And what Frenchman could forget what he owes to the Prince Regent of England; to that noble people which has done so much to deliver us? Elizabeth's flags waved in the armies of Henri IV.; they reappear among the battalions that restore Louis XVIII. to us. We are too sensitive to glory not to admire Lord Wellington, who has reproduced in such a striking manner the virtues and talents of our Turenne. Are we not moved to tears when, at the time of our retreat from Portugal, we see him promising two guineas for every French prisoner brought to him alive? By his moral strength, still more than by military discipline, he has miraculously suspended, on entering our provinces, both the resentment of the Portuguese and the vengeance of the Spaniards; in a word, it was under his standard that the first cry of 'Long live the King!' awakened our unhappy country."

Such apologies are distressing. But at that period men were so weary of the despotism and wars of Napoleon, that many said, like the author of *Buonaparte et les Bourbons:* "Reflect that all the woes we experience, the loss of our property and our armies, the miseries of invasion, the massacre of our children, the trouble and tearing asunder of all France, and the loss of our liberties, are the work of a single man, and that we shall owe the contrary benefits to a single man. Let us hear then, from all sides, the cry which can save us; the cry our fathers raised in defeat as well as in victory, and which, for us, will be the signal of peace and happiness: Long live the King!" This cry was everywhere heard along the route of Louis XVIII., on the 26th of April, at Boulogne-sur-Mer; on the 27th at Abbeville, and on the 28th at Amiens. On entering the cathedral of the chief town of Picardy, the sovereign exclaimed, as he looked with emotion at the immense multitude that cheered him: "What a magnificent day!" During the banquet, several young girls, dressed in white, sang before the Duchess of Angoulême Gluck's fine chorus, which had been sung so often in honor of the Queen, her mother. The next day, the 29th of April, the daughter of Louis XVI. and Marie Antoinette arrived with Louis XVIII. at Compiègne.

II

COMPIÈGNE

AT an interval of only four years, from the 27th of March, 1810, to April 29, 1814, the château of Compiègne presented two widely different spectacles. The decorations were hardly changed. Many of the same actors appeared, but the piece was altered from top to bottom. On the 27th of March, 1810, Napoleon arrived at Compiègne with his young wife, and made arrangements there for the entry of the new Empress into Paris. On the 29th of April, 1814, Louis XVIII. arrived at Compiègne with the Duchess of Angoulême, and made arrangements there for his formal entry into his capital. The same marshals figured both times in the first rank of courtiers; but in 1810 they called themselves Marshals of the Empire, and in 1814, Marshals of France. In 1810, the chief figure among them was Marshal Berthier, Prince of Wagram and Neufchâtel, who, as ambassador extraordinary, had gone to fetch the Empress from Vienna. In 1814, it was the same Marshal Berthier, Prince of Wagram and Neufchâtel, who was to felicitate the Most Christian King in the name of his colleagues. The flatteries, the ceremonial, the incense, were the same; nothing was changed except the idols.

Louis XVIII. might have made but a single stage from Calais to Paris, but he would not. This monarch by divine right thought that a king should never wait, but that it became him to be waited for. Persuaded that his subjects ardently desired his return, he took pleasure in deferring his triumphal entry into Paris, in order to augment the impatience and curiosity of the populace. He travelled by short stages. A slow and majestic progress suited his tranquil nature.

People wondered how Napoleon's marshals would behave towards a sovereign whose manners, physique, and character bore so little resemblance to those of their former master. "I feared the effect of his appearance," M. de Chateaubriand wrote in reference to Louis XVIII. "I hastened to arrive before him at that city in which Joan of Arc fell into the hands of the English, and where a book was shown to me pierced by a bullet aimed at Bonaparte. What would people think of the aspect of the royal invalid who was to replace the bold rider who might have said with Attila: 'Grass never grows again where my horse's hoofs have been'? Without mission or inclination (the lot had fallen to me), I undertook a sufficiently difficult task: that of describing the arrival at Compiègne, and of representing the son of Saint Louis such as I had idealized him by the aid of the Muses."

The marshals, also, were awaiting, and not without a certain anxiety, the moment when they should be confronted with the new sovereign on whom their destinies, titles, places at court, and military commands must henceforward depend. They met at Compiègne and decided that two of their number, Ney and Marmont, should go to meet and congratulate the King and the Duchess of Angoulême. The two marshals met the sovereign and his niece on the hither side of the last station. The royal carriage stopped. The two marshals alighted. Ney, who was to be shot the following year, being the eldest, was spokesman. "The King replied in a gracious and benevolent manner," says Marmont in his Memoirs, "but he closed his remarks with a phrase which, to me, seemed silly. Naturally he talked about his ancestor, Henri IV. It was the time to do so, doubtless, but this is what he said, in pointing to his hat, in which there was a small, white heron feather: 'Behold the plume of Henri IV.! It shall always be in my hat.' I wondered what sense there was in these words, and whether any relic of the sort had been preserved by the royal family."

In other respects, the impression Louis XVIII. produced upon the Duke of Ragusa was favorable: "The sentiments of my childhood and early youth," he adds, "rekindled in full force and powerfully addressed my imagination. A sort of prestige accompanied his illustrious race. From the most remote antiquity the origin of its grandeur has been unknown. From generation to generation, the transmission of its blood marks the epochs of our history, and serves to make them recognized. Its name is linked with all that is great in our country. His descent from a saint, who, six hundred years ago, was a man of superior intelligence and a great king, gave him a special halo. All these considerations acted powerfully on my mind." Comparing his two masters with each other, the marshal goes on to say: "I had lived on an intimate footing with a mighty sovereign; but his elevation was our own work. I entertained toward him the feelings naturally begotten by our former relations and the admiration his great qualities awakened; but that chieftain was a man like myself before he became my superior; while he who now appeared before me seemed a part of time and fate."

Meantime the whole town of Compiègne was impatiently awaiting the King, whose approach was hourly announced by successive couriers. Suddenly the drums beat the general alarm. A carriage drawn by six horses entered the courtyard of the palace, and drew up before the door; it was not yet the King, but the Prince of Condé and his son, the Duke of Bourbon, father of the unfortunate Duke of Enghien, who preceded the monarch. A few minutes afterward, Louis XVIII. and his niece arrived. Read the lyrical account published in the *Journal des Débats* by Chateaubriand: "When the King alighted from his carriage, assisted by the Duchess of Angoulême, France seemed to behold its father once more. Neither the King nor Madame, neither the marshals nor the soldiers, could speak. They could express themselves only by tears. But still those least affected cried: 'Long live the King! Long live our father!' The King wore a blue coat, distinguished only by a star and epaulettes; his legs were enveloped in large, red velvet gaiters bound with a narrow gilt ribbon. He walked with difficulty, but in a dignified and affecting manner; his figure was not at all extraordinary; he had a superb head, and his glance was at once that of a king and a man of genius. When he sat down in his armchair, with his old-fashioned gaiters, and holding a cane across his knees, one could imagine himself beholding Louis XIV. at the age of fifty."

And the great royalist author, working himself up, perhaps a trifle in cold blood, exclaims as if in a burst of enthusiasm: "Such is the force of the legitimate sovereign in France; such the magic pertaining to the name of king. A man arrives all alone from exile, despoiled of all, without attendants, guards, or riches; he has nothing to give, and almost nothing to promise. He alights from his carriage, leaning on the arm of a young woman; he shows himself to captains who have never seen him, and to grenadiers who hardly know his name. Who is this man? It is the King! Everybody is at his feet."

Here the illustrious writer exaggerates. He will recognize it himself, for in his *Mémoires d'Outre-*

Tombe he will say: "What I wrote about the warriors, and with a special end in view, was true with regard to the leaders; but I lied about the soldiers." At Compiègne Louis XVIII. was no longer an outlaw. He had a great deal to give and to promise. Never had any prince more petitioners and courtiers. The great dignitaries of the Empire stood in as much need of him as the chiefs of the army of Condé. He was not despoiled of all. He had honors, riches, rank, and decorations to bestow, and all who saluted him, saluted in him the rising sun.

The Duchess of Angoulême, dressed in a simple white frock, attracted all eyes. Her head was covered with a little English bonnet. Her features seemed a happy blending of those of her father and mother. An expression of gentle sadness witnessed to the sufferings she had endured with so much resignation. Even in her somewhat foreign costume evidences of her long exile might be seen. She constantly repeated: "How happy I am to be in the midst of the good French people!"

As soon as Louis XVIII. had entered his apartments, Marshal Berthier, in his own name and that of the other marshals, addressed him in a discourse, which would not have been out of place in the mouth of an ardent royalist. He interspersed it with the white plume of Henri IV. and besieged Paris, succored by its King: "Sire," said he, "after twenty-five years of uncertainty and storm, the French people have again delivered the care of their welfare to that dynasty which eight centuries of glory have consecrated in the history of the world as the most ancient in existence. As soldiers and as citizens, the marshals of France have seconded this outburst of the national will. Absolute confidence in the future, admiration for greatness in misfortune, all, even to ancient souvenirs, concur to excite in our warriors, who are the upholders of the glory of French arms, the transports Your Majesty has witnessed on your journey."

Louis XVIII. replied to Berthier's harangue: "It pleases me to meet you, gentlemen, and I rely upon the sentiments of affection and fidelity which you express toward me in the name of the French army. I am happy to find myself amongst you." Then he stopped and said over again, emphasizing each word: "Happy, happy and proud." After saying a few kindly words to each of the marshals, Macdonald, Ney, Moncey, Sérurier, Mortier, Brune, Berthier, Lefebvre, Oudinot, and Kellermann, he stood up, although suffering from the gout. His principal officers approached to assist him, but, seizing the arms of the two marshals who were nearest, he exclaimed: "It is on you, marshals, that I always desire to lean; come near and surround me; you have always been true Frenchmen. I hope that France will have no further need of your swords. But if ever — which may God avert — we are forced to draw them, gouty as I am, I will march with you." "Sire," replied a marshal, "let Your Majesty consider us the pillars of the throne! We will be its firmest supports."

Dinner was served at eight o'clock. The King, the Duchess of Angoulême, the Prince of Condé, the Duke of Bourbon, the marshals, the generals, the gentlemen-in-waiting to the King, the ladies of the Duchess of Angoulême, Mademoiselle de Montboisier, the daughter of Madame de Malesherbes, the Duchess of Duras, the Countess of Simiane, and several other distinguished personages, invited by order of the King, sat down at the same board. The crowd of persons standing in the dining-room was so great that the servants could hardly wait on the table. At the beginning of the repast the King said to the marshals: "Gentlemen, I am sending you some vermouth; I wish to drink with you to the health of the French army." According to the *Moniteur*, a sentiment of respect prevented the marshals from proposing the King's health in return, as their enthusiasm prompted.

After dinner, the sovereign returned to the drawing-room. Every one wished to remain standing, but Louis XVIII. obliged the marshals and generals to seat themselves at his right hand. The article in the *Débats*, which we have already quoted, says: "These brave captains appeared singularly moved by this kindness on the part of the sovereign. They remembered that the foreigner" — so they called Napoleon at this time — "without regard to their age, their labors, and their wounds, had forced them to stand for hours in his presence, as if he measured the respect of his servants by the pains he made them endure." The King showed polite attentions to each of the great dignitaries of the army. As he noticed that Marshal Lefebvre walked with difficulty, being tormented with gout like himself, he said: "Well, marshal, are you one of ours?"

Then, turning to Marshal Mortier, he said: "Marshal, when we were not friends, you had an esteem for the Queen, my wife, which she did not conceal from me, and I recall it to-day." . . . Then, addressing Marshal Marmont: "You were wounded in Spain and came near losing an arm."— "Yes, Sire," replied the marshal, "but I have found it again for Your Majesty's service."

All these lieutenants of Napoleon were enchanted. They seemed no longer to think of anything but the King. On all sides one could hear: "He shall see how we will serve him! We are his for life." *Émigrés* and former commanders in the imperial army clasped each other by the hand like brothers. No more factions, said they, no more parties! All for Louis XVIII.!

The marshals showed themselves profoundly moved by the attentions of the King, and even the reception given them by his courtiers, the great personages of the old régime, touched them more than we could easily believe. In his *Histoire de la Restauration*, that impartial and masterly work which has done him so much honor, Baron Louis de Viel-Castel thus estimates the attitude of the Emperor's chief companions-in-arms: "Nowadays, when the names of these warriors, aggrandized by time, shine through the magic memories of the Empire with that brilliancy which in reality belongs only to some among them, it is hard for us to conceive that they should have been so sensitive to the condescension of courtiers whose only claim to distinction was derived from their ancestors; but at that time the lieutenants of Napoleon did not yet appeal to the imagination; they did not consider themselves in so important an aspect. They found difficulty in believing that their fortunes could survive those of the great Emperor who had made them what they were, and they needed to be reassured. In the days of their youth, when they were still private soldiers, and their most ambitious hopes did not aspire to aught beyond the epaulettes of a sub-lieutenant, they remembered having seen these elegant and polished courtiers, who now treated them as equals, already in the uniforms of colonels and general officers. The prestige of the past was not yet so completely effaced that such a change in situations could fail to make a marked impression on them, and these men who had unconcernedly commanded armies, gained battles, and conquered and governed provinces, were surprised and intoxicated by the advances made by these great lords. Their pride was not of a sufficiently lofty nature to preserve them from the trivialities of vanity."

The court was reconstituted at Compiègne. The Count of Artois and his son, the Duke of Berry, who had left Louis XVIII. several weeks before, came there to offer him their homage. On the 13th of April, the King went to Mass in the palace chapel, passing through the hall of the Guards. He was followed by the Duchess of Angoulême, dressed very simply in a white silk robe, her head covered with a wreath of flowers and a lace veil. When the King left the chapel, the market-women presented him with a bouquet and a wreath of lilies and orange flowers. Afterwards, the Duchess of Angoulême, accompanied by the Count of Artois and the Duke of Berry, went out to walk in the park without other attendants. Possibly she would have preferred ignorant bourgeois and poor peasants to great dignitaries of the Empire, whose conversion to the royalist faith seemed to her a trifle sudden, and more especially a trifle selfish.

Among the personages who repaired to Compiègne to pay their court to the King, was Bernadotte, that former marshal of the Empire who had become Prince-Royal of Sweden, and, for an instant, had aspired to the crown of France. As the Count of Artois was conversing with him concerning the difficulties of home politics, he said: "Monseigneur, to govern the French, you need an iron hand in a velvet glove."

The arrival of Prince Talleyrand created some sensation. "People were curious," says Baron de Vitrolles in his Memoirs, "to see how he would present himself and how he would be received. They expected to see him complaisant, adroit, flattering, and caressing; but he chose quite another rôle. He was cold and serious, and made advances to nobody, acting like a man who had nothing to accuse himself of and who stood in no need of support. . . . This rôle of independence was carried so far that instead of going to meet his uncle, Cardinal de Périgord, grand-almoner of France, returning in the suite and favor of the King, M. de Talleyrand waited for the august old man, who, in his haste to absolve him, took the first steps toward this nephew, so insolent in his cleverness."

The pious Duchess of Angoulême could not have found the presence at Compiègne of the former vice-grand-elector of the Empire very agreeable. This unfrocked priest, this ex-bishop of Autun, who at the time of the fête of the Federation, on the 14th of July, 1790, had said a Mass on the Champ-de-Mars which boded ill to royalty; this great revolutionist lord, this apologist of the 18th Fructidor, could but awaken painful thoughts in the daughter of Louis XVI. And under what aspect could he be regarded by the Prince of Condé and the Duke of Bourbon, the grandfather and the father of the unhappy Duke of Enghien; he who was the First Consul's Minister of Foreign Affairs when the young prince was murdered; he who had given a ball three days after the outrage at Vincennes?

M. de Talleyrand was received with extreme politeness by Louis XVIII., but without much cordiality. He was obliged to wait two or three hours before being admitted to the King's presence; and even then was forced to seek the intervention of M. de Blacas. The sovereign reminded him, not without a spice of malice, of the divergence of views which had arisen between them since the Revolution began, and then added, after saying that his own foresight had been justified by events: "If you had proved in the right, you would say to me: 'Let us sit down and have a talk.' As it is I who have triumphed, I say to you: 'Sit down, and let us talk.'"

On the 1st of May, the Emperor Alexander, that autocrat who had made himself the champion of liberalism at Paris, came to Compiègne to recommend the Constitution elaborated by the Senate. "Contrary to all that has been invented by the historians of that epoch," says Baron de Vitrolles, "the interview between the two sovereigns was nothing but graces and compliments. Now, in that line, Louis XVIII. certainly had the advantage. The Emperor of Russia had too high a sense of the proprieties to seem to wish to give lessons to the old King, while the latter's mind was too pliant and his character too easy to permit him to put himself in opposition to the Czar. I don't know whether the Emperor Alexander placed much confidence in this easy way of looking at things, a way which entailed no positive consequences; but for the moment it was all that the most skilful politician could have advised."

Thoroughly satisfied with his stay in Compiègne, Louis XVIII. left there on the 2d of May, and halted for one day at Saint-Ouen, his last resting-place before entering Paris.

III

SAINT-OUEN

LOUIS XVIII., accompanied by the Duchess of Angoulême, arrived on the morning of May 2d, at Saint-Ouen, a village on the Seine, between Saint-Denis and Paris. He lodged there in the little château which he was to present, some years later, to his favorite, the Countess of Cayla. The nearer he approached his capital, the more did the multitude of his courtiers increase. He alone made no haste while all the world was in commotion around him. He wanted to appear as tranquil as Napoleon had been unquiet. It was not until half-past seven in the evening that he admitted the ministers to his presence in a dimly lighted hall. "It seemed," says Count Beugnot, "as if they wanted to accustom us very gradually to the spectacle of a king lying in his armchair, — us, who were coming away from him who passed over Europe with the stride of a giant. But already, even from his armchair, the King made himself felt by each of us; a calm dignity, a caressing glance, a flattering voice, questions put most apropos, revealed to us a sort of power whose importance we had never yet felt."

Baron de Vitrolles has thus described this audience: "We found the King sitting in the middle of the salon; his attitude and person conveyed the impression of his supreme rank; his head still preserved a youthful appearance, and his fat cheeks diminished somewhat the prominence of his aquiline nose; his large forehead sloped back a little too much; he had a quick and penetrating glance which seemed to light up his face; his hair was dressed in the fashion of his youth — cut short and combed up over his forehead into a sort of brush, and powdered and tied behind in a cue with a ribbon. He wore a perfectly simple blue coat, with gold buttons engraved with lilies, and no distinctions save epaulettes embroidered with a crown; he wore the blue ribbon on his waistcoat, and at his buttonhole the cross of Saint Lazarus, which was called the Order of Monsieur, because he himself had revived the institution when he bore the title of Monsieur. . . . One would have had to see the King in order to get any idea of the dignity which he was able to impart to such an ungainly body and so awkward a gait. Madame (the Duchess of Angoulême) stood up, hardly distinguishable, if one may say so, from the persons in waiting on the King."

The Senate, which had essayed at first to take a high tone with the sovereign and dictate conditions to him, had become pliant very promptly. On the evening of the 2d of May, they came to Saint-Ouen, headed by M. de Talleyrand, who mentioned the charter in his address. Deputations from the constituent bodies came next, and spoke neither of the Constitution nor of liberty. It was a real storm of adulations, a rivalry of dithyrambs. The first president of the Court of Cassation celebrated "the sublime and rapid movement" which, by re-establishing the King on his throne, had "effaced twenty-five years of error and ruin, and terminated the evils of a too disastrous revolution."

Meanwhile, only a few hours remained in which to elaborate the Royal Declaration which must be published before Louis XVIII. entered Paris, and which was awaited by the public, not merely as the programme of the new reign, but as a guarantee of liberty. The King contented himself with sketching the chief outlines of this Declaration, which was destined to become celebrated under the name of the Declaration of Saint-Ouen, but he did not take the trouble to write it out. He left that care to three of his advisers, MM. de Blacas, de Vitrolles, and de La Maisonfort, and went quietly to sleep until they should have accomplished it. When the three editors had succeeded in coming to an agreement, M. de Blacas, in spite of the entreaties of M. de Vitrolles, refused to waken the King, knowing so well the value he set on his repose. In the same way, later on, they hesitated to arouse him on the fatal night when his nephew, the Duke of Berry, was assassinated. The liberal Declaration of Saint-Ouen, that prelude to the charter, was taken to Paris at two in the morning, without even being submitted to Louis XVIII.; it appeared in the *Moniteur* at seven o'clock, and was shortly afterwards placarded on the walls of the capital, and produced a good impression.

The preparations for the formal entry had been very skilfully arranged. Everything had been so managed that the ceremony should present that dramatic aspect which is so agreeable to Parisians. The season was favorable, and the weather superb. Royalty was about to renew itself together with the spring. Count Beugnot, who at the time of the entry of the Count of Artois, had invented the famous phrase attributed to the Prince: "There is simply one more Frenchman," had just found an excellent inscription for the base of the plaster statue of Henri IV., placed provisionally on the Pont Neuf while awaiting the bronze which was to succeed it. He had chosen these four Latin words: "*Ludovico reduce, Henricus redivivus*, Louis having returned, Henry comes to life again." In his Memoirs he says: "I had conceived and executed tolerably well the scheme of replacing the statue of Henri IV., a plaster one at least, on the platform of the Pont Neuf. There was nothing left in Paris from which a horse could be cast, and I was obliged to send in haste for the horses of that wretched chariot which we had carried off from Berlin in 1806, and which returned there in 1815, in both cases by the right, not to be gainsaid, of the strongest. At last the horse and the statue reappeared as if by enchantment."

M. Beugnot next considered the inscription: "I puzzled my brains all the morning," he adds; "I made twenty different versions on the paper; but no sooner had I re-read what I had written than I cancelled it as too long, or too short, or as unintelligible or stupid. Finally, by dint of essaying French versions, I was delivered of the Latin word *resurrexit*. It was good, but it was trite. I remembered that it had been placed on the pedestal of Henri IV.'s statue when a prince, a hundred times worthier than he, Louis XVI., had come to the throne, and that it remained there until a joker took a notion to write underneath it: —

> "*D'Henri ressuscité j'approuve le bon mot,*
> *Mais, pour me le prouver, il faut la poule au pot.*[1]

"I could think no more about my *resurrexit* and, moreover, the same quiz, had he still been alive, would have returned to demand his chicken, and the Cossacks had arranged all that."

In his perplexity, Count Beugnot bethought himself of consulting the class of inscriptions and belles-lettres at the Institute. They sent him four, which were not devoid of merit, but which failed to satisfy him completely. "At last," he adds, "I gave a final glance at the sheet, covered with my attempts

---

[1] I approve the witticism about Henry's resuscitation, but, to make me believe it, a chicken in my dinner-pot would be necessary.

and erasures, and made out this version: 'The return of one causes the other to revive.'[1] It lacked dignity in its wording, and the construction was too commonplace; and yet, as the idea I wanted was there, I attempted to Latinize it in these words: *Ludovico reduce, Henricus redivivus.* I was struck at once with the felicity of my version, and awarded myself the prize without further ceremony."

Every detail of the formal entry was arranged beforehand. Baron de Vitrolles remarks that the white apple-wood cane of the grand-master of ceremonies presided over everything; for the Marquis of Dreux-Brézé had resumed his functions by the same right that the King had to his throne. Feeling all his official importance, he came to interview the baron concerning the ancient and solemn custom observed at the entry of kings, of having heralds-at-arms scatter small gold and silver coins, stamped with the sovereign's effigy, among the people. "I made haste," adds M. de Vitrolles, " to have forty or fifty thousand of these pieces struck off at the mint, some of them in gold, but the majority in silver, and they were scattered in front of His Majesty's carriage. The people showed alacrity in picking them up, but not the sort of eagerness that leads to disorder. When I went to Saint-Ouen to take my place in the procession, I took with me some handfuls of these gold pieces and gave them to the King

---

[1] "*Le retour de l'un fait revivre l'autre.*"

and the Princes. The Duchess of Angoulême approached and took out of my hand some of these medals which I could have desired to present in a more respectful manner; and she was so gracious as to seize this occasion to say some words expressive of that favor and kindness of which I have experienced such affecting evidence."

It was not the men of Coblentz who displayed the greatest eagerness to decorate their houses with white flags. The persons who showed most zeal were those who had been accustomed to live at the expense of the budget. They all wished a share of the booty, under the Bourbons, as they had done under the Empire. Let us hear M. de Chateaubriand: "A filthy rope," says he, "was put around the neck of the statue on the column in the Place Vendôme; there were very few royalists to hoot at glory and to haul at the rope; it was the authorities, all Bonapartists, who cast down the image of their master with the aid of a gallows-bitt. The mighty image had to bow its head; it fell at the feet of those sovereigns of Europe who so often had prostrated themselves before it." And the author of *Mémoires d'Outre-Tombe* exclaims: "Imperialists and liberals, it is by your hands that power fell; it is you who bent the knee to the progeny of Henri IV. It was wholly natural that royalists should rejoice at recovering their princes and ending the reign of him whom they deemed a usurper; but you, who owe your all to that usurper, you would outdo the sentiments of the royalists. . . . Who was it that drew up those proclamations, those accusatory and outrageous addresses with which France was flooded? Was it the royalists? No; it was the ministers, the generals, the authorities chosen and maintained by Bonaparte. Where was the Restoration plotted? At the houses of royalists? No; at the house of M. de Talleyrand. With whom? With M. de Pradt, almoner of the *Dieu Mars* and mitred mountebank. . . . Where were fêtes given to the *infâmes princes étrangers?* At the châteaux of royalists? No; at Malmaison, at the home of the Empress Josephine."

Is it not strange to find the author of the brochure, *Buonaparte et les Bourbons*, writing these ironical phrases: "Madame de Talleyrand, whom Bonaparte had pasted on her husband like a placard, rushed through the streets in an open carriage, singing hymns about the pious family of the Bourbons. Some sheets that fluttered from the windows of the domestics of the imperial court caused the innocent Cossacks to think that there were as many lilies in the hearts of the Bonapartists as there were white rags at their casements. It is wonderful how contagion spreads in France, and so when people heard their neighbors bawl, 'Off goes my head,' they bawled it likewise. The imperialists even entered the houses of us Bourbonists, and forced us to hang out, in the fashion of spotless flags, whatever white articles were locked up in our linen rooms. This happened at my house, but Madame de Chateaubriand would not hear of such a thing, and valiantly defended her muslin."

And now let us recount the triumphal entry of Louis XVIII. into his capital.

IV

THE ENTRY INTO PARIS

SINCE the morning of the 3d of May the whole population of Paris has been astir. Everywhere the drum is summoning the National Guard to arms. Around white standards ornamented with blue tassels of the fleur-de-lis gather the legions which shall soon form in lines between which the King will pass. Red has been excluded, as it is the color of blood. In his writing entitled *De l'Esprit de Conquête et d'Usurpation*, Benjamin Constant thus cursed the tricolor: "Do not," he said, "indecently forsake the oriflamme of your fathers for a banner bloody with crimes and stripped of every success." The plain of Saint-Ouen, the hills of Montmartre, the avenues of Paris, the banks of the Seine, are covered with an innumerable multitude. No clouds are in the sky. The sun is resplendent. Windows and roofs are lined with spectators. White flags are on all the houses.

The royal procession has just left Saint-Ouen. Salvos of artillery resound on the air. A detachment of mounted national guards and another of cavalry of the line head the procession. Behind them come in the same carriage Cardinal Talleyrand-Périgord, Grand Almoner of France; the Duke of Duras, First Gentleman of the King's Bedchamber; the Count of Blacas, Grand Master of the Wardrobe, and the Marquis of Dreux-Brézé, Grand Master of Ceremonies. Marshal Berthier, Prince of Wagram and Neufchâtel, rides on horseback before the King's carriage, accompanied by a number of general officers. The royal coach, drawn by eight horses taken from the Emperor's stables and led by grooms who wear his green livery, advances with majestic slowness. The future Charles X., Monsieur, the Count of Artois, and his son, the Duke of Berry, with the Marshals of France and the Dukes of Gramont and of Havre, both captains of the guard, are on horseback, one on the right side of the coach, and the other on the left. On the back seat of the coach may be seen Louis XVIII. with the Duchess of Angoulême. On the front seat are the Prince of Condé and his son, the Duke of Bourbon, father of the unfortunate Duke of Enghien. Behind the royal coach is Marshal Moncey, Duke of Conegliano, with a party of general officers of the army and a detachment of the old Imperial Guard.

Such is the procession which reaches the Barrier Saint-Denis. M. de Chabrol, Prefect of the Seine, surrounded by some dozen mayors, presents to the King the keys of the city on a golden plate. "Sire," he says, "the municipal body of your good city of Paris lays at the feet of Your Majesty the keys of the capital of the kingdom of Saint Louis. . . . The image of Henri IV., of the sight of which we have so long been deprived, appears once more on this solemn day. It recalls to us days of affliction, to which shall soon succeed days of public rejoicing. This day his reign begins once more. All France, France blessed by his trust and his love, turns, too, its glance upon those beloved princes, upon an august princess whose name awakens so many feelings and emotions, and it exclaims with transports of joy and tenderness: 'Long live the King! Long live the Bourbons!'" — "At length," replies the monarch, "I am in my good city of Paris! I am greatly moved by the evidence of love she gives me at this moment. Nothing could be more grateful to my heart than to see erected the statue of him who, among all my ancestors, is most dear to me. I touch the keys, and I restore them to you; they can be in no better hands, nor can they be confided to magistrates more worthy to bear them."

The procession continues on its way. A magnificent coronal falls into the royal coach as it passes under the triumphal arch at the Porte Saint-Denis. The shouting is very enthusiastic. The cry of "Long live the Guard!" mingles from time to time with the shout of "Long live the King!" which is heard continually. When the Market of the Innocents is reached, two orchestras are found there which play the tune, "Vive Henri IV." The King stops his carriage, that he may receive the congratulations of the market-women. At the same instant a most lovely little child presents a basket of flowers to the Duchess of Angoulême, and releases two young turtle-doves which fly about the Princess. It is half-past two o'clock when the procession draws up before the church of Notre-Dame. Louis XVIII. is received by the metropolitan chapter under an awning spread before the great gate. The Abbé de La Myre speaks. "Sire," says he, "one of the illustrious ancestors of Your Majesty here poured out at the foot of the altar of our august Patron Saint his prayers and his vows with pious trust, and to him was granted the birth of a son, Louis XIV. For many long years we, too, in silence and in sorrow, have laid on the same altar our prayers and our tears, and to-day Heaven gives us back our King, our father, Louis XVIII. The God of Saint Louis has raised your throne; you will strengthen His altars. 'God and the King' is our device; it has always been the motto of the clergy of France, whose mouth-piece the Church of Paris now felicitates itself on being."

The sovereign responds: "Upon entering my good city of Paris my first concern is to come to thank God and His Holy Mother, the all-powerful Protectress of France, for the marvels that have ended my misfortunes. I, the son of Saint Louis, will imitate his virtues."

Then the monarch is borne into the sanctuary on a throne carried by four canons. At his right hand is Monsieur, at the left the Duchess of Angoulême. The Duke of Berry, the Prince of Condé, and the

Duke of Bourbon follow the throne. Monseigneur de Talleyrand-Périgord, Archbishop of Rheims, and Grand Almoner of France, hands the prayer-book to the King. *Domine salvum fac regem nostrum Ludovicum* is sung. Then the *Te Deum* is intoned.

At this solemn moment there is but one thing that disturbs the joy of the royalists; it is the presence of regicides in the cathedral. Listen to the indignation of the Baron of Vitrolles: " Places," he says, " had been reserved at the right and left of the nave for all the constituted bodies, the municipal council, members of the courts of justice and the treasury courts, the Corps Législatif and the Senate, — that Senate which still counted among its members several regicides of the Convention. I was disturbed by the idea that perhaps some of these great criminals, taking advantage of their high positions, would slip in among those who were engaged more immediately in the ceremonies, and I had spoken to M. Pasquier, the Prefect of Police, about the matter, begging him to use all the means in our power to prevent the scandalous anomaly of murderers coming, as it were, to welcome the brothers and the daughter of their victim. But it became evident that his intervention was useless; these persons set at naught the instructions of the official, and insolently came to affront God, the King, the daughter of Louis XVI., and, so to say, all France, which recoiled from them with horror.

" The King was in the choir, Monsieur the King's

brother and Monseigneur the Duke of Berry, at his right hand, and Madame at his left, all kneeling at prie-dieus, on cushions that had been arranged for them. The members of the Council and the ministers stood along the stalls on both sides of the choir. I found myself one of those who were nearest to Madame; she absorbed all my thoughts, and I pondered deeply on all that must be passing through her mind. I saw that she was disturbed, pale, trembling, and weak to the point of swooning. Once I even took a step forward to support her; my imagination represented to me all that the daughter of Louis XVI. must be experiencing as vividly as hers could have felt it."

The orphan of the Temple was not the only one who suffered at that moment. The King and his retinue had but now left Notre-Dame to return to the Tuileries. A regiment of the Old Guard stood in line from the church to the Pont Neuf. Hear what M. de Chateaubriand, an eye-witness of the scene, has to say of it: "I do not believe," says he, "that human beings ever before formed so menacing and terrible a spectacle. Those grenadiers covered with wounds, the conquerors of Europe, past whose heads so many thousands of bullets had whistled, who had known fire and powder, — those same men, bereft of their captain, were obliged to salute an old king, invalided by time, not by war, and were watched by an army of Russians, Austrians, and Prussians in the capital of which Napoleon had been robbed. Some, by knitting their brows, brought their huge hairy hats down over their eyes so that they might not look; others curled their lips in angry scorn, and others tigerishly showed their teeth under their mustaches. When they presented arms it was with a furious movement, and the rattle of the weapons made one tremble. Never, surely, had men been put to such a trial or suffered such torture."

And to the orphan of the Temple what anguish even at the moment of her triumph! While the grenadiers of the old Imperial Guard were trembling with rage, she was pale with grief. During the progress from Notre-Dame, she had to pass the Palace of Justice from which her mother had been led to the scaffold, in a vile cart, and amid the curses of the furies of the guillotine. There loomed up the gloomy turrets of the Conciergerie, the last prison of the Queen-Martyr. The Duchess of Angoulême was suddenly agitated. Tears rose to her eyes. The procession has now stopped on the Pont Neuf before the statue of Henri IV. Madame Blanchard, the aeronaut, makes an ascent in a balloon, holding a white flag in each hand. The singers of the Conservatory strike up the national air, "Vive Henri IV.," and soldiers and people repeat it in chorus. Two small temples have been erected on either side of the statue, one dedicated to the Harmony of the French, and the other to the Peace of Nations. Great is the enthusiasm of the people. But nothing attracts the attention of the Princess, oppressed as she is with gloomy thoughts and mournful memories. The nearer she draws to the Tuileries, the more agitated she becomes, for she is returning to that majestic and fatal palace which she left on August 10, 1792, and which, since then, she has never seen. It is not the present acclaims that she hears, but the far-off echoes of mourning and massacre. She seems to see the red caps of pikemen and the corpses of the murdered Swiss. The Tuileries is to her not the abode of pride and joy, but a place accursed. She treads the threshold with feelings of repugnance and horror alone. On this splendid day when the sun sinks in refulgence below the horizon, and its brightness, like the flame of an apotheosis, illuminates the triumphal return of the brother of Louis XVI., she, the child of martyrs, is sad at heart. Nevertheless she alights from the carriage. But, despite all the firmness of her nature, she is unable to endure such emotion, and swoons when two hundred women, robed in white, and decked with lilies, kneel before her and say: "Daughter of Louis XVI., grant us your blessing!" Borne half-dead to her apartments, she recovers only to weep and pray.

Louis XVIII. remains calm. He, who had seen neither the 20th of June nor the 10th of August, is assailed by no such emotions. He is escorted to the room on the first floor, between the Throne Salon and the Gallery of Diana, which but a few days before was known as the Emperor's Salon.

The royalists congratulated themselves on the

outcome of the day. "Never," says the Baron of Vitrolles, "had Paris been so greatly moved. I had seen Bonaparte's entrance into the Tuileries: it was cold, silent, and solitary. Upon his return from his greatest victories I had seen him received with utter indifference, and at most but slightly applauded when he attended the theatre. When he rode on horseback along the boulevards, only a few children could be seen trotting along beside him and crying, 'Long live the Emperor!' There were not enough of them to make one think that they were not all doing their best under the pay of the police. We rejoiced without stint in this triumph of the ancient race of our kings."

But there were shadows in the picture drawn in such brilliant colors by M. de Vitrolles. "Already," says Count Beugnot, "we could see what a sorry leave of all our victories we had been forced to take. The comrades of Napoleon deeply lamented him, and derided a king lolling in his easy-chair." The appearance of the King was, indeed, exceedingly singular to a nation of soldiers which for fifteen years had had a man of devouring activity for its chief. One would hardly believe to what an extent this comparison injured Louis XVIII. Bourrienne, another witness of the royal entry, says: "On the day of the entry of the King, there was no such enthusiasm as on that when Monsieur, the King's brother, came to Paris. When I walked about, I noticed a curious kind of wonder everywhere."

The enthusiasm was indeed far from universal. Under a foreign invasion there could be no real festivities. A dismembered nation, which but now has lost the fruit of so many glorious efforts, has no right to rejoice. The good sense of the public had observed, and not without severe reflections upon them, the over-sudden recantations of Napoleon's marshals. "I was in the crowd, watching the procession," says Savary, Duke of Rovigo, in his Memoirs. "If the men who had shared the misfortunes of his exile had been seen on horseback beside the King's carriage, it would have seemed perfectly natural; but it impressed one as a somewhat indecent thing that men should figure in the suite of Louis XVIII. who had been most prominent in the Emperor's triumphal processions. The common people, who have more sense of propriety than would be supposed, treated Berthier without ceremony. I frequently heard the crowd cry out at him: 'To the island of Elba! To the island of Elba!'"

By a singular coincidence, on that very 3d of May, 1814, at nightfall, when all Paris was ablaze to celebrate the King's return, the English frigate *Undaunted*, bearing the Emperor, who had now been transformed into the sovereign of the island of Elba, approached Porto-Ferrajo and hove to, a quarter of a league from the town. France for Louis XVIII.; for Napoleon, the island of Elba! The King entered his capital on the 3d of May, and Napoleon was to enter his on the day following.

V

THE ALLIES

LOUIS XVIII. had had the tact to ask, and the good fortune to have his request granted, that no foreign troops should be present at the celebration of his return to his capital. The patriotism of the Parisians had enabled them for a moment to forget the affliction of the nation. On the next day, which was the 4th of May, their conquerors held a grand review. Following is the comment made by the *Moniteur* of May 5th, in its report: "Yesterday there was a grand parade of all the allied troops. They formed in line on the right bank of the Seine. At three o'clock they defiled, infantry, cavalry, and artillery, under the King's windows; they were commanded by S. A. I., the Grand Duke Constantine. Their Majesties, the Emperor of Russia, the Emperor of Austria, and the King of Prussia, and their Royal Highnesses, Monsieur and Monseigneur the Duke of Berry, were close to the King. The Duchess of Angoulême was beside them. The public, which flocked under the windows of the Pavilion of Flora, constantly cried: "Long live the King! Long live the Allied Sovereigns!" Louis XVIII.

thought that he had saved the national dignity by taking precedence of the foreign monarchs. "His Bourbon pride was so exaggerated and absurd," said Marshal Marmont, " that he, who was so much indebted to the sovereigns of Europe, contrived on two occasions to take precedence of them, and at his own house. He gave a dinner to the Emperor Alexander and the King of Prussia, and sat down first at the table. On another occasion, having gone to a balcony to see the troops pass, he ordered an easy-chair for himself and simple chairs for them. The sovereigns remained standing, and it was commonly thought that the King sat in the easy-chair because of his infirmities."

The pride that amused Marmont excited a certain degree of admiration in Chateaubriand, who says: "When Louis XVIII. accorded to the triumphant monarchs the honor of dining with him, he unceremoniously preceded princes whose soldiers were encamped in the court of the Louvre; he treated them like vassals who had done only their duty in bringing armed men to their lord suzerain. All royal families are but of yesterday when compared with the family of Hugh Capet, and nearly all of them are the offspring of that family. The more impolitic was that same superb haughtiness of the descendant of Saint Louis (it was disastrous to his successors), the more it pleased the national pride. The French were delighted to see sovereigns who, when vanquished, had borne the chains of one man, bear, when conquerors, the yoke of one race."

The allied monarchs were modest in their triumph. In Paris they lived the life of ordinary people, with no pretence of superior power or any show of royalty. "They declined," as we are told by the Baron of Vitrolles, "to occupy any of the royal mansions, — the Tuileries, the Luxembourg, or even the Palais Royal, — a simplicity of good taste which is in strong contrast with the lordly vanity of Bonaparte, who, at Vienna, Berlin, and Moscow, strutted in the dwellings of kings as if to signalize his victories. Ordinarily they went through the streets without wearing any distinguishing costume; and sometimes on foot without any escort, as if they wished to keep all tokens of defeat from the eyes of the Parisians; and for this they received their reward. The good wishes of the public surrounded them everywhere — in the streets, when they were recognized, with shouts and vivas; at spectacles, with rounds of applause and, when their presence was foreseen, with couplets in their honor, the frequent exaggerations of which surprised even ourselves." The foreign sovereigns became popular. They amused themselves by mingling in the crowds and going incognito to the shows at small theatres. The King of Prussia found pleasure in going alone to the "Montagnes Russes," and rolling up and down their steep inclines in a double-seated car, side by side with a woman he did not know. "Who were they who spent their time with the autocrat Alexander?" says Chateaubriand. "Scholars of the Institute, savants, men of letters, philosophers, philanthropists, and the like. They were delighted and went away loaded down with eulogies and snuff-boxes."

It must be said that the French officers did not share this infatuation for the foreigners. They kept away from the theatres as long as the allied troops occupied the capital. They walked about dejectedly, like civilians, without uniforms or decorations. There were royalists, too, who shared in their dejection. Madame de Staël says that when she landed at Calais after ten years of exile, she counted on the great pleasure she was to have in seeing once more the beautiful land of France which she had so much regretted. Her sensations were utterly different from what she had expected. The first men she saw on the shore were dressed in Prussian uniforms; they were masters of the city, and had gained the right to it through conquest. As she neared Paris, Russians, Cossacks, and Bashkirs met her sight on every hand: they encamped around the church of Saint-Denis in which reposed the ashes of the French kings. When she entered the capital in which she had passed her happiest and most brilliant days, she felt as in a painful dream. "Was I in Germany or in Russia?" she says. "Had they imitated the streets and public squares of France in order to recall it to memory when it existed no longer? My whole being was troubled; for, notwithstanding my intense suffering, I esteemed the strangers for removing the yoke from our necks. I admired them beyond measure at that time, but it was an insupportable grief to me to see Paris occupied by them, and the Tuileries and Louvre guarded by soldiers brought from the confines of Asia, and to whom our language, our history, and our great men were less known than the last Tartar Khan."

Listen once more to Madame de Staël as she gives an account of a representation at the Opera during the foreign occupation: "Some days after my arrival," she tells us, "I wished to go to the Opera; many a time during my exile had I recalled that daily fête in Paris as being more pleasing and brilliant than all the wonderful pomps of other lands. The play was the ballet of 'Psyche,' which had been rendered continuously for twenty years, under circumstances of great difficulty. The stairs of the Opera were lined with Russian guards. On entering the house I looked about to find some face known to me, and I saw only foreign uniforms. There were some few old citizens of Paris in the parterre, who had come so as not to break up their old habits; for the rest, all the spectators had changed; the spectacle alone remained the same; the decorations, the music, the dancing, had lost none of their charm, and I was humiliated to see French grace thrown away on these sabres and mustaches as if it had been the duty of the vanquished to amuse their conquerors."

The Emperor Alexander was somewhat distant to

Louis XVIII. without becoming embroiled with him. The Czar could not forget that he had only to say the word, and the Restoration would be overthrown, and the King of Rome proclaimed. He considered Louis XVIII. an ingrate, ill advised, and infatuated as to the superiority of his royal line. He was hurt at not having received the cordon of the Holy Ghost, which was given to the Prince Regent of England, and at not having obtained a seat in the Chamber for his protégé, the Duke of Vicenza. So he very seldom appeared at the Tuileries. He preferred the society of Prince Eugène de Beauharnais to that of Louis XVIII., and became the intimate friend and courtier of the Empress Josephine and Queen Hortense, for whom, by dint of persistent application, he had obtained the title of Duchess of Saint-Leu. These two Princesses pleased him far more than the austere Duchess of Angoulême. Not long ago the Emperor William said that he perfectly well remembered one evening that he spent, in 1814, with the Empress Josephine at Malmaison, in company with his father, Frederick William III., and his brother, Frederick William IV., the Emperor Alexander, and the Russian Grand Dukes Constantine and Nicholas. Queen Hortense sang a romanza of her own composition, and it seems that as she sang she smiled with special favor on the handsome Grand Duke Nicholas, the future Czar.

On the 16th of May, Prince Schwarzenberg, the Austrian field marshal, gave a fête at his headquarters, the château of Saint-Cloud, at which the Emperor Alexander, the Grand Dukes of Russia, the Prussian King and Princes, the Duke of Berry, and a large number of general and superior officers, both foreign and French, were present. The *Moniteur* reported this fête, which the Duchess of Angoulême had the good taste not to attend. The palace of Saint-Cloud was illuminated most splendidly. Members of the Comédie-Française played " The Legacy " and the " Suite d'un Bal Masqué" on a stage specially put up at the lower end of the great gallery painted by Mignard. After the play there was a ball in the Salon de Mars. The Czar took part in the dancing. The assembly then adjourned to a large hall in which a magnificent dinner was served. This hall, which communicated with the Orangery, was filled with shrubs and flowers, the sight of which, according to the *Moniteur*, reminded the Emperor of Russia of the beautiful conservatories of Saint Petersburg.

On the 29th of May, the Day of Pentecost, the attendance at the palace of the Tuileries was very large and brilliant. The princes of the royal family and the blood royal met. There for the first time the Duchess of Angoulême appeared in the new court costume, which consisted of a white silk dress with a long train and a lace head-dress with hanging lappets. On the same day died the woman who had been Empress of the French and Queen of Italy. On the next day the *Journal des Débats* announced at the same time the royal audience at the Tuileries and the death of the former Empress. The royalist journal thus expressed itself: " The mother of Prince Eugène died at noon in the château of Malmaison, after an illness which first showed itself as a catarrhal fever and then suddenly assumed such a malignant character that she succumbed to it at the end of three days. She received all the aids of religion with as much piety as resignation. . . . Some hours before her death she counted with pleasure upon the regret of the many families whom she had had the pleasure of assisting, and the hope of this regret seemed much to alleviate her sufferings." On the day after that on which the companion of Napoleon's happy days received the last sacraments, France signed the treaty by which it relinquished all the conquests of the Revolution and the Empire.

Having nothing further to wish for, the foreigners decided to take their departure. On the 1st of June the Emperors of Russia and Austria went to the Tuileries to take leave of the King and the princes of his family. On the following day the Czar was represented at the funeral of the Empress Josephine and left the capital; the Austrian Emperor set out on the same day; on the 4th of June the King of Prussia also departed, and all the allied troops which yet remained in Paris and its vicinity followed on the next morning.

The Czar was dissatisfied with the whole affair. In conversation with Prince Eugène de Beauharnais, to whom he displayed the most intense sympathy, he said: "I do not know but I shall repent having re-seated the Bourbons on the throne; we have had them in Russia, and I know how to conduct myself so far as they are concerned." To the great scandal of the royalists, he had pretended to delight in the society of liberals. Once when he met M. de Lafayette in the salon of Madame de Staël, he complained — he, the autocrat — of the prejudices of the old régime which were at the bottom of the government of the Bourbons and, when the old revolutionist seemed to think that misfortune would have some corrective effect on them, "They corrected!" exclaimed the Czar. "They are uncorrected and incorrigible. There is only one of them — the Duke of Orleans — who has liberal ideas; as to the rest of them, never allow yourself to hope for anything from them." "If that is your opinion, Sire," replied M. de Lafayette, "why have you restored them?" "It is not my fault," replied the Emperor. "They were pressed upon me from all sides. I wished to keep them back in order that the nation might have time to impose a constitution on them. They overwhelmed me like a flood. You know that I went to Compiègne to see the King: I wanted to get him to give up his nineteen years of reign and pretensions of that sort. A deputation from the Corps Législatif was there as soon as I was, to recognize him at all times and without conditions. What could I do when the King and the deputies were of the same mind? The whole thing was a failure, and I went away much distressed."

Before leaving Paris this autocrat, absolute at home, liberal abroad, and mystifying everywhere, had caused a religious service to be held in the Place de la Concorde. Chateaubriand says: "An altar was erected on the spot where the scaffold of Louis XVI. had been put up. Seven Muscovite priests celebrated, and foreign troops were drawn up before the altar. The *Te Deum* was sung to one of the beautiful tunes of the ancient Greek Church. Soldiers and sovereigns knelt to receive the blessing. The minds of the French reverted to 1793 and 1794, when cattle refused to walk on the stones rendered hateful to them by the smell of blood. To this feast of expiation what hand had led these men from all lands, these descendants of old barbarous invaders, these Tartars, some of whom dwelt in sheepskin tents under the great Chinese wall?"

VI

THE COURT

THE court was established at the Tuileries on the 3d of May, 1814. It was to remain there till the 19th of March, 1815. Louis XVIII. occupied the chamber of Napoleon on the first floor, which opened on the garden and adjoined the large apartments overlooking the Carrousel. Monsieur, the King's brother, and the Duke of Berry were installed in the Pavilion de Marsan. The Duchess of Angoulême lived in the Pavilion of Flora, where she could recall mournful memories of Madame Elisabeth and the Princess of Lamballe, who had also dwelt there.

Court etiquette was about the same under royalty as under imperialism. But the general appearance of the palace underwent some modifications; there were more courtiers, and especially was there much more domesticity. Types the most diverse met there. An old *émigré*, the Count of Puymaigre, gives this description of it: "What a singular mixture I saw in 1814 when I reached Paris in July!— a mixture of courtiers of all epochs; of military men of the times before, during, and after the Revolution! Here was an officer escaped from the disaster at Moscow; there another who had put on again the uniform of the army of Condé; yonder a Vendéan dressed in green, or a Chouan in iron gray; and then one of those young men who, wishing to keep out of harm's way, had enlisted as soon as peace came. The old régime and the new were face to face, and it should also be said that, aside from some wise men, — and there were very few such, — everybody remained fixed in his old prejudices, in his antipathies, and in his political theories, and all, nevertheless, besieged the Tuileries and the offices of the ministers with the same importunity."

A strange and particolored court filled with heterogeneous and diverse elements; a court confused and contradictory; a true picture of a France thus divided! How many people could say to themselves at the Tuileries what the Doge of Genoa said to himself at Versailles: "What most surprises me here is to find myself here at all." What a singular gathering! Volunteers of 1792 side by side with the soldiers of Condé; defenders of the throne and the altar mingling with regicides, and Vendéans with men who had been the mere tools of Napoleon. Etiquette always prevents controversies at the Tuileries, and men who at bottom are agreed in mutual hatred, have officially for each other only polite phrases. "The fear which the imperial government inspired," says Madame de Staël, "had entirely destroyed the customary freedom of conversation; under that government nearly all Frenchmen became diplomatists, so that society indulged only in insipid talk which never recalled the bold spirit of France. Assuredly no one had anything to fear in 1814, under Louis XVIII.; but the habit of reserve had become fixed and, besides, the courtiers thought it would not be 'good form' to talk politics or to discuss any serious subject; they hoped that in this way the nation might be made frivolous again, and, consequently, submissive; but the only result they accomplished was to render conversation insipid, and to deprive themselves of all means of getting at anybody's opinions."

And yet there was one theme upon which every one was allowed to touch, and that was satire of the imperial government. Listen to Madame de Staël again: " The most moderate party was made up of the royalists who had returned with the King and who had never forsaken him during his exile, — the Count of Blacas, the Duke of Gramont, the Duke of Castries, the Count of Vaudreuil, etc. Their consciences bore witness that they had acted in the most noble and disinterested manner from their point of view, and they were quiet and kindly disposed. But those who had most difficulty in restraining their virtuous indignation against the party of the usurper were the nobles or their adherents who, while that same usurper was in power, had asked for place, and had left him at once on the day of his downfall. The enthusiasm for legitimacy which was displayed by such persons as the chamberlain of Madame Mère and the tiring-woman of Madame Sœur knew no bounds."

The King did not re-establish the conditions which under the old régime had been exacted in order to be received at court. He politely received all who were presented, no matter what camp they had belonged to or what cockade they had worn. Sometimes they were old republicans, sometimes they were even members of the Convention, and again they were deputies of the West, wearing the white emblems of their party, or precinct captains from La Vendée wearing hats of the style of Rochejacquelein. Chateaubriand says: "Uniforms of Napoleon's Guard intermingled with those of the body-guard and of the Maison-Rouge, cut precisely after the old patterns. The aged Duke of Havré, with his powdered wig and his black cane, walked with trembling head as captain of the body-guard, near Marshal Victor, limping in the manner of Bonaparte; the Duke of Mouchy, who had never witnessed the firing of a gun, went to Mass side by side with Marshal Oudinot, riddled with wounds; the château of the Tuileries, so precise and military under Napoleon, was now, instead of smelling of powder, redolent of the odors of food cooking on every hand; under messieurs the gentlemen of the bedchamber and messieurs the gentlemen of the wardrobe everything assumed an air of domesticity." The author of the *Mémoires d'Outre-Tombe* also places before our eyes ladies of the imperial court introducing the dowagers of the Faubourg Saint-

Germain and showing them the intricacies of the château; Conventionists who had by turns become counts, barons, and senators under Napoleon and peers under Louis XVIII., relapsing, now into the republican dialect, which they had almost forgotten, and now into the idiom of absolutism, which they had learned thoroughly; lieutenant-generals raised to game-keepers; aides-de-camp of the last military tyrant discussing the inviolable liberties of the people, and regicides with pious warmth upholding the dogma of legitimacy.

The court functionaries had been re-established. M. de Talleyrand-Périgord, Archbishop-Duke of Rheims, was Grand Almoner; the Prince of Condé was Grand Master of France; the Count of Blacas, Grand Master of the Wardrobe; the Marquis of Dreux-Brézé, Grand Master of Ceremonies; the Dukes of Richelieu, of Duras, of Aumont, and of Fleury, First Gentlemen of the Bedchamber; the Marquises of Avaray and of Boisgelin, Masters of the Wardrobe; the Duke of Mortemart, Commander of the Hundred Switzers; the Marquis of Vernon, Chief Equerry; the Count of Cossé-Brissac, First Pantler; the Marquis of La Suze, Grand Master of the Lodges; the Count of Escars, Grand Maître d'Hôtel; and the Marquis of Mondragon, Maître d'Hôtel Ordinaire.

The military household of the King was revived on the same footing that it had held previously to the reforms which reasons of economy had suggested to Louis XVI. The companies of the body-guard, each of which had hitherto been four hundred men strong, including their supernumeraries, were enlarged to six hundred each, instead of four hundred. The first were commanded by the old titularies, — the Duke of Havré-Croï, the Duke of Gramont, the Prince of Poix (Noailles), and the Duke of Luxembourg (Montmorency). The King gave the other two to Marshal Berthier, Duke of Wagram and Neufchâtel, and Marshal Marmont, Duke of Ragusa. Each of these six officers bore the title of Captain of the Body-guard. The two companies of light-horse and gendarmes of the guard, which were called "the red companies" because of their uniforms, were given, one to Count Charles de Damas, Lieutenant-Captain of the Light-horse of the Guard, and the other to Count Etienne de Durfort, with the title of Lieutenant-Captain of the Gendarmes of the Guard. Both of these men had been aides-de-camp of the Count of Artois. The companies of Royal Musketeers, the gray and the black, — named so, because of the color of their horses, — were placed under the command of two generals who had belonged to the Imperial Army — the Count of Nansouty and the Marquis of Lagrange. The Marquis of Rochejaquelein had command of the company of mounted grenadiers, which was made up of a hundred men chosen from the ranks of all arms. There were, besides, two other corps in the royal household — the guards of the gate and the guards of the provostship of the hotel, whose business it also was to act as Guards of the Seals. The Count of Vergennes commanded the former, and the second were under the orders of the Count of Monsoreau, who acted as Grand Provost, holding the office in reversion from the Marquis of Tourzet, the titulary commander.

Although he was one of the chiefs of the military household, Marshal Marmont criticised the institution very severely: "That establishment," said he, " gave occasion for the creation of five thousand officers, — subaltern, superior, or general. One may judge, at a glance, of the effect thus produced on the army at the very moment when the most far-reaching and least-understood reforms had struck at a multitude of brave officers, covered with glory and in the full vigor of manhood. The Abbé Louis, with hard and sordid calculation, applied the reform to a great number of men at the very time when it was most important to attach the army to him, to make it feel secure, and to soften any hardships that the changes might impose upon it. And all this was done in order to save two millions when the military establishment of the King was to cost more than three millions. One can hardly understand a course of conduct so unjust and so impolitic."

Notwithstanding this, the Restoration, at the start, met with so much sympathy, especially from the middle classes of Paris, that the very military establishment, which was destined so soon to become unpopular, was at first looked upon with favor. "It is difficult," says the Baron of Vitrolles, "to show the extent to which the revival of those figures of times past pleased the people and public opinion. I saw the crowd press around the first detachments of light cavalry and gendarmes of the guard, and applaud their splendid uniforms overlaid with sleeveless white jackets, on which, both on breast and back, was a large red cross that seemed to date from the Crusades. Detestation of souvenirs and ancestor-worship had not yet been sown in their hearts."

A thing that produced still more discontent in the army was the truly ridiculous prodigality with which rank was lavished on a few privileged persons. A question of etiquette, of dress, was the first cause of this scandal. Monsieur, the King's brother, told the Baron of Vitrolles one day, that his sons, the princes, had asked him to keep his hair cut and not to use powder. "Who could have foreseen," adds the Baron, "that the granting of this request would have important consequences? There exist in nature no germs so hidden as the infinitely small causes of human events. The result was, that short and unpowdered hair precluded the use of dress coats at court. Dress coats having gone, men took to wearing uniforms; a uniform makes epaulettes necessary; old men of rank could not be content with the epaulettes of a sub-lieutenant; so military rank was demanded, not for military services, but as due to one's station or age."

General Dupont, the Minister of War, and the

man who capitulated at Baylen, was, according to the
severe expression of M. de Vitrolles, "the pander in
this prostitution of rank and military crosses." During the exile the Bourbons had bestowed neither
military rank nor promotion. This wise abstention
was observed so scrupulously that in 1814, when all
the old general officers once more appeared upon the
scene, there were only three lieutenant-generals in
the royal army, — MM. de Viomesnil, de Vaubecourt
and de Béthisi. Then General Dupont distributed
many promotions which were connected with times
long gone. Extreme confusion in all grades was the
result of this. Louis XVIII., wishing to please the
army, had adopted military dress instead of wearing
the dress coat which the kings of France wore in all
the courts of the last century. Following his example, every officer of the court wanted a military
uniform. It was, as Marshal Marmont observes, an
economical way of furnishing one's wardrobe. But,
as not one of them had been in the service for twenty
years, each found at first, that he had only a low-grade epaulette which he did not deem in harmony
with the dignity with which he had been newly
arrayed. The Marquis of Dreux-Brézé, who was only
a captain and grand master of ceremonies, had himself dubbed a lieutenant-general, and drew the salary
of a man of that grade in active service. M. Just de
Noailles received as his first grade, the title of major-general, when he was sent as ambassador to Russia.
Count Blacas, opposed to this shameful distribution

of titles, had the good taste repeatedly to decline the promotion with which General Dupont thought to please him. But the generality of the court habitués longed for braveries and big epaulettes. The officers of the Empire, who accepted without difficulty the grades of the army of Condé and the army of La Vendée, had no patience with the court titles.

Nevertheless it must be granted that the task of Louis XVIII. was very difficult, and that it would have been impossible at the same time to please the men of the two régimes, who bore so little resemblance to each other. With the best will in the world Louis XVIII. could not make the titles of the Empire as old as those of the Monarchy. Napoleon's marshals were exceedingly sensitive in regard to matters of precedence and etiquette. These parvenus of glory sometimes displayed the pettiness of tradesmen. In the matter of aristocratic pretensions they were perhaps more touchy than the dowagers of the Faubourg Saint-Germain. Having been accustomed under the Empire to lord it everywhere, the marshals especially desired to keep up their splendid position at court. The attitude of the men of the old régime disturbed them beyond measure. They took umbrage at everything. If one was reserved towards them, they thought he wished to keep them at a distance; if familiar with them, they thought him lacking in respect. A thousand unbecoming speeches that were made by the lords and ladies of the court are recounted, these being either invented or exaggerated.

One of these ladies who, at a gathering in the Tuileries, asked a stranger the name of a beautiful woman who had attracted her attention, received the answer: "We don't know those persons; they are wives of marshals." An old-time duke, after a long conversation with Marshal Ney, is said to have remarked to him in a caressing tone: "What a pity it is that you have not, as one of us, what it is impossible to give you!" Louis XVIII., who liked M. Decazes as much as MM. d'Avaray and de Blacas, and who set prodigious store by his own claims to nobility but cared little for those of others, could not keep from smiling at dissensions like these, which had their basis in heraldry.

On the whole, nobody was perfectly satisfied at court — neither the second-hand royalists, as the old followers of Napoleon were called, nor even the true royalists, who had always been faithful to their cause and to the white flag. The men of the Revolution and the Empire always wanted to be the masters. As Madame de Staël says, many who called themselves patriots thought it strange that the King did not make up his council of men who had judged and condemned his brother. Carnot, the mouthpiece of the malecontents, said in a lampoon which had a wide circulation: "To-day if you want to appear with distinction at court, you must be very careful to keep from saying that you are one of the twenty-five millions of citizens who so gallantly defended their country against invasion by enemies; for you will be told that those twenty-five million pretended citizens were twenty-five million rebels, and that those pretended enemies were always friends. Say that you were lucky enough to be a Chouan or a Vendéan, a refugee or a Cossack or an Englishman, or that though you remained in France, you sought place under the governments that preceded the Restoration only that you might the better betray them, and then your fidelity will be lauded to the skies, and you will receive delicate congratulations, decorations, and touching responses from the whole royal family."

On the other hand, the old legitimists, the partisans of the throne and altar, said to themselves: "Was it worth while to suffer so much merely that we might be present at the spectacle that we witnessed on the very day of our triumph, — that day so long and so impatiently expected? We who so ardently desired the Restoration at bivouacs of the army of Condé and amid the woes and humiliations of exile, — were we dreaming of such things? Could we ever have believed that the escorts of our kings would be made up of coryphées of the Revolution, of the satellites of Bonaparte? One would have said that it was we who had been defeated. What! we cannot even make the Jacobin spoliators disgorge? We must not recover the so-called national property, which is our property, precisely as the throne is the property of the King. With what are we reproached? With having emigrated. But did not the King and the princes emigrate also? Was not emigration a duty that we owed to honor and fidelity? Bonaparte may be excused for making us suffer for it, but it is absurd and intolerable that Bourbons should bring it as an accusation against us. Did we impose upon ourselves so many privations, so many sacrifices, that we might put heart into Jacobins, butchers, and thieves? Should not the day of the King's return have been the end of our misfortunes? We have suffered, — should we not share in the triumph? True, we receive a few barren honors, a few court positions, but to whom go the real offices — those that give power? Who is Minister of Foreign Affairs? A bishop whose so-called wife is his concubine. Who is Minister of Finance? A married priest. Who is Minister of War? One of Napoleon's generals. Who are installed in the prefectures and military commands? Republicans, Bonapartists. It is they who receive every trust, every employment, every favor. It is we who are deceived and mortified, and ours is the ridicule of having expected so much from a government that treats us so badly! We were better off at Coblentz, since at Coblentz we had illusions which here we have no longer. There are times when we have to look back with longing even to the days of our exile. What we see is no true Restoration; it is a prolongation, or, rather, a parody, of the Revolution and the Empire."

Such was the language of extremists on both sides, and to look at a court apparently so calm, so united, and so well disciplined, no one would have suspected the intrigues, jealousies, dissensions, and passions that were hidden within it.

VII

THE CITY

WE have just taken a view of the court, and now let us cast a glance at the city. Paris was quiet enough at the beginning of the Restoration. After so much commotion and disturbance the masses were well pleased to have a little repose. When they thought of their children, mothers especially were delighted at the return of peace.

Tradesmen favored the Bourbons, and the people were not hostile to them. Commerce and industry began to look up, and, to judge from the general feeling of the city when the allied troops had departed, one would say that it was entirely normal.

Some salons were open once more, but as spring was not then the fashionable season, there were very few fêtes. Moreover, it required some time for society in the Faubourg Saint-Germain to reassume its splendor. In the words of Madame de Staël, very few agreeable members of the old régime were in Paris, for the aged were for the most part broken down through long-continued misfortunes or soured by inveterate indignation. The nobles who returned from exile were like shipwrecked sailors cast on the shore and still bewildered by the storm. Such as had been courtiers of Napoleon, and who but a short time before had frequented his house or that of the Empress Marie Louise, hoped to have their genuflections before the imperial throne pardoned, should they be royalists for a few weeks. If they were to justify their sudden change, they must call the Emperor "Buonaparte" an appreciable number of times.

On the other hand, all were not of one mind in that society which called itself well disposed. Some people favored the charter; others opposed it. Liberal monarchists were continually criticised at court by legitimists more royalist than the King. Nobles might be met with who in their own minds looked upon Louis XVIII. as a revolutionist, not to say a crowned Jacobin, because he had been imprudent enough to give his people their rights. "Parbleu!" said an old soldier of the army of Condé to Count de Puymaigre, "the King is really kind to bother himself so much about his charter. In order to put a stop to all our disputes I would have only one law, with two sections." — "Ah! that's singular; and what would your two sections be?" "Well! the first would run as follows: 'Everything is re-established in France just as it was on the 13th of July, 1789.'" — "And the second?" "The second? It is even simpler: 'My ministers of war, of the interior, of finance, etc., are charged with the execution of the above ordinance.'"

"And this man," M. de Puymaigre adds, "was not

lacking in intelligence; but he was fixed in one idea, and thought that nothing had undergone any change."

Salons in which such subjects were daily mooted could not have been very agreeable to men of the Revolution and the Empire. In the words of Madame de Staël: "A society as insipid as this was regarded, however, with strange jealousy by many of Napoleon's old courtiers, and, like Samson, they would willingly have used their mighty hands to pull down the edifice, if so they might ruin the hall of feasting which they might not enter."

Among the salons famous at the beginning of the Restoration were those of the Duchess of Duras, Madame de Staël, and Madame de Récamier. M. de Chateaubriand and his admirers frequented that of the duchess. Madame de Staël, always independent, and a furious enemy of Napoleon, though enthusiastic for Louis XVIII., held a liberal salon. That of Madame de Récamier, who was, above all, a pretty woman, was eclectic. Mathieu de Montmorency, who became gentleman-in-waiting to the Duchess of Angoulême, was often there, and was one of the chief admirers of the mistress of the house.

There also might be seen a friend of Madame Récamier's childhood days, Madame Moreau, the widow of the conqueror at Hohenlinden, and the wife of Bernadotte when he became Prince Royal of Sweden. After the death of her husband, who was struck by a French bullet while in the Russian army, Ma-

MME. DE RÉCAMIER

dame Moreau received from the Emperor Alexander a pension of a hundred thousand francs. Louis XVIII. offered her the title of duchess; she refused it, and would accept only such dignity as would have been her husband's had he been alive in 1814. The title "Maréchale de France" was bestowed on her. She is, we think, the only woman who ever received that designation. Madame Bernadotte, or rather the Princess Royal of Sweden, who in France bore the title of Countess of Gothland, had come to live at Paris after some experience of the climate of her future kingdom.

To sum the whole matter up, the ways of the world were not as yet greatly changed. The appearance of Paris had undergone but few modifications. The attendance at theatres, cafés, and on the promenades, was as large as it had been before. The galleries of the Palais-Royal were still a hotbed of corruption. The populace was neither more nor less moral under the Kingdom, than it had been under the Empire, and the inhabitants were not sensibly altered.

However, two new elements might be observed in Paris, — office-seekers from the provinces and half-pay officers. Both should be carefully examined if one would have a correct idea of the appearance of the capital. It swarmed with a host of people who might be called honorable mendicants. Every small country squire innocently imagined that for him Paris was a land of promise, where all his dreams would be turned into realities. Chouans covered with scars, Vendéans reduced to penury, poverty-stricken *émigrés* unable to find either their former dwellings or their families, passing before their old fields, now furrowed by alien ploughs, and eating the bread of charity at the doors of their former homes, — all had hoped that the Restoration would be for them a golden age at the end of an age of iron. They assailed the ministers with requests of all sorts. Representatives of the camp of Jalès came in the costume of their province and period. The streets thronged with these old *émigrés* whom the officers called Louis XIV.'s light-infantry. These relics of a former time might be seen strutting about in blue coats with two fleur-de-lis embroidered on the collar, a frill, a sword worn at right angles with the body, and small epaulettes which looked like sword knots cut in two. All these poor legitimists, threadbare in their convictions as in their coats, came to the city filled with confidence. What illusions did they not create for themselves! It is in the nature of modern monarchies that they should coquette with their enemies rather than their defenders. They say to themselves about their most ardent partisans: What is the use of paying particular attention to them? We shall always be sure of them, — and then they lavish their favors on persons who owe their success solely to the swiftness of their conversion, and to their cynical recantations. The unfortunate legitimists were soon called upon to meditate on a caricature which represented the King as holding out his hand to the Bonapartists and saying to them: "Union," and turning his back on the Vendéans, whom he seemed to dismiss with a disdainful gesture, while the motto written for them was: "Forgotten."

M. de Vitrolles himself, ardent a royalist as he was, and favorite of Charles X. as he was to become, was the first to amuse himself with certain defenders of the throne and altar, and to speak ironically of the deluge of petitions, a few of which had some basis of right, but most of which were inadmissible or extravagant. He tells how, one day, the Minister of Marine, Baron Malouet, came to the Council with a number of petitions and, among them, that of an old naval officer who asked for the rank of a rear-admiral. The petitioner established his rights in this way. In 1789, he had been a cadet in the navy, and so the crime of having served the Revolution could not be imputed to him. He calculated that if he had remained in the service, and without reference being had to the extraordinary promotions which he would have been sure to obtain, he would by this time, if only through seniority, have risen to the rank of rear-admiral, a grade which he claimed from the justice of the King. "What shall I tell him?" asked M. Malouet. "It seems to me," replied M. de Vitrolles, "that you may perfectly well admit all this gentleman's logic and even the conclusions he draws with it, as well as his rights in the matter; but you should add that he has forgotten just one essential fact, which is, that he was killed at the battle of Trafalgar." King and courtiers burst out laughing, and the petition was thrown into the waste-paper basket.

Apropos of such requests, Louis XVIII. used to say, by way of joke that in the *Spectator* Addison had told the story of a pronounced Tory who, on the accession of Charles II. to the throne, solicited a place in the King's household, on the ground that he had betrayed the wife of one of the opponents of the Stuarts. Louis XVIII., who was sly, was even the collaborator of M. de Vitrolles and M. de Jouy in a certain anonymous satirical article which appeared in the *Journal des Débats* on the 29th of May and the 2d of June, to the great disgust of more than one royalist. It was called: *Lettres du Cousin et de la Cousine.* "How happy I am, my friend," wrote the lady, "in the events that bring our illustrious princes back to the throne. What good fortune! You have no idea of the confidence which these events and your sojourn at Paris give me here. The prefect is afraid of me, and his wife, who had never before noticed me, has invited me twice to dinner. But we must lose no time, and we count on you. Would you believe it possible that as yet my husband has not taken a single step to have himself re-instated in his old place, on the pretext that the place no longer exists, and that he has been reimbursed for his office in assignats. He is the most apathetic man in France. My brother-in-law has received his cross of Saint Louis. He was not over nine years old when the Revolution broke out. It wouldn't have been right for them to refuse to add to the number of his services the twenty years of trouble and misfortune that he had spent on his estate."

Then the lady mentioned her protégés to her influential cousin: "You remember poor N. . . . He really was noted in the days of the Revolution; but, on my word, it is a full month since he recanted! You know that he is penniless, and that he is ready to sacrifice his all for our masters. His devotion to them leads him to desire the office of a prefect, for the duties of which he is well fitted. You remember the pretty song he composed for me. . . . I must not forget to recommend B. to you. . . . He is accused of having served all parties because he was employed by all the governments which have succeeded each other in France during the last twenty years; but, believe me, he is a good fellow; he was the first person here to don the white cockade. Besides, he only wants to keep his place as postmaster. Be careful to write to me under cover to him."

The cousin's answer, in which is shown all the caustic verve of the sovereign whom Talleyrand called the "*roi nichard*," is a small masterpiece of witty malice. "You cannot think, my dear cousin, with how much interest I read the letter you did me the honor to write, and how anxious I have been to further the interests — interests so just and so legitimate — of everybody you recommend to me. You will not be more astonished than I was at the obstacles that stood in my way, and which you would deem insurmountable if you did not know as well as I the people with whom we have to deal. When I spoke of your eldest son, who always wished to enter the army, and when I asked that he should be appointed major of the regiment in which his father formerly served, I was met with the objection — as if it had any weight! — that we are now at peace, and that before thinking of making an officer of M. de S. F., provision would have to be made for twenty-five thousand officers, some of whom — would you believe it? — had taken advantage of their campaigns, and their scars, and even gone so far as to base their claims on the score of the battles in which they had fought, while the rest, who were more closely associated with the misfortunes of the royal family, had come back to France with no other prospects than the favors and promises of the King. I inquired, with some heat, what they intended to do for your son and the host of royalists who had grieved in secret over the woes of the State, and had always desired the return of the Bourbons to the throne of their ancestors. The answer was that they would have the pleasure of seeing their misfortunes ended and their desires accomplished."

So there is little hope for the protégés of the lady. In fact, her cousin gives her very little encouragement. "I am sorry," he adds, "that your brother-in-law regained the cross of Saint Louis before he had ever worn it; for it is possible that the King would not have relinquished the right to confer it himself or recognized the justice which certain persons are bent on doing to themselves. I presented a petition in favor of N., at the end of which I had inserted the little song that he made for you, but they insisted very strongly upon it that such things were not sufficient to entitle a man even to an insignificant prefecture."

And the cousin comes to the following mournful conclusion: "The upshot, my dear cousin, is, you see, that you must arm yourself with patience. I will even say that it is to be feared that your proposed visit to Paris will not greatly expedite matters. At the time when I am writing to you there are a hundred and twenty-three thousand provincials of every class and age and of both sexes on the police lists, who have come here to prefer claims, armed with titles nearly as unquestionable as yours and having an inestimable advantage over you in the fact that their claims were put in before yours."

And the unfortunate legitimists were sad at heart over this satirical piece of work which was due to the witty collaboration of the King, M. de Vitrolles, and M. de Jouy. "What's this?" they cried. "The Restoration does nothing in our behalf. It is powerless to mend the evils we have endured for it, and yet it permits us to be publicly insulted in newspapers which it ought to suppress!"

Demands, however, continued to pour in in numbers not less than fabulous. "On the day of the downfall of Bonaparte," says Madame de Staël, "they were as busy all over France as at Paris, and at Paris there were thousands of people asking the government for money and places of all sorts. How incredible is the madness of the desire for power! The first article in 'the rights of man' in France is that every Frenchman shall have public employment. The importunate class do not know how to live save on government money. No industry or business could make life tolerable to them." But among these importunate persons how many interesting people there were! Of how many thousands of employees of all sorts, custom-house officials, assessors of taxes, police officers, and departmental functionaries was not France left bereft who, having neither salary nor asylum, died of starvation in Paris, together with their wives and children!

The most dangerous, bold, and popular of the malecontents were the half-pay officers, the former conquerors of Europe, now much astonished at finding themselves conquered. Can one not see them strolling about in civilian dress, but always with a military look, gait, and manner of speech, with an aspect fierce in spite of their misfortunes, a bitter smile on their lips, felt hats on their heads, and walking-sticks in their hands? Can you not see, can you not hear, them at the Palais-Royal, on the Boulevard des Italiens, in the cafés, sneering at men and things, railing pitilessly at everybody and everything except the Emperor and the Empire, making merry over the impotent Louis XVIII. and his well-known infirmities, and treating as renegades and traitors the marshals and generals who throng the antechambers of the King and his ministers?

The Duchess of Abrantès tells us that one morning five persons gravely entered Tortoni's and seated themselves at a table. They called for the bill of fare and looked around disdainfully, without seeming to pay any attention to the surrounding company, which laughed at the strangeness of their clothes and general appearance. They were all dressed alike, in little threadbare coats, half-gilt epaulettes of marigold color, short breeches, checkered hose, small hats, and long swords worn diagonally across their coat-skirts. After a long time spent in poring over the landlord's bill of fare, these grave personages ended by calling for a cutlet for five. The waiter looked at them in total bewilderment. The cutlet was brought, and they breakfasted on it, accompanying their repast with conversation as singular as their appearance. These five self-styled *émigrés* were officers in disguise, and among them was the future general de Lawœstine, an ardent Bonapartist in spite of his old-time name and his title of Marquis. Jests and pleasantries from the barracks are the prelude to military sedition. It will not be long before the half-pay officers will enter the Tuileries as conquerors and replace the tricolor on the Pavilion of the Horloge.

VIII

THE KING

WE have just cast a rapid glance at the court and the city. Let us now endeavor to draw a picture of the King, the royal family, and the princes of the blood. We shall begin with Louis XVIII., whose personal appearance, character, and habits we wish to describe accurately. We shall ask ourselves these questions: Was Louis XVIII. religious? Was he moral? Was he good? Was he intelligent? Was he able? and we shall answer by drawing the elements of our response from the memoirs of men who knew the King exceedingly well. We think that their testimony, when grouped and compared, will enable us to arrive at the truth and paint a true instead of an imaginative picture.

Lamartine, whose magic pen embellishes beyond measure all that he writes about, has displayed Louis XVIII.'s personal appearance in colors which, in our opinion, are too brilliant. The poet more than idealizes the King. "In studying him," says he, "one could not fail to admire him. . . . His large eyes of celestial blue, with sockets oval at the bend and high at the top, were luminous, sparkling, liquid, and frank. The nose was aquiline, as it always is among the Bourbons; his lips were usually slightly parted, his mouth smiling and refined, and his cheeks full, though their fulness did not efface the delicacy of their outlines and the suppleness of their muscles. A healthy complexion and the vivid freshness of youth tinged his face. In beauty the features were those of Louis XV., but they were illuminated by larger intelligence and a more concentrated power of thought in the whole countenance. Even majesty was not lacking to them; his physiognomy spoke, questioned, answered, controlled."

And the singer of the "Harmonies" adds in his customary lyric way: "In whatever aspect one regarded that presence, thoughtful and self-contained, dominating yet sweet, severe yet attractive, one would not have said: 'He's a sage, he's a statesman, he's a pontiff, he's a legislator, he's a conqueror,' for his natural repose and quiet majesty removed all likeness to such professions, which make the face pale and the features sunken; one would have said: 'He is a king! but he is a king who has not yet experienced the cares and the fatigues of the throne.'"

M. de Lamartine began his career as a member of Louis XVIII.'s body-guard. The founder of the second republic was then an enthusiastic royalist. When, in his old age, he evoked the image of the King of his early days, he became a royalist again for a moment, and his imagination called up a

Louis XVIII. handsomer than the reality. In 1814 republicans and Bonapartists regarded the King in an utterly different light. The prince whom the royalists found so majestic, appeared to their vision as a gouty old man, dressed in superannuated clothes, awkward in carriage, without prestige, and almost ridiculous.

In our opinion the truth lies between these two exaggerations. Without being so handsome as his admirers said it was, the physiognomy of Louis XVIII. was both charming and dignified. His countenance was animated, his mouth refined, his voice sonorous, and his movements symmetrical. Born on the 17th of November, 1755, he was fifty-eight years old at the outset of the Restoration. His body, borne down by infirmities, and especially by gout, was that of an aged man, but his face still retained something of youth. We do not think that Lamartine exaggerates when he thus expresses himself: "One would say that time, exile, fatigues, infirmities, and his unwieldy obesity had attacked his feet and body only to bring out more fully by contrast the perennial and vigorous youthfulness of his face." Marshal Marmont, who is harsh rather than sympathetic when speaking of the King, says: "There was something winning in his manners, gracious in his way of speaking, alluring in his words, and strong and authoritative in his whole aspect. I have never met it to the same degree in anybody else."

We think M. de Vitrolles equally right when

he says of Louis XVIII.: "The noble expression of his features, his beautiful and sonorous voice, and his whole regal appearance commanded respect in spite of his ill-proportioned figure. Even the disadvantages under which he labored by reason of his infirmities, the difficulty with which he walked and his excessive fatness, seemed to give a sort of dignity to his person. He knew how to make them nobler than grace and agility. In the eyes of men who had been attached to the hardy chieftain who but lately had dominated France, he was in strong contrast with their old leader." As M. Thiers says in his account of the formal entry of the King into Paris: "However much enamoured of peace he may have been, as everybody was at that time, one could not help regretting that the prince who had been recalled to govern France was unable to mount a horse, and public fancy naturally reverted to a picture, reproduced at the time, of an aged father coming in, surrounded by his children."

Obliged by his infirmities to remain constantly seated in an armchair, Louis XVIII. was artist enough to make the chair a sort of throne. I see him gravely installed there, in clothes half-military and half-civilian. He wanted to wear boots, for a king is a general, and a general should be booted. But leather boots hurt his legs, which were gouty. So he had to be content with velvet boots reaching to his knees. He never laid his sword aside, even in his armchair, for a sword is the distinctive sign of a nobleman, and the Most Christian King is the first nobleman not only in France and Navarre, but in the whole world. His breast is covered with heraldic orders. The blue cordon of the Holy Ghost stands out in relief on his white waistcoat. His blue coat is neither civilian dress nor uniform. Two small golden epaulettes glitter on his shoulders to remind people of the military nature of kingship. His hair, dressed with white powder according to the old fashion, and crimped at the temples by the barber's curling-irons, is brought together at the nape of the neck and bound with a black silk ribbon that falls down over the collar. A three-cornered hat, adorned with a cockade and a small white plume, is now on the monarch's knees and now in his hand. His entire costume, reminding one of two different eras, is at one and the same time that of a man of the court of Versailles and that of a man of the nineteenth century.

After having examined Louis XVIII.'s personal appearance, let us examine his character and bring forward the questions mentioned at the opening of the present chapter. Was Louis XVIII. religious? Although he showed himself respectful toward the faith of his fathers both in speech and act, the author of the *Génie du Christianisme* represents him as a sceptic; Chateaubriand says: " Affected with the spirit of his time, it is to be feared that to the Most Christian King religion was only an elixir fit for use in compounding the drugs that go to make up royalty." Enthusiastic royalists and ultra-Catholics accused Louis XVIII. of being at bottom a Voltairian. It is not necessary to penetrate into the recesses of his soul and determine the extent of his religious faith. But it should be said that he believed in the necessary connection of the throne and altar, that he went to Mass not only on Sunday, but on every other day of the week, that he showed great respect for the clergy, that he would allow of no jest at religion in his presence, and that he died a very good Christian.

Was Louis XVIII. moral? He was less devoted to women than his predecessors. Let us listen to Chateaubriand, who was so enthusiastic in his subventioned writings and so caustic in his *Mémoires d'Outre-Tombe:* " The libertine imagination that he inherited from his grandfather," says he of Louis XVIII., " must have aroused some distrust in regard to his exploits; but he understood himself and, when he made positive affirmations, he laughed at himself for the boasting he was doing. One day I spoke to him of the necessity of a new marriage for the Duke of Bourbon in order to restore the race of the Condés to life. He strongly approved of the idea although he did not trouble himself about the said resurrection. But apropos of the subject, he mentioned the Count of Artois, and said: 'My brother might remarry and still not change the royal succession; he could beget only younger sons; as to myself, all who might be begotten by me would be eldest sons; I do not choose to disinherit the Duke of

Angoulême.' He bridled up with an air of whimsical importance, but I did not pretend to deny any sort of ability to the King."

To sum up, perhaps there was not much merit in the tranquil life led by Louis XVIII., but it is certain that in the early times of the Restoration the general appearance of the court was rather austere than lively. There was as yet no question of a favorite.

Was Louis XVIII. kind and good? Opinion is divided as to this. Let us see how Chateaubriand contradicts himself. What does he say in one of his perfunctory writings: *Le roi est Mort, vive le Roi?* "In the presence of Louis XVIII. one had feelings of mingled confidence and respect. The benevolence of his heart was shown in what he said; the greatness of his race appeared in his aspect. Indulgent and generous, he reassured those who might accuse themselves of wrongdoing; ever calm and reasonable, one might tell him everything, for he could understand everything." And how does the same writer speak in regard to the King in his *Mémoires d'Outre-Tombe?* "An egotist and without prejudices, Louis XVIII. wanted peace at any price. He upheld his ministers as long as they were with the majority; he dismissed them as soon as that majority began to totter and his repose might be disturbed! He did not hesitate to draw back as soon as it would have been necessary to take but one step forward in order to gain the victory. . . .

Without being cruel, this King was not humane. Tragic catastrophes neither surprised nor touched him. To the Duke of Berry, who excused himself for having had the misfortune to disturb the king's slumber by dying, he was content to say: 'I had my sleep out.' Nevertheless this imperturbable man flew into a horrible rage whenever he was contradicted, and, in fine, this prince, so cold and insensible, had mental affections that closely resembled passions; thus Count d'Avaray, M. de Blacas, M. Decazes, Madame de Balbi, and Madame du Cayla were in turn his intimate friends; all these beloved persons were favorites; unfortunately too many letters fell into their hands."

These criticisms seem to us a little harsh. Was not the favoritism of which Louis XVIII. is so often accused a necessity of friendship? A childless widower, his essential need was that of a friend, a confidant, another self, whom he could admit to all his thoughts, to all his troubles; and the persons whom he definitively honored with close affection, received only benefits from him in return for what they gave. Let us add that Louis XVIII. was an accomplished host; it was he who made the celebrated remark: "Punctuality is the politeness of kings"; he had the gift of saying amiable and pleasing things, and, besides this, he was generous and delicate in making presents. There was a depth of moderation, wisdom, and indulgence in his character. He was not cruel; he did not like war; he did not even punish criminals, except when he believed their chastisement not only necessary but indispensable from a political point of view; and we think that Marshal Marmont was right in saying: "His heart was generous and kindly when the passions of the people about him did not hinder him from showing his true character."

Was Louis XVIII. intelligent? All are agreed on this topic. Had he not been King, still Louis XVIII. would have held his own among the most intelligent men of this epoch, — even beside M. de Talleyrand himself. Unlike those *émigrés*, of whom it was said that they had learned nothing and forgotten nothing, he had learned much and retained much. It was always noticed that in familiar conversation, as well as in his responses to addresses and public speeches, his expressions were appropriate, and his ideas to the point. He was well educated, and no one was better versed than he in Latin authors, especially Horace, his favorite poet, and one whom he quoted with great propriety. He was a fine conversationalist. Being a man of ability, he was fond of literature, and, as sovereign, he protected it. Nevertheless Marshal Marmont, though he recognized the King's intelligence, makes some exceptions: "His intellect," says he, "which was far too highly praised, was often at fault. His prodigious memory and exceedingly wide reading afforded him the means of making the most extraordinary *tours de force* and astonishing his auditors, but, so far as serious discussion is concerned, his abilities were of the flimsiest. His brain, which could retain everything, produced nothing. He never went so far as to give three reasons in defence of a preconceived opinion. Serious in the most trifling matters, he had a notion that he could rouse admiration by employing pretentious and often very ridiculous phrases. . . . Having seen much, he had a great store of anecdotes which he told agreeably; but persons who, like myself, had long been on intimate terms with him, knew them by heart, but though he was perfectly aware of this he never failed to repeat them."

It has been said that no man is great to his valet. May it not be added that no sovereign is wise to his courtiers? The Duke of Ragusa saw Louis XVIII. too frequently, and that is why he criticises him. Moreover, his criticisms seem to us somewhat overstated. He accuses Louis XVIII. of being at a loss for arguments during a discussion; kings do not discuss, they decide. The Marshal accuses him of telling the same story over and over again; but what anecdotist does not repeat himself? He says that his brain was incapable of originating anything; but one does not expect a wit to create works of imagination. In any case it is certain that everybody who came to the court felt the charm of the King's conversation. The Duchess of Abrantès, who was intelligent herself, says in her Memoirs: "I found Louis XVIII. a man of great learning and profound wisdom, and endowed with large knowledge of men. On one occasion, especially, I was with him for three-quarters of an hour, and assuredly I do not regret the attention I gave to what he said to me. He conversed with rare talent." In fine, we do not hesitate, in answer to the question: "Was Louis XVIII. intelligent?" to reply that he was very intelligent.

Was Louis XVIII. able? His ability is as incontestable as his intelligence. In an era of scepticism he had from the outset the great merit of believing and making others believe in himself and his cause. On this essential point Chateaubriand, even in his *Mémoires d'Outre-Tombe*, does him full justice: "Louis XVIII.," says he, "never forgot the pre-eminence of his birth; he was everywhere king, as God is God everywhere; in a crib or in a temple, on a golden altar or on one of clay. Evil fortune never wrested from him the least concession; his haughtiness gained assurance even, by reason of his low estate; he had the appearance of saying: 'Kill me! You will not kill the centuries written on my brow.' The fixed idea of the grandeur, the antiquity, the dignity, and the majesty of his race gave to Louis XVIII. a veritable empire. Even the generals of Bonaparte acknowledged its dominion. They were more intimidated when in the presence of this impotent old man than in the presence of the terrible master who had commanded them in a hundred battles. The unshaken faith of Louis XVIII. in his blood is the real force that put the sceptre into his hand. The exile without an army made his appearance at the close of all the battles which he had not fought. Louis XVIII. was legitimacy incarnate; when he disappeared, legitimacy was no longer to be seen."

This faith in the monarchical cause was a supreme ability. The first merit of a priest is belief in religion. The first merit of a king is belief in royalty. Louis XVIII. had another secret, fit for kings. He never hurried. Most politicians exhaust themselves in fruitless excitements. He was disturbed neither by the inexpediency of impatience nor the dangers of hasty action. His sluggishness was the result of calculation, his temporizing was a force. Nothing intimidated, nothing took him by surprise. He was not always master of others, but he was always master of himself. No one knew better than he the hardships of being an *émigré*, and no one ever found him falling into the exaggerated way of speaking common among those about him. He never went to extremes, but was, if one may so express himself, a "golden mean," a sovereign, an umpire, a moderator, a king, and a philosopher at the same time. As Lamartine says: " He was obliged, by complaisance and weakness, to feign more hatred and contempt for the Revolution than he really felt. At bottom he was well disposed towards a revolution that had restored him to his throne, and which agreed with him in establishing it firmly through the power of the opinions which had of late come into vogue. His mind was rejuvenated by reflection, just as his body had grown old by years. He was a king of the past, but he was a man of his day. Let us say the word: his memories came from habit; his forecasts from genius. At need, he was energetic and could enforce his will." "King Louis XVIII. had a cold heart and a liberal mind," said M. Guizot. "The anger and bad temper of his relatives had little effect, when once he had decided not to let it trouble him. It was his pride and his pleasure to think himself more clear-headed and more politic than the rest of his family, and to act on his own opinion with entire independence."

Although, in general, Louis XVIII. was very highly esteemed for his sagacity, yet he had his detractors among noted statesmen who judged with great severity of his work. Prince Metternich thought that the author of the Charter was thoroughly in error, and that a liberal Restoration could be nothing but an expedient and not a solution. He wrote to Count Apponyi on the 2d of July, 1827: "Napoleon, of whom it cannot be denied that he had the sentiment of power, said to me one day: 'You see me master of France. Well, I would not undertake to govern it for three months under a free press.' Louis XVIII., seemingly thinking himself stronger than Napoleon, was not content to allow freedom to the press, but expressly made it free by the terms of the Charter."

According to the Austrian statesman: "In 1814

everything should have been done in France except what actually was done. Grant that Louis XVIII. was Frenchman enough to have all the national defects, grant that, little by little, he could have gained popularity without exposing the throne and the nation to another revolution by evoking the principles in which the Revolution had its rise, it is still certain that he was mistaken in either case, and that the results of his error would of necessity have been disastrous. By resting the restored throne on the principles of the Constituent Assembly, applied, indeed, with moderation, he caused the return of the Revolution which Napoleon had overthrown. This was to erect a throne surrounded with republican institutions — an invention of which Louis XVIII. is the author."

Did Prince Metternich, then, wish for the reestablishment of the old régime? No. What he desired was the imperial régime enforced by royalty. He says: "Louis XVIII. had the choice, not between the return of what had come to be called the old régime, — impossible now, since men cannot return to things the very principles of which have been destroyed, — but between a new monarchical order applied on monarchical bases and a state of affairs which, under the name of monarchy, surrounded the throne with republican institutions. Instead of establishing the throne, as Bonaparte did, on frankly monarchical foundations, Louis XVIII. founded it on the *moderate* principles of the liberalism of 1789.

... It is the misfortune of France to be ungovernable, and she is in this lamentable condition because the fragments of a social revolution are poor materials for reconstruction, and because Louis XVIII. was a wretched architect. In the last and longest conversation accorded to me by the King before my departure from Paris, I said to him: 'Without wishing to do so, your government is substantially on the way to revive the Revolution of 1789. The Restoration seems to have come to life only to give the seal of legality to doctrines and acts which had not that sanction till the Restoration was brought about.' The mind of Louis XVIII. was strongly impregnated with the good and bad characteristics of the French mind in general, — that strange amalgam of serious qualities and an amount of levity that renders actions incalculable and stands in the way of foreseeing what will happen."

And so to the Austrian statesman Louis XVIII. was a mere Utopian, a doctrinaire. But the ideas of Prince Metternich have to be discounted. He was the born enemy of parliamentarism, against which he waged a war from which he did not come out victorious. We are inclined to believe that since it was not in the power of the Restoration to give glory, it ought to have given liberty. However that may be, the fact should be remembered that the system inaugurated by the author of the Charter was followed by all succeeding governments, and that this prince remains the type of a constitutional sovereign.

Having studied Louis XVIII. in his physique and morals, let us now see how he lived at the Tuileries. The King's life was regulated most methodically, and every hour had its regular and invariable use. He rose at seven o'clock, received the first gentleman of the bedchamber or M. de Blacas till eight, held his business meeting at nine, breakfasted at ten with attendants and persons who had been authorized, once for all, to come at all hours; that is to say, with the titularies of important court offices and the heads of the various departments of the royal household. The Duchess of Angoulême and one or two of her ladies were present at this breakfast and withdrew at five minutes to eleven. From five minutes to eleven till the clock struck, the royal amphitryon often told some rather broad story to cheer up his convives. Exactly at eleven o'clock he dismissed them, and gave audiences till noon, when he received men of the most prominence and the distinguished foreigners who were passing through France. "Here," says Lamartine, "this prince really enjoyed his throne. In order to appear less great, he descended to all the familiarities of conversation. . . . He liked to please and charm those with whom he talked; he reigned by his attractive qualities; he felt and made others feel that he was the brightest man in the kingdom. This was the sceptre personal to himself; he would not have exchanged it for that to which he was born." At noon the King went to Mass attended by his retinue, which was always composed of at least twenty persons. Upon returning from the chapel of the château, he received his ministers when they wished to consult him, or his council, which he held once a week, and which never remained in session for more than an hour. When it was two, three, or four o'clock, according to the season, he went for a drive in his large travelling-carriage, and sometimes made four, five, or even ten leagues, the horses running at full speed; for he considered rapid driving indispensable to his health. He felt stifled if the horses went slowly or even at a trot. He must have full gallop. And this dizzy speed tired his numerous escort greatly. Relays of steeds and detachments of troops stationed at intervals gave employment to nearly three hundred horses for these daily drives of the King. He dined at six o'clock with the Duchess of Angoulême and members of the royal family, and ate with good appetite. He was a gourmet, and his pretensions in the line of gastronomy were perfectly justified. **Dinner** lasted till seven o'clock. The royal family were together till eight. Then people who had the entrée might ask for admittance; they were received, sometimes individually and sometimes in groups. At nine, Louis XVIII. went to the council-room and gave out the countersign; that is to say, the countersign of the château. A few persons had the right to be present at this time. They profited by it to pay court to the sovereign. This business commonly occupied five minutes, and then the King retired, after saying a few words, always kindly, to every person present. To-morrow was like yesterday, and the royal life went on with majestic monotony.

IX

MONSIEUR

BORN at Versailles on the 8th of October, 1757, and, since the 2d of June, 1805, the widower of Marie Thérèse of Savoy, Monsieur — for so the Count of Artois, who was subsequently to reign under the name of Charles X., was called by virtue of his position as brother of Louis XVIII. — was fifty-six years old at the beginning of the Restoration. While the King already looked like an aged man, Monsieur, who was only two years younger, still preserved the grace and elegance of youth. The two brothers resembled each other in morals no more than in physique. Their appearance, their bearing, their faces, and their ideas were in absolute contrast. The Count of Artois, slender and handsomely formed, accustomed to bodily exercise, was not only a great pedestrian and huntsman, but an accomplished horseman. The face of Louis XVIII. was grave; that of the Count of Artois always pleasant and smiling. There were certain modern aspects in the character and opinions of Louis XVIII.; the Count of Artois was essentially a man of the old régime, a *grand seigneur* of the court of Versailles, a prince after the *émigrés'* own heart. The one looked upon the reforms that had been brought about as necessary and even indispensable; the other was convinced that the Revolution had been the most disastrous, as it was the most sterile, of convulsions. One looked forward to the future; the other shut himself up in the past. One wished to be a man of the times; the other would have been glad had he been able to go back to the days of the Crusades. One emigrated only when nothing else was left for him to do; the other was the first to give the signal for flight. In exile as at the court of Louis XVI., and at the Tuileries as in exile, they had pursued different courses. The liberal royalists extolled Louis XVIII.; the Count of Artois was the idol of the absolutist royalists.

The two opposed systems, which first were face to face at Versailles, and then again during the exile, again found themselves at war after the return of the Bourbons to France. The Count of Artois, whose lieutenant-generalship had given him a taste for power, did not wish to give up politics. At the Pavilion de Marsan he had organized, or at least had tried to organize, a sort of State within the State. For the sake of Monsieur, the King's brother, a bureau of information was established at the entresol of the Pavilion, under the direction of MM. de la Maisonfort and Perrier de Monciel. M. de Vitrolles had put this bureau into operation on the very day when the Count of Artois entered Paris. According to

Lamartine, the whole policy of the King's brother consisted of secret intrigues, police espionage, contingent plans of government, encouragement for ultra-royalist writers, and court subsidies for sycophantic and hungry authors. This was only a policy of mystification. When his brother was not present, the Count of Artois allowed bitter criticisms of the course of the government to be made. In the King's presence he was submission itself. Louis XVIII. had established strict discipline at court, and no member of his family dared to censure him. The petty intrigues of the Pavilion de Marsan were carried on surreptitiously, and sometimes even the King was ignorant of their existence, so greatly did people fear to disturb him in his repose.

Being an extreme optimist, the Count of Artois did not understand the political difficulties of the situation, and innocently imagined that if he had been allowed to act, he would have satisfied everybody. The magnificent reception given to him in Paris on the 12th of April, 1814, had dazed him. He judged the Restoration by that first day, just as some people judge of a marriage by the honeymoon. When he entered the Tuileries he was in an ecstasy. Everything filled him with joy; everything ravished him. "Would you believe," said he to Count Beugnot, "that I heard a hundred times at Versailles that there was not elbow-room at the Tuileries, that it consisted of garrets and holes, and behold! the rooms are commodious and magnificent!" He was so happy that he thought everybody else must be happy too. The miseries of exile had not weakened his bent for seeing everything in a rose-colored light. He was a man perpetually under illusions. When he left Versailles, in 1789, he imagined that he was to return within three months. At the outset of the Restoration he was convinced that the Revolution had forever disappeared, and that France and the Bourbons were to be indissolubly in accord. Heedlessly prodigal of fair words and promises, carrying courtesy to the point of exaggeration, affable even to the extent of making himself commonplace, a man of the world rather than a prince, he had the gift of pleasing, and the liberals themselves pardoned his retrograde opinions because of his kindly deportment. Superficial and not well educated, he was not without some intelligence, and, notwithstanding his great piety, his worldly conversation pleased the ladies more than the learned quotations and harmonious periods of his brother. Before all, he was a courtier, a man of the salons. He was affable to his acquaintances, good to his sons, affectionate to his niece and daughter-in-law, the Duchess of Angoulême, and had the art of consoling with a smile the poor *émigrés* who returned to their provinces without having been able to obtain anything from the King and his ministers, and he enjoyed real popularity among the ultra-royalists by reason of his disposition, his manners, and his courteous language.

The household of Monsieur was composed of men

who were faithful personal attendants and sincere admirers of his political ideas. His chief equerry was Count Armand de Polignac; his first gentlemen of the bedchamber were the Duke of Maillé and the Duke of Fitz James; and his first almoner, the Abbé de Latil. By his conversation this virtuous ecclesiastic recalled to him touching and mournful memories; for the Prince, who, at the end of the old régime, had led a very idle and dissolute life, became a pious and exemplary Christian during the emigration. The death of his well-beloved, the beautiful and poetic Countess of Polastron, had wrought this change as by miracle. In her curious and still unpublished memoirs the Duchess of Gontaut, who was a relative of Mme. de Plastron, describes the last moments of that clever and affectionate woman: "The doors of the salon were open; Monsieur did not venture to enter; I was with her, I held her hand, she was trembling. She saw Monsieur, who was about to spring to her side. 'Don't come in!' said the Abbé de Latil in a loud voice. Monsieur did not dare to cross the threshold. His agitation increased. She raised her hands, and said: 'A boon, monseigneur, a boon! Be God's, all God's!' He fell on his knees and exclaimed, 'God, I swear it!' She said again: 'All God's!' Her head sank on my shoulder. This last word was her latest sigh; she had passed away. Monsieur raised his arms toward heaven and uttered a dreadful cry. The door was then closed."

From that hour the worldly man disappeared and gave place to the man of piety. The Prince never failed in the promise made at that deathbed and sealed with a vow. Thereafter, he who had been so fond of women led a life of the utmost propriety, and thought chiefly of his salvation. As Lamartine says: "The cause, the efficacy, and the enduring nature of the change in his life showed that he possessed a power of loving and a strength of resolve which no one had ever suspected under his habitual weakness and inconstancy. It proved that had he been better advised by those who surrounded him, he might have displayed political heroism as well as the heroism of love and piety." Some indulgence should be granted to the memory of the brother of Louis XVI. and Louis XVIII., for his faults were those of the head, and not those of the heart. Even when he was the victim of self-deception in regard to politics, he thought he was acting for the best. The criticisms that he made do not prove jealousy, but genuine conviction and unswerving faith in the theory of throne and altar. His mistakes will be pardoned because of the goodness of his heart and his sincerity.

X

THE DUKES OF ANGOULÊME AND OF BERRY

THE King's two nephews, the Duke of Angoulême and the Duke of Berry, one born at Versailles on the 5th of August, 1775, and the other on the 24th of January, 1778, were, respectively, thirty-eight and thirty-six years old at the advent of the Restoration. Unlike their father in personal appearance and disposition, they had neither his elegance, nor his affability, nor his charm. The Count of Artois looked the *grand seigneur* as much as his sons comported themselves like plebeians. At first sight no one would have said that they belonged to two of the most illustrious families in the world, — the houses of Savoy and Bourbon. Yet they had traits that were serious and worthy of their line, — rectitude, honesty, and courage. They were not men of courts, but men of heart.

The Duke of Angoulême was not at Paris during the first days of the Restoration. He did not arrive till the 27th of May, 1814, and came from the south of France, where he had been the first to raise the white flag. A brilliant reception was given to him. The Duchess of Angoulême, escorted by the Duke of

Berry wearing the uniform of the chasseurs, and by a large staff composed of French marshals, lieutenant-generals, major-generals, and other high officers, went as far as the Grand Montrouge to meet him. The national guard, both infantry and cavalry, several detachments of troops of the line, and gendarmes went to the barrier of the Maine. These troops were preceded far beyond the barrier by an immense number of Parisians, on foot, on horses, and in carriages, which lined both sides of the road. The boulevards, the public squares, the quays which the Prince must pass, were equally crowded with a sympathetic multitude. When the carriages of the Duke and the Duchess met, husband and wife seemed delighted to see each other again. They alighted and conversed together for a few minutes. They then proceeded to the Tuileries, the Prince on horseback, and the Princess in her carriage. In the words of the *Moniteur:* "It touched the people to see the auspicious change in the face of the Duchess, the happiness and satisfaction wrought by the whole scene. His Highness responded with remarkable affability to the cheers which, in consequence, became still more enthusiastic." When the barrier was reached, the Prince received the congratulations of the prefect of the Seine. Then, preceded by the members of the municipal corps in state carriages, and accompanied by the Duke of Berry and the entire staff, he traversed the new boulevards, the rue de Sèvres, and the rue du Bac, and arrived at the château of the

Tuileries, through the great gate of the Palais-Royal. The *Moniteur*, ever enthusiastic, adds: "All the homage and devotion that the inhabitants of the capital had rendered to the King and to the princes of his house when they came within the walls, were renewed with the same enthusiasm and the same unanimity during the entry of the Duke of Angoulême. This Prince, who, in our southern provinces, had so often witnessed the enthusiasm inspired by his presence, could not but think that he was still surrounded by that same quality of Frenchmen who can express their feelings only by the liveliest sort of excitement. The speech and the animated accent of Bordeaux and Toulouse reappeared in Paris to honor and welcome him."

At court the Duke of Angoulême was but a moderate success. He had neither the good qualities nor the faults that please courtiers. His household was made up of members of the nobility. Count de Damas-Crux was his first gentleman of the bedchamber; the Duke of Guiche, his chief equerry; and Baron de Damas, Count Melchoir de Polignac, and Count Louis de Saint-Priest were his gentlemen-in-waiting. But this was not the society he preferred. As Baron Louis de Viel-Castel says: "He had no predilection for courtiers, and more than once he even let them see that their society was not very agreeable to him. This aversion, strange in a man in his position, may have been due to his natural clumsiness; he was ill at ease in refined and polished society, which, though it is lavish of respectful and devoted homage to princes, requires from them consideration and respect in return. Whatever may have been the cause of such conduct, it might have resulted, and later on it did result, in making the Duke of Angoulême popular for some time, in that it brought him into closer relations with generals of the Empire and men of the new régime, who annoyed him less than the old courtiers because they more readily accommodated themselves to the inequalities of his disposition."

Notwithstanding his natural vivacity, the Duke of Angoulême was an admirable husband. Full of respect for his wife, to whom he had been married since the 10th of June, 1799, and whose barrenness he lamented without even complaining of it, he was always faithful to her. The wedded pair, perfectly at one in thought and feeling, entertained for each other an affection based on the highest esteem. The Duke of Angoulême was a pious man without being "clerical." As regards political matters, he was favorable to a just and wise liberalism. Sincerely devoted to Louis XVIII., with whom during the exile he had lived much more than with his father, he held absolute obedience to the King to be the first duty of a prince.

The Duke of Berry did not lead so regular a life as his brother. He was extremely fond of pleasure. He had had mistresses in London. At Paris he was dissipated. His capricious and violent temperament could not endure quietude. His conversation was more interesting than that of his brother. When he chose to take the trouble, he talked agreeably, and he was by no means devoid of a certain sort of wit. Naturalness and connectedness are shown in his correspondence. He had artistic tastes, was fond of music, and understood painting. He had a fund of loyalty, generosity, and kindliness, but the intemperance of his language, his rudeness, his vehemence, and his fits of rage made him many enemies.

At great ceremonies, when he donned a white satin costume embroidered with gold, the Duke of Berry, with his big neck and his portly figure, looked awkward and constrained. But uniform did not become him badly, and he had a martial air. He had greatly distinguished himself in the army of Condé by his rash valor. Interested in military matters rather than in politics, he affected to prefer barracks to salons, and a trooper to a courtier. When he held a review he had a mania for imitating the rude behavior and the familiar language of the Emperor Napoleon. He retained his affection for the noblemen who had shared his exile. His first gentleman of the bedchamber was Count de la Ferronnays; his chief equerry, Count de Nantouillet; his commander of the horse, Chevalier de Ségur; his gentlemen-in-waiting, Count de Mesnard and Count de Clermont-Lodève; but he was still better pleased to be in the company of the young officers who had shone in the court of Napoleon.

"The Duke of Angoulême," says Marshal Marmont, "seemed lacking in grace and intelligence. The Duke of Berry appeared to be greatly his superior. The latter possessed nobility, gaiety, and a liking for pleasure and the fine arts. The young general officers who had been on the Emperor's staff; the courtiers who had carried the court spirit into the army — a spirit a thousand times more dangerous and shocking on the field of war, where truth, frankness, and devotion should alone prevail, — these military gentlemen, I say, who had already secured favors without sharing in dangers, thought that there was still good quarry to be got out of the new state of affairs. So they followed and flocked around the Duke of Berry, who was at first much flattered by their attention. But it was not long before the Prince's habitual rudeness, and his mania for aping Napoleon in his blunders and defects, which nothing in the Prince could justify or excuse, together with the signs which shortly seemed to show how little solidity there was in the Restoration, chilled their ardor for the new master of their choice."

Yet the princes had many followers, in spite of their imperfections. As the Duchess of Abrantès observes: "The Duke of Berry was, they said, the worthy descendant of Henri IV. Poor Henri IV. was ever present to serve as a criterion. The distribution of qualities was made according to character. The Duke of Angoulême descended from Saint Louis because he was a godly man; the Duke of Berry descended from Henri IV. because he had worldly tastes; and the Count of Artois from Francis I. because twenty years previously he had been what was called a *vert-galant*."

As the health of Louis XVIII. and the duties which required his presence at the seat of government would not permit him to visit the different portions of France, it was thought needful to send the princes there. In July and August, the Duke of Angoulême went through the west, the Count of Artois through the east, and, in September and October, the Duke of Berry went northward. Of the three princes, the Duke of Angoulême produced the most favorable impression. Sensible people were won by his moderation and the fact that he displayed no aristocratic prejudices. He showed himself prudent and conciliating everywhere. The ultra-royalists found him a little lukewarm. In his book, *Vendée Militaire*, M. Crétineau-Joly says, on the road from Cholet to Montagne, all that were left of the insurrectionists joined in welcoming the Prince with enthusiasm. But these warlike agriculturists were told that the King's nephew did not wish to see them under arms. They piled their weapons at the roadside, and then stepped back five paces. Surrounded by squadrons of cavalry, the Duke of Angoulême passed these worthy royalists without his presence being indicated by anything save a cloud of dust. As they walked back to their cottages as sadly as if they were returning from a funeral, the villagers said to each other: "Poor Prince! He has been forbidden to say that he loves and esteems us."

On his part, the Duke of Berry wrote as follows to M. Louis de La Rochejaquelein on the 21st of May: "The love of the Vendéans for the King, which they have retained owing to you, gives me good reason to hope that the species of ferment that seems to exist in this province will not have any unpleasant consequences. You will give the brave and good inhabitants of Poitou to understand that zeal too ardent and ill-considered often occasions as much trouble as insubordination. The way in which they demand the repudiation of the civil authorities is unseemly and even seditious. These outcries against the prefects and the gendarmes have a revolutionary tone, and can be the result only of inconsiderate zeal, or rather the outcome of the intrigues of secret enemies of the King and the public good."

If the Duke of Angoulême was unsatisfactory to the royalists of the west, the Duke of Berry did not produce a pleasant effect on the old Bonapartists of the north. It is said that at Lille, during a review, an officer stepped from the ranks and asked for the cross of Saint Louis. "What have you done to deserve it?" asked the Prince. "I have served for thirty years in the French army." "Thirty years of brigandage!" exclaimed the Duke of Berry, turning his back on the officer. It is added that on the next day the Duke wished to make amends for his imprudent speech, but it had gone the rounds and produced its effect. The soldiers complained that the princes distributed the cross of the Legion of Honor during their tour so lavishly as to dishonor it. They indignantly repeated to each other that when at a ball, at the prefecture of Lille, a woman who danced with the Duke of Berry asked for her husband that cross for which so many brave men had paid with their blood, the Prince, without further inquiry, gave himself the pleasure of bestowing it on the man.

In spite of his irregularities, the Duke of Berry possessed noble qualities. His youthful escapades did not prevent him from preserving his respect for religion, and, although he was not pious like his father and brother, he remained true to the faith of his ancestors. He loved France sincerely and wished to see her great and glorious. He was regarded as the hope of the Bourbons, and people looked forward with impatience to the time when he should marry and perpetuate his line. His was an energetic and intrepid nature, and the wretch Louvel well knew, when he smote the Duke, that his knife was hewing down the most vigorous branch of the royal tree. All the faults of the Duke of Berry were expiated by his sublime death. No hero, no Christian, could have more courage when, in presence of the last agony, he gathered all the strength that was left him to pardon his murderer, and exclaim: "Have mercy, have mercy on the man!"

XI

MADAME

AT the outset of the Restoration, the royal family, properly speaking, was composed of only five persons, four of whom were men, — the King; the Count of Artois; his elder son, the Duke of Angoulême; and his younger son, the Duke of Berry. There was but one woman, the Duchess of Angoulême (the members of the Orleans and Condé families bore the title of princes and princesses of the blood, but were not members of the royal family). Doubly niece of the King, — by blood as the daughter of Louis XVI., and by alliance as the wife of the Duke of Angoulême, — the Duchess was called Madame during the reign of Louis XVIII., while, when Charles X. was King, she was styled Madame la Dauphine, and the abbreviation Madame served to designate the Duchess of Berry.

Born at Versailles on the 19th of December, 1778, the Duchess of Angoulême was thirty-five years old at the commencement of the Restoration. In a preceding study we have endeavored accurately to depict her escape from the Temple after more than three years of captivity, on the 19th of December,

1795, the very day on which she became seventeen years old. She was then a charming young girl of truly ideal beauty. Since then she had greatly changed. Her voice had grown somewhat coarse, and her face somewhat grave. Her features had become accentuated. The valiant woman of the Scriptures had succeeded to the type of the tender and timid maiden.

The freshness of youth having departed, Louis XVI.'s daughter lost charm, but majesty still was hers. Her presence at Paris produced at once universal sympathy and veneration. In every class of society, from the greatest personage to the humblest laborer, all recognized the features of the orphan of the Temple. It may be said of this elect lady that, even while living, she became legendary. In looking upon her, every one, no matter what might be his party, was touched. The only fear was that her austerity might prevent her from attending fêtes and appearing at theatres; and therefore the public was delighted when it learned that she would be present with the King and princes when gala pieces were played at the royal theatres.

"The infirmities of Louis XVIII.," says Marshal Marmont, "made it difficult for him to move. On this account a large box, easy of access, and in which he could be comfortable, was arranged for him at every place of entertainment. This contrivance and the brilliancy of the preparations for his appearance made veritable fêtes of the performances.

The attendance was very large. The King's box was placed at the centre of the first tier, was carefully ornamented, and was large enough to accommodate the whole royal family. The King, Madame the Duchess of Angoulême, and the princes commonly came in a single coach in which there was ample room for five persons."

The performance given at the Opera on the 17th of May, 1814, was, so to speak, the apotheosis of the daughter of Louis XVI. and Marie Antoinette. The play was *Œdipe à Colone* in which the principal female character is Antigone. On seeing Ducis again, the King quoted the following four lines from the tragic poet: —

> "Yes, thou through every coming age shalt prove
> The perfect symbol of true filial love;
> Long as unhappy fathers shall remain,
> Thy name shall solace them in every pain."

And the King added: "You can certainly divine who is the Antigone to whom I have often quoted those verses. They are worthy of her; I can make no finer encomium upon her." "The New Antigone" came to be the sobriquet of Louis XVIII.'s niece, and the drama played at the Opera gave rise to many allusions to the devotion and filial affection of the Princess.

All the boxes were secured three weeks in advance. Only tickets for the parterre and gallery were to be had, and tickets and other cards giving admission only to the corridors were sold for fabulous prices at the door. At five o'clock a great multitude thronged to the theatre, although it was known that only a few seats could be bought. Hardly a twentieth part of the crowd could gain admittance. The Duchess of Abrantès, who was present at this representation, afterward said: "The hall itself was an extraordinary spectacle: the women wore no diamonds and were all dressed in white. Their only ornaments were plumes, sprigs of lily, and bunches and garlands of white lilac. All the bouquets were white; the hall was enchanting, adorned as it was with flowers and women. There was about it an elegance for which I could not at first account, and which I afterwards explained by that gracious hue, white, and the perfume of the budding year which penetrated everywhere."

Just as the curtain rose, the King, followed by his family, appeared in his box, and was greeted with acclamations and a flourish of trumpets. The play abounded with allusions, for which the public waited impatiently, and which they seized upon with enthusiasm. This was the case, for example, with these lines: —

> "Thou august victim of mischance and woe,
>   End the regrets within thy heart that burn,
> The soul that naught but innocence doth know
>   To brave the face of Fortune still should learn.
> Possess thy soul in peace, the while we prove
>   By that most jealous care we'll show for thee
> That thou alone shalt be our liege and love, —
>   Our zealous care, that of Antigone."

At the name of Antigone, the King, somewhat anticipating the emotion of the spectators, and turning to his niece, who sat beside him, for a long time mingled his plaudits with those of the public. Cries of "Long live the King! Long live Madame the Duchess of Angoulême!" resounded through the hall. The beautiful air which begins thus: —

"On me she lavished her tenderness and care"

was tumultuously encored.

During the entr'acte the orchestra played the tune "Vive Henri IV.!" which was sung in chorus by the whole assembly. The spectacle ended with a new ballet by Gardel, in which the two fashionable dancers, Mademoiselle Bigottini and Mademoiselle Clotilde, appeared, always to the air of "Vive Henri IV.!" The re-birth of the lily, and the return of peace, were represented in a clever allegory, in which the favorite dances of the various nations of Europe were introduced.

"This representation," said the Duchess of Abrantès, "was more serviceable than might have been expected. It had been reported that Madame would not attend the theatre, and the announcement of such a rupture with the fashionable world had done her much harm. Madame the Duchess of Angoulême was gracious, though melancholy, on that day, and this melancholy impressed on one who sacrificed on the altar of the living God every resentment and every remembrance of affront, was a sentiment at least permissible in a woman who mourned for those whom she had lost by a death more frightful than death itself."

In spite of the ovations she received, the daughter of Louis XVI. was profoundly sad at heart, and neither flatteries nor so-called pleasures could dispel her grief. She attended fêtes and spectacles only from a sense of duty. Her return to the Tuileries, far from assuaging her sorrows, had brought them more vividly before her. Upon entering this château, the Count of Artois and Louis XVIII. were in a triumphant mood, and filled with thoughts of grandeur and satisfied ambition. Intoxicated with happiness, the Count of Artois went into ecstasies over the luxuriousness of the palace, adorned and embellished by Napoleon. On seeing the walls of which he had so often thought during the long hours of his exile, the King congratulated himself upon the success of his enterprises. On the contrary, the daughter of the martyred King and Queen seemed to herself to be surrounded by mournful phantoms and scenes. When she looked upon the court of the Carrousel, she dreamed of the 10th of August and the massacre of the Swiss. On the balcony of the Hall of Marshals overlooking the garden she dreaded to look before her, for in the distance appeared the square of the crime, that unhappy square which, all through the Restoration, she refused to cross. When she paced the large apartments, she passed the spot where pikemen placed the red cap on the heads of the King and the Dauphin. The chambers of her father, her mother, and her brother were to her so many sanctuaries which she hardly dared to enter. She lodged in the Pavilion of Flora, where her aunt, Madame Elisabeth, resided from the 6th of October, 1789, to the 10th of August, 1792. Thoughts of this saint constantly occupied her mind. In reading the correspondence of Madame Elisabeth, — those really admirable letters in which much religion blends with so much resolution, — one perceives that the tastes, the ideas, the sentiments, and the principles of the Duchess of Angoulême were on every subject entirely the same as those of her aunt. Never was pupil better fashioned in the image of her instructress. The lessons that the sister of Louis XVI. had given to the young girl in the dungeon of the Temple were never forgotten by the woman at the Tuileries. Upon the occurrence of any political event, the Duchess of Angoulême said to herself: How would this be looked upon by my aunt Elisabeth? And at once a secret voice answered the question thus put.

It is easily understood that a woman habituated to thoughts so grave and meditations so austere would have no inclination for the distractions, trivialities, meannesses and intrigues of the court. The proceedings of the government, besides, displeased her in many respects. Doubtless she did not deem a reconstitution of the old régime possible. Her husband, with whom she lived in perfect community of ideas, was looked upon almost as a liberal. He encouraged neither the utopian opinions of the ultra-Catholics nor the exaggerated zeal of the ultra-royalists. Like him, she held the red and the white Terror in equal aversion. She did full justice to the heroic qualities of the lieutenants of Napoleon, and her courtesy to them was never less than perfect. But she had a horror of treason, apostasy, recantation, and baseness. She did not feel at home at the Tuileries, since she saw about the King men who, in her opinion, were out of place there. For example, she could not admit that the man who had been Bonaparte's Minister of Foreign Affairs when the Duke of Enghien was assassinated, and who had given a ball to the diplomatic corps three days after the murder, ought to be Louis XVIII.'s Minister of Foreign Affairs. It pained her to see that the Restoration, so long and ardently desired by the royalists, was chiefly beneficial to men who were once enemies of the throne and altar.

The talk at court seemed to her objectless, superficial, and little in keeping with the unhappy state of affairs. She could have wished for a graver, a more moral, and a more religious society. Preaching by example, she afforded only edification by her piety as well as by her charity, and she liked nobody whose morals were not absolutely irreproachable. The Bishop of Nancy was her first almoner: his assistants were the Abbé Grimaldi and the Abbé de

Vichy; her chaplain was the Abbé Cacqueray; her lady-in-waiting, the Duchess of Sérent; her lady-in-waiting in reversion, the Countess of Damas; and her tiring-woman, the Countess of Choisy. As ladies-in-attendance, she had the Countess of Béarn, the Countess of Gontaut-Biron, Marchioness de Saint-Maure, Viscountess de Vaudreuil, the Countess of Goyon, and Marchioness de Rougé. Her gentleman-in-waiting was Viscount de Montmorency; her chief equerry, Viscount d'Agoult; and her commander of the horse, Count de Lastours. She confided in the few persons whom she honored with her special esteem, but the high-flown and almost idolatrous flattery of which too zealous courtiers sought to make her the object seemed intolerable to her. She understood the human heart thoroughly and recognized at once what was false and selfish in the protestations of devotion that were lavished upon her. Past apostasies gave her a presentiment of those which were to come. What made her little pleasing to the courtiers was that, notwithstanding her civility, they saw perfectly well that she was not the dupe of their flattery. Deeply sincere and always simple-hearted, she despised factitious and theatrical emotions. As M. Louis de Viel-Castel remarks: "She had passed through realities too terrible to allow her to acquire a taste for those romantic encomiums which her misfortunes inspired in the poets and orators of her time."

In character as in physique she resembled her

father much more than her mother. She had neither the irresistible magnetism nor the surpassing elegance of Marie Antoinette. She felt a strong antipathy against a fashionable life and a frivolous society like that of the Petit-Trianon. Her tastes were those of a nun rather than a princess. M. de Vaulabelle said of her: "Her character was masculine and firm, and her courage, submitted to the harshest trials, was always equal to the situation. A devoted relative, a steadfast and trusty friend, and endowed with all the virtues that go to make up an honored wife, she possessed much benevolence and goodness of heart, whatever has been said to the contrary. Unfortunately, her awkward bearing and her rough and heavy voice rendered all her movements and her slightest expressions disagreeable; every word she uttered gave a galling tone of severity to her voice. It was only the habitual sombreness which a long life of sorrow had impressed on her face that gave it, in the eyes of the multitude, an expression of haughtiness and disdain."

Frivolous people would have liked to see her joyous, gay, and smiling when the very utmost that she could do was to repress the tears that rose to her eyes and keep down the sobs that oppressed her breast. While everybody about her forgot, the daughter of Louis XVI. remembered. Grave, self-collected, and austere, she watched over the memories hidden in the deepest recesses of her heart. To lay her afflictions before the eyes of courtiers seemed to her a profanation. To her, silence was a species of modesty. The gushings and trickeries of sentiment were repugnant to her. Many persons would have liked to hear her tell the story of the days she had passed in the Temple as an actress declaims her part. She never gratified their wish. To God alone she told her sorrows. One of her contemporaries, M. Fiévée exclaimed: "Can she regard the judgment of men or attach the least value to it? Has not this intrepid soul been led to look on God alone as its judge? It is said she is not gay, is not confident, has forgotten nothing; upon returning from exile her manners recall the country where she found the hospitality which was refused her by her own. Ah! if she were light-minded, if she were imprudent, if in her eyes there were no distinction between crime and virtue, between treachery and fidelity; if she were not religious; if her experiences had not profoundly affected her; if, before she knew you, she had, following a natural bent, sacrificed to the frivolities that to you seem so important, you would find her more worthy of your love and respect, and would rely upon her more, simply because her whole being would be contrary to the moral laws of Providence."

Although the Duchess of Angoulême was but little pleasing to the courtiers, she made a strong impression on the masses whenever she appeared in public. On the 12th of June, 1814, which was the day of Corpus Christi, she attracted universal attention when she appeared on the balcony of the Hall of the Marshals. On that day, in all the parishes of the capital, great crowds of the faithful joined the priests in the procession of the Blessed Sacrament. The inhabitants adorned the fronts of their houses with tapestries, hangings, and decorations in which religious emblems were intermingled with those of monarchy; for the partisans of the throne and altar did not sunder God and king. National guards, troops of the line, and Paris guards, preceded and closed the procession. Altars glittering with gold and covered with flowers stood at various places. While the processions were entering the churches, an immense mass of people was at the château of the Tuileries, awaiting in the garden the moment when the King and his family should come from Mass and appear on the balcony. When the people caught sight of the Duchess of Angoulême, they were enthusiastic. They said to themselves: "This is a fête after her own heart."

In June, the Princess was forced by the state of her health to take the waters at Vichy, and her journey to that place was a continuous ovation. We quote from the *Moniteur* passages which show the feeling of the day very well.

"Vichy, June 29. — Madame, the Duchess of Angoulême, has arrived and been warmly welcomed by the local authorities and the multitude that gathered to see her pass by. She received everybody with infinite grace and kindliness and drew all hearts to her. She is very careful to hurt no one's feelings."

"July 15. — The Duchess of Angoulême continues to make salutary use of the waters of this place. Her health has singularly improved. Her Royal Highness walks out frequently and makes excursions into the neighboring rural districts, during which her ready charity and great beneficence secure for her the acknowledgment of the local authorities and the blessings of the unfortunate."

"July 19. — It is hoped that the waters of Vichy will respond to the prayers of all the French people, who implore Heaven for the complete restoration of their tutelary angel. Since the arrival of Her Royal Highness, Vichy has assumed the appearance of a populous city. Every day witnesses the arrival of numerous deputations, not only from the department of Allier, but from all departments. From noon till one o'clock, which is the hour at which Madame receives the respects that they are so anxious to pay her, she frequently sees fifty or sixty persons who lay at her feet the vows and the homage of the cities and communes which they represent. Sometimes the spokesmen are overcome by emotion. One of them, in despair of being able to say a word, fell sobbing at the Princess's feet and begged pardon for being unable to deliver his address. Bidding him rise, Madame said in a voice that showed how greatly she was touched: 'Why do you regret that you cannot speak to me? What better could you say?'

Every word of Madame's bears the impress of penetrating insight and of that close perception of things which causes them to appear in their true light."

On the 19th of July, the guard of honor from Moulins came to Vichy, and thereafter it constantly accompanied Madame to divine service and when she went out for an airing. Among the deputations, that from the inhabitants of the mountains, the members of which were dressed entirely in white, attracted special attention. "They," adds the *Moniteur*, "addressed Madame with so true and touching a feeling that they left the presence bathed in tears and causing everybody to share their emotion. As they withdrew they pressed to their hearts the decoration of the fleur-de-lis which Her Royal Highness had kindly given them."

Let us read further the account sent by the correspondent of the *Moniteur*: —

"Vichy, August 3, 1814. — Madame, the Duchess of Angoulême, left this morning, after having filled with joy and happiness all who have seen and had access to her. Wherever she goes, she excites the same feelings. In her the angel of the reconciliation of past and present wins admiration. Her journey is a triumphal progress."

The Princess goes from Vichy to Lyons. There is a fête champêtre in even the rural districts through which she passes. She seems to take her way only over hills of verdure and a carpet of flowers. Lyons awaits her with impatience. The city wishes to give her a fête; commerce claims the same honor; the national guard aspires to take the lead in all; the citizens of the Bellecour quarter demand the preference. In zeal and enthusiasm there is common emulation. On Saturday, the 6th of August, the daughter of Louis XVI. enters the walls of Lyons. Triumphal arches have been erected along her way. A troop of young girls, dressed all in white, presents her with flowers. Marshal Augereau, Duke of Castiglione, — Augereau, once an ardent republican, Augereau, the man of the 18th Fructidor, — has gone past Écully to meet her. At the faubourg of Vaise, at the Pyramid, another triumphal arch appears. In a semicircle is an amphitheatre adorned with ladies elegantly dressed. The streets, the bridges, the public squares, the quays along which the Princess is to pass, have been decorated with white draperies and festoons of grasses. She advances slowly in an open carriage drawn by six white horses, and salutes the crowd affably and with emotion. On the Pont de Change she sees an Ionic temple bearing this inscription: "Love to Madame." As she passes the temple, the doors are flung open and she sees the flame on the tripods. The porters of the temple, dressed as at the famous siege of Lyons, pay their respects to the Princess. At nine o'clock in the evening, there are fine fireworks on the Pont du Bois, before the Archbishop's palace. Immediately afterwards the city is illuminated as if by magic.

On the 7th of August, the Princess attends solemn

Mass in the primatical church of Saint-Jean. On the same day, at the desire of the city, she drives along the Saône as far as the isle Barbe. She goes in a coach to the harbor of Serin, passing the square Louis-le-Grand. In the middle of this square an open octagonal temple, consecrated to the Bourbon family, has been constructed on the spot where the statue of Louis XIV. once stood. Medallions of Saint Louis, Henri IV., Louis XIII., Louis XIV., Louis XV., Louis XVI., Louis XVII., and Louis XVIII. adorned the various sides of the temple. In the centre of this sanctuary of royalty appears an altar covered with an offering of flowers. At the Hôtel de Ville, on the great balcony of the side overlooking the square des Terreaux, is a design representing the city of Lyons, in the form of a woman whose head is adorned with a mural crown, and who holds in her hands a portrait of Louis XVIII. These lines from Delille's poem called *Pitié* are on the pedestal: —

> "In exile drear, and in adversity,
> Still wast thou here to my fidelity."

When the harbor of Serin is reached, the Duchess of Angoulême enters a boat adorned with the city arms, and accompanied by two other boats beautifully decorated, and in which are the authorities and the persons invited to take part in the procession. A vessel with an orchestra on board follows the flotilla. The Saône is hidden in the great number of gondolas. The weather is magnificent. When they land at the isle Barbe, the mayor, in his oration, speaks of four epochs memorable on the island: it was the refuge of early Christians in the days of persecution; there Charlemagne established the first library; Pius VII. visited the place; and now the daughter of the martyred King honored it with her presence.

When they re-embark they hear the cry: "Farewell, Madame!" The sun no longer shines on the hilltops. In the evening, the Princess goes to the Grand Theatre of Lyons, where she sees a play composed for the occasion and entitled *Fête du Bonheur*. The public seize with transport upon the allusions in it. All the houses are illuminated as on the foregoing evening.

On Monday, the 8th of August, Madame was at the plain of Brotteaux to see a review of the horse and foot national guards, the 13th dragoons and the 24th of the line. At the entrance to the bridge on the city side was a verdure-clad triumphal arch bearing warlike emblems. At the summit was this inscription: "The Road to the Field of Honor." A shield surrounded with military trophies bore this device: "Our Blood has flowed for the King." On another shield was this second device: "The Siege sustained for sixty-three days in the year 1793." The Princess drove through the lines in the midst of *vivas;* then the troops defiled before her. After the review Marshal

Augereau invited her to breakfast. "It is not on the fine appearance of the troops that I wish to congratulate you," said she to the marshal. "It is on the spirit that animates them. I shall tell it all to the King, but I fear he will be jealous of the pleasure I have had."

Upon her return, the Duchess of Angoulême found the streets and quays ornamented with white draperies and garlands of flowers. In the evening she attended the fête of Commerce and Arts which was given in her honor at the palace of Saint-Pierre. After the concert, she went to see the exhibition of silk stuffs that had been mounted for her in one of the rooms of this palace. The workmen wrought under her eyes a brocaded tissue upon which, when it was shown, she recognized her own features most faithfully reproduced. Afterwards she witnessed the ball that followed the concert, and, before withdrawing, she descended to the garden, where she moved about amid general applause. People had come to Lyons for twenty leagues about, to join in the magnificent rejoicings. Despite her experience of human vicissitudes, the orphan of the Temple never suspected that, a few months subsequently, she would be forced to begin once more her life of exile. On the 13th of August she set out for Paris without having for an instant been intoxicated by the odor of the incense which during the whole of her trip had been burned before her.

At the time when the Duchess of Angoulême was

taking the waters at Vichy, another princess, whose name was on every lip a few weeks before, and about whom no one was concerned, was taking the waters of the Aix-en-Savoie. It was said in the *Journal des Débats:* " Aix-les-Bains, July 18 (Mont Blanc).— The concourse of strangers at the waters of the Aix is very considerable. The Archduchess Marie Louise arrived yesterday, the 17th. Since many apartments had been reserved for Her Highness, it was supposed that she would have a large following. For a long time we have had no weather so fine and suitable for bathing." Savoy was as yet a part of France, and the little town of Aix-les-Bains was comprised in the French department of Mont Blanc, whose chief city was Chambéry. Four months previously, Marie Louise had been its ruler. She went there now merely as a private person, save that her domestics still wore the imperial livery. To understand the fact that she was authorized to live in this way under the reign of the Bourbons and in her old Empire, it must be considered how little she was devoted to her husband. She was, besides, entirely forgotten. It was to the Duchess of Angoulême that the general attention of France was then directed.

Beyond question there was some exaggeration in the encomiums which at that time were lavished in profusion on the daughter of Louis XVI. Those dithyrambs showed marks of the declamatory tone which was as fashionable under the Restoration as it had been under the Empire. But the virtuous Princess really deserved distinguished praise, for in the highest degree she was precisely what Marie Louise was no longer, — a woman devoted to duty. Louis XVIII. often sought the advice of his niece. Napoleon said of her, that she was the only man in her family. In truth, she possessed great elevation of mind, great generosity of heart, and a most courageous character.

Certainly the Duchess of Angoulême may have deceived herself, but the policy which she would have caused to prevail would under all circumstances have been the policy of virtue and honor. She had the energy of her grandmother, Maria Theresa, that powerful-minded woman to whom the Hungarians cried out: *Moriamur pro rege nostro*. Taught in the school of adversity, she understood better than anybody else how to guard herself against the snares of flattery. In the darkest of their days, Louis XVIII. and the Count of Artois were always surrounded by courtiers. Even in exile they lived the life of courts, in palaces with chamberlains, favorites, and office-seekers. The Duchess of Angoulême, on the other hand, having known prison life, and been submitted to the rigor and loneliness of prison rule, had learned how very hard are adversity and captivity. No woman of the people had been more harshly treated, or had suffered more cruelly. That experience gave her her power.

In studying the virile character of this woman, one is sometimes forced to regret, on her account, that France should have been governed according to the Salic law. Perhaps the orphan of the Temple would have made a better sovereign than either of her uncles. It is said that she strongly disliked the defects of the Restoration, and was opposed to the ordinances that caused the downfall of Charles X. However that may be, the granddaughter of Maria Theresa possessed qualities that fitted her to be a ruler. Her conduct at Bordeaux during the Hundred Days showed her presence of mind and the vigor of her character. She was a bold horsewoman, and could have reviewed troops better than Louis XVIII. There was not a single French soldier who would not have respected a sovereign possessing the virtues and the decision of character that marked the daughter of Louis XVI. There was no necessity that she, who already bore the crown of sorrow and misfortune, should be crowned at the cathedral at Rheims. If, instead of being a princess without influence, she had been the real queen of France, perhaps Napoleon would have hesitated to return from the island of Elba.

XII

THE ORLEANS FAMILY

THE Duke of Orleans had not yet come to Paris when Louis XVIII. made his triumphal entry. Instead of following the example of the Count of Artois and the Duke of Angoulême, who returned to France before the abdication of the Emperor, he remained at Palermo with his family under the protection of his father-in-law, King Ferdinand IV., awaiting events. On the 23d of April, 1814, the news of the Restoration reached Sicily by the English vessel *Aboukir*. The Duke of Orleans, abruptly entering his wife's room, exclaimed: "Bonaparte's day is over, Louis XVIII. is re-established on the throne, and I am about to set out in an English vessel that has been sent to carry me back to France." Husband and wife threw themselves into each other's arms. The Duke then went to the Colli palace, where his father-in-law, the King of the Two Sicilies, could not restrain himself for joy. "Faccia in terra, per ringraziare Dio!" cried the chief of the house of the Neapolitan Bourbons, prostrating himself to render thanks to God.

Nevertheless, the Duke of Orleans was, perhaps, not certain as to the reception that Louis XVIII. might give him. He desired, however, personally to see how the land lay and to go to Paris without his family, intending to return to Palermo and fetch them, should he be satisfied with the treatment he received from Louis XVIII. On the 1st of May, 1814, which was the day of the feast of his patron, Saint Philip, he embarked at the port of Palermo on the *Aboukir*, and his Duchess, who was a very pious woman, congratulated herself upon the date of her husband's departure, which seemed to her to be a happy presage for the voyage.

The Duke of Orleans reached Paris on the evening of the 17th of May. Instead of taking immediate possession of the Palais Royal, his ancestral home, he went quietly to the hotel Grange Batelière. His first visit was to the King. On the 29th of May, the day on which the Empress Josephine died at Malmaison, the Duke went to the Tuileries, where the King, with his own hands, bestowed on him the decoration of Saint Louis. The *Journal des Débats* gives the following account of the ceremony of investiture: " The King stood with drawn sword in his hand, while the Duke knelt before His Majesty. The King gave him the accolade in the customary forms of chivalry. When His Majesty raised the Duke in order to embrace him, His Highness bowed and respectfully kissed His Majesty's hand."

The Duchess of Angoulême was well disposed toward a prince whose wife, a niece of Marie Antoinette, was her cousin-german. On the 1st of June, she visited the beautiful gardens of the Duke of Orleans at Monceaux.

The Duke, perfectly satisfied in regard to the amicable intentions of the King, installed himself at the Palais Royal. He at once became popular. The *Débats* of date June 7, 1814, contains the following: " Monseigneur, the Duke of Orleans, first prince of the blood, has occupied the Palais Royal for several days. Yesterday, while leaving the palace at noon, he was greeted with applause by a large number of people who were waiting for him at the foot of the grand staircase. His Most Serene Highness appeared gratified with this reception and saluted the public."

The Duke left Paris on the 2d of July and returned to Palermo to fetch his wife and his three children, who had all been born in that city, — the Duke of Chartres, on the 3d of September, 1810; the Princess Louise (who became Queen of the Belgians), on the 3d of April, 1812; and the Princess Marie (the future Princess of Wurtemburg), on the 12th of April, 1813. He embarked on the French man-of-war, the *Ville de Marseille*, which bore the flag of Rear-Admiral L'Hermite, and entered the roadstead of Palermo on the 14th of July. The population gave him a hearty reception from the shore. On the 27th of the same month, he set out for France with his family on the *Ville de Marseille* and set foot on French soil on the 18th of August, after a few day of quarantine. His wife, then pregnant with the child who became the Duke of Nemours, learned, during the voyage, of the death of her mother, Queen Marie Caroline, at Vienna. The Duke had with him also his sister, born on the 23d of August, 1777, who was unmarried, and was known as Madame Adélaïde. The Prince was everywhere received with great honor. The *Débats* of the 10th of September, 1814, says: —

"Lyons, Septemper 5. — Yesterday, at two o'clock in the afternoon, the Duke of Orleans, his wife, the Princess of Sicily, and Mademoiselle d'Orleans entered Lyons amid manifestations of public delight. At two o'clock to-day the Prince held a review in the plain of Brotteaux."

"Paris, September 9. — The Duke of Orleans reached Paris at eleven o'clock. His first act was to render his respectful compliments to his mother, the Dowager Princess. His Highness preceded his wife and children to see if all was ready to receive them at his palace. He returns for them to-morrow."

On the 22d of September the Duke came back to Paris with his family. M. Trognan, the biographer of Queen Amélie, says of the Princess: "She reached the Palais Royal, greatly moved to find herself at Paris once more, offering to God the tears that incessantly rose to her eyes and at the same time giving Him thanks for having brought her long voyage to an end so much desired. Moreover, she was received only with joy and confidence in the world she entered. People were still in the first emotions that came from peace succeeding long wars, and the morn of liberty following the greatest despotism. Happy in existing, the government of the Restoration had the appearance of walking forward without looking behind. Old French society, finding itself again on its feet at the Tuileries, as also in the mansions of the Faubourg Saint-Germain, did not dream of the perils its own imprudence was preparing for it. The mourning which the Duchess of Orleans wore in her heart as well as in her garments, and the demands of a pregnancy the end of which was at hand, alone prevented her from mingling from that time with what was going on at court, and in Parisian life."

Marie Amélie was born on the 26th of April, 1782, and was, at this time, thirty-two years old. She was the daughter of Ferdinand IV., King of the Two Sicilies, and Queen Marie Caroline, Archduchess of Austria, and sister of the Queen of France, Marie Antoinette. On the 25th of November, 1809, she married the Duke of Orleans, then exiled at Palermo, the marriage being a love match. An irreproachable and devoted mother, she bore a great reputation for virtue and piety. The Duchess of Angoulême, who liked only persons whose morals were pure, gave her pious cousin a specially friendly welcome. She was god-mother to the Duke of Nemours, who was born at Paris on the 5th of October, 1814. The *Journal des Débats* contains the following account of the baptism: —

"Paris, October 26, 1814. — The King and Madame the Duchess of Angoulême to-day held at the baptismal font in the chapel of the Tuileries, the Duke of Nemours, second son of Monseigneur the Duke of Orleans. The ceremony was performed by Monseigneur the Archbishop of Rheims, Grand Almoner of France, assisted by M. the Curé of the parish of Saint-Germain-l'Auxerrois. Madame the Duchess Dowager of Orleans, Monseigneur the Duke of Orleans, and the principal personages of the court were present. The Count of Blacas drew up the civil certificate."

The Duchess Dowager of Orleans had, like her daughter-in-law, a great reputation for piety. Born on the 23d of March, 1753, Louise-Marie-Adélaïde de Bourbon, daughter of the virtuous Duke of Penthièvre, sister of the unfortunate Princess de Lamballe, and widow of the Duke of Orleans (Philippe Egalité), had borne a long series of catastrophies with great fortitude. She was married at the age of sixteen and appeared to great advantage at the court of Louis XVI., which she left only when her husband became embroiled with the King and the princes. She remained in France during the most perilous epoch of the Revolution and was imprisoned at Paris in 1793. Having lived till the 9th Thermidor without anybody caring what became of her, she was placed in a private asylum, where she remained till the 12th of September, 1797. Then she was deported to Spain and did not return to Paris till the 7th of August, 1814. Her residence was in the rue Tournon, at the Nivernais mansion. In spite of the recollections attached to the memory of her husband she met with an excellent reception at court, and passed a life of tranquillity, devoted to religion and good works.

Her son, Louis Philippe, Duke of Orleans, who was born on the 6th of October, 1773, had already undergone many vicissitudes of fortune. In his early youth, in 1789, he had been led into the Revolution through the example and by the authority of his father, whose illusions he shared, and he even took a not inglorious part in the first battles of republicans in arms against foreign invasion. Subsequently condemned to exile by the government of the Terror, and already an object of hatred to all parties, he had travelled for a long time in Europe and America, where he was sometimes obliged to conceal his name and to take pupils in order to procure the necessaries of life. Misfortune had given him precocious wisdom, and when afterwards he was a refugee in Sicily he had the adroitness to secure the hand of the daughter of King Ferdinand IV., and in a delicate situation he displayed rare prudence and address. He went to see Louis XVIII. in England and retracted what he then called the political errors of his youth. He divined, too, the future, and laid his plans for the situation he desired at court in case of a restoration. So he was very well received at the Tuileries, and for some time pursued a course of conduct not displeasing to the royal family, and the way in which he did so was wholly agreeable to the liberals.

The salon of the Duchess of Orleans was very select. "Court homage," says M. Trognon, her biographer, "caused her to be sought at the Palais Royal. Only a small number of *émigrés*, faithful to their old enmity to the name she bore, were lacking. Together with the élite of old families of the kingdom, marshals, generals, and senators converted into peers of France, presented themselves to her, certain to meet with a better reception than they ever found at the Tuileries. Independently of all these people to whom the apartments of the Palais Royal were open, there was a closer and more restricted circle in which the first rank belonged to the Duchess Dowager and her sister-in-law, the Duchess of Bourbon. After these figured the few that still remained of the old familiars of the house of Orleans, to whom were added the new officers whom the Prince had attached to his person, — General Albert, Colonel Athalin, Count Camille de Sainte-Aldegonde, Viscount de Rohan-Chabot, Count Thibaut, and Baron Raoul de Montmorency. The honorary title of tutor to the young Duke of Chartres was given to Count de Grave, one of the constitutional ministers of Louis XVI. during the last days of his reign.'

Already, and in spite of the Duke's reserve, is seen the birth of what has been called Orleanism. As M. de Viel-Castel observes: "The Prince restored to the favor of Louis XVIII., and, so to speak, amnestied, remained nevertheless an object of aversion and distrust to the royalists. It was known that in renouncing the exaggerated notions of his youth, he had not abjured all thought of liberty, reform, and improvement, and was not alien to the spirit of the times. It was remembered that on several occasions the idea of raising him to power had occurred to men who were looking about for means of re-establishing the throne without causing alarm, and without endangering new interests. His somewhat bourgeois manners, his familiar and easy address, forming, as they did, a very strong contrast to the almost oriental etiquette of the Bourbon court, seemed to many people a stroke of policy to win popular favor. Louis XVIII. did not like him, perhaps because he suspected him of ambitious designs, and perhaps because he foresaw that even involuntarily and by the sheer force of circumstances he would one day become the rallying-point of the malecontents. On the other hand, the Count of Artois, who had at the same time less perspicacity and a more affectionate disposition than his brother, showed great kindness to the Duke of Orleans, who had taken occasion to render him a number of personal services during their sojourn in England."

In the words of M. Thiers, the Orleanist party

existed of itself, without any help from the Duke of Orleans, who, "well educated, bright, cautious, understanding the *émigrés* perfectly well and joking about them in the privacy of his family, was so much pleased to be in his country once more and to regain there a princely position and a large fortune, that he thought of nothing else, and never dreamed that he was giving good occasion for the hatred of the royalists, which remained as bitter against him as it had been against his father."

A proof that there was no connivance between the Prince and his partisans is that, since 1814, there had been an Orleanist party in abeyance, which, perhaps, had nothing whatever to do with the actions of its natural head. After the return of the Bourbons, the instinct of the people seemed to forecast the fate which the hazard of revolutions held in reserve for the future King, Louis Philippe I. "In vain," says M. Vaulabelle, "did he try to make people forget him; no matter how great might be the pains he appeared to take to efface himself, the court, as well as the official public, was soon disquieted about him. The royalists, being unable to make up their minds to pardon him the vote which his father had cast in favor of the execution of Louis XVI., nor the revolutionary opinions which he himself had professed for a long time, were suspicious of his cautious attitude, and accused him of cherishing designs to place himself on the throne of his Bourbon ancestors. The way in which he received at his house all the chief notabilities of the Empire and the early days of the Revolution, his polite, caressing, and almost too popular manners, his conversation, exempt as it was from the prejudices which dominated at court and in the government, sufficed to point him out as the hope of the liberals."

In Louis Philippe there were two distinct men, the prince and the revolutionist, and he played two different parts with equal ingenuousness. He was, as Montaigne would have said, an undulating and diverse man, whose fluctuations were explainable by the wavering epoch in which he lived. Perhaps he did not acknowledge even to himself the contradictions that existed in his character as in his destiny. He was — involuntarily, likely enough, and by the force of circumstances rather than from premeditation — the representative of that fickle France which, while believing itself sincere in its mobility, changes its opinions and its flags as an actress changes her costumes. The prince and the revolutionist that were incarnate in the same man could each make use of a different language, — the prince at the Tuileries, the revolutionist at the Palais Royal.

At the Tuileries the prince might say: "I am not responsible for my father's faults. He expiated them cruelly and repented of them before his death. His fate, and that of Dumouriez, my old general, set me to thinking in a way that opened my eyes to the truth. I retracted all the errors of my early youth, and during the whole duration of the Empire I remained faithful to the cause of kings. I asked the Spanish Cortes for a command against Bonaparte, and it is not my fault that England prevented me from warring against the usurper, against whom I had already issued a strong proclamation. I have the honor to be the husband of the niece of Queen Marie Antoinette, and no household is more closely united than mine. I am on the best of terms with my father-in-law, King Ferdinand, who assuredly does not suspect me of too liberal tendencies. I shall always be faithful to my duties as a prince of the blood. My devotion to the person of Louis XVIII., my sovereign, my benefactor, is absolute."

At the Palais Royal the revolutionist might say: "My father died a victim to his devotion to the cause of liberty, and I have never disavowed my father. I had the honor of fighting under the shadow of the tricolor. I am a soldier of Jemmapes and Valmy. I belong to the present and not to the past. The friend of progress, the foe of reaction, and French before being prince, I shared in none of the whims and prejudices of the *émigrés*. I am not a man of the old régime; I am a man of the principles of 1789. I will instruct my children as I myself was instructed, in the new ideas. Liberals, you have a pledge in my antecedents, and you can count upon me."

XIII

THE FAMILY OF CONDÉ

IF in the House of France the Duke of Orleans was the representative of the new ideas, the old régime was, on the other hand, personified in the aged Prince of Condé and his son, the Duke of Bourbon, who was father of the unhappy Duke of Enghien. Both these princes, who had never compromised with the Revolution, and who had combated it in arms from the first, were fine types of the *émigré*. The ultra-royalists admired these two veterans of the monarchical cause, whose life was a model, but whose race, on the point of becoming extinct, already seemed but a memory of the olden times. The Palais Bourbon, where they lived, and which, by irony of fortune (for both father and son detested parliamentarism), stood side by side with the Chamber of Deputies, was the rendezvous of reactionaries who bitterly opposed the government of Louis XVIII. because, in their opinion, it was too liberal. They reproached the King with having entertained advanced ideas from the beginning of his political career; with his connection with the philosophers; with his tardy emigration (he did not emigrate till

1791, while the flight of the Condés dated from 1789); with his ministry composed almost exclusively of men of the Revolution and Empire; and with his partiality for those who had taken possession of the national property; and, above all, did they blame him on account of the Charter, which the old defenders of the throne and altar looked upon as an unintelligent and useless concession to the most subversive principles. The King cared but little for the opinion of the two Condés. He treated them civilly and allowed them to figure at his side in ceremonies, but their political rôle was confined to these official public appearances.

Born on the 9th of August, 1736, Louis Joseph de Bourbon, Prince of Condé, was seventy-seven years old at the beginning of the Restoration. His military reputation was fully established. At the age of sixteen he entered the profession of arms, and at once became known for his distinguished gallantry. In 1762, he fought the Prince of Brunswick and took him prisoner, together with all his artillery. His popularity was then so great that once, when he appeared at the Théâtre Français after the battle of Johannisberg, the entire audience turned their faces to the Prince and greeted him with applause, when an actor spoke the words: "I drink to Mars!" Even his reverses themselves inured to his fame. The French cannons that he saved on the day of Rossbach were set up for ornaments in his magnificent gardens at Chantilly. During the last years of the old régime he had the reputation of being one of the bravest, most affable, and most hospitable princes in all Europe. He often gave what he called military dinners, and delighted to surround himself with whatever recalled to him the great martial deeds of his ancestors, and the battles at which he himself had fought. Extremely devoted to ancient traditions, he put no faith in the philosophers. "Good men," said he, "are more to my liking than brilliant men."

The Prince of Condé was married twice. At the age of seventeen he became the husband of Charlotte Godefride-Elisabeth de Rohan-Soubise, by whom, in 1756, he had the Duke of Bourbon and, in 1757, Mademoiselle de Condé, who died in 1760. He was married again on the 24th of October, 1798, to Catherine de Brignole, Princess-Dowager of Monaco, who died in 1813.

During the whole Revolution and Empire, the Prince remained steadfast to his ideas. After the events of 1789, he issued a manifesto inviting royalist gentlemen to join him in his warring exile. As creator and head of the little army which bore his name, and in which three generations of his family had fought for the royal cause, he held it as a patriotic deed to cast in his lot with the foreigners who were at war with republican France. When his army was disbanded in 1801, he retired to England, which country he left only to return to France with Louis XVIII.

All the officers and soldiers of the old army of

Condé came to the Palais Bourbon to pay their respects to their chief and, generally, to seek aid, since they were nearly all poor. The Prince passed a considerable part of his time in signing papers and acknowledgments of services rendered. For some weeks the applicants were nearly all gentlemen who were survivors of the army of Condé. But soon the number of his visitors became so large that the aged Prince said: "It is strange that all these gentlemen pretend they know me; this can hardly be the case, for down there I had only a few regiments, and now a whole army is flocking to see me."

In his *Souvenirs*, Count Alexandre de Puymaigre says: "As to the Prince of Condé, my old general, and the patron of my father and my family, he was always faithful to his chivalrous traditions, and exhausted himself in endeavors to get a place for me; but his great age, the political insignificance of his son, and the approaching end of his illustrious race, unfitted him for having much influence. The intelligence of the Prince was sometimes clouded, and then he confused men and epochs, — an excusable thing in a man of his years. I remember being with him one Sunday, when the Duke of Dalmatia (Marshal Soult) was announced, together with Count Beugnot, both of whom the King had just called to the ministry, — 'Who are these people?' the Prince asked us; but before any one could reply, they were introduced. 'Monsieur,' said the Prince to the Marshal, 'I trust that you will continue to serve the King as you have always done, and with the same zeal.' This confusion of ideas amused us very much, and especially so did the embarrassed air of the new Minister of War, who was never noted for bashfulness."

Another anecdote, somewhat touched up, perhaps, but in any case diverting, is related. One day, M. de Talleyrand-Périgord was announced at the salon of the Prince of Condé. The Prince rose, received his visitor, and recognized him perfectly well. He was the famous Talleyrand, the Minister of Foreign Affairs. But the Prince pretended to take him for Monseigneur de Talleyrand, Archbishop of Rheims and Grand Almoner of France. This prelate was the famous diplomate's uncle, and, like the Prince of Condé, had emigrated, been the companion of the Prince's exile, and returned with him from England, along with the King. "Ah, my dear Archbishop," exclaimed the old Prince, "how delighted I am to see you!" Then, entering into conversation and speaking of the past, he inveighed against the Revolution, the Empire, and all who had served these two abhorred régimes. "It pains me to say so," he added, "but of all those rascals the most odious, my dear Archbishop, is unquestionably your own nephew, who, doubly apostate as gentleman and as priest, was one of Bonaparte's chief ministers when my grandson, the Duke of Enghien, was assassinated." The King's Minister of Foreign Affairs said not a word, and remained unmoved. At length he rose to go; "Adieu, Mr. Archbishop," said the Prince; "come to see me again, but, I conjure you, never bring with you that scamp whom you have the misfortune to call your nephew; for if he comes, I shall be obliged to have him thrown out of the window."

The Duke of Bourbon, son of the Prince of Condé, held the same ideas and sentiments as his father. He was born on the 13th of April, 1756, and married Louise Marie Thérèse Bathilde d'Orléans, on the 24th of April, 1770. The Duke of Enghien was born of this marriage, in 1772. Associated with the destinies of his father, the Duke of Bourbon had followed him, first in the army of Condé, and then on his exile to England. The two returned to France together. Caring very little for politics, and surrounded with some women and a few friends who had shared his exile, he spent the greater part of his time at the château of Chantilly, and distracted his attention from his troubles by going on continual hunts in the forests, that recalled his infancy and early youth. (Upon the death of his father, on the 13th of May, 1818, he took the title of Prince of Condé, and died on the 27th of August, 1830, by suicide, some say, although, according to others, he was assassinated. By a will, dated on the 30th of August, 1829, the Duke of Aumale was made his heir.)

His wife, Louise Marie Thérèse Bathilde d'Orléans, was born at Saint Cloud on the 9th of July, 1750. She was the daughter of Louis Philippe, Duke of Orleans, grandson of the Regent, and was the sister of Philippe

Égalité, and aunt of the Prince who became King
Louis Philippe. When the Duke of Bourbon was
hardly fifteen years old, he fell in love with the Princess, who was six years his senior. This marriage,
of which the Duke of Enghien was born, was not
happy. The couple soon separated. The Duke returned her dowry to the House of Orleans, and made
a small addition to it. Left alone, the Princess gave
herself up to a mixture of mystical and revolutionary
notions. She became intimate with Catherine Théo,
who wanted to be called the "Mother of God," and
she paid much attention to the predictions of the
Carthusian friar, Dom Gerle. On the outbreak of
the Revolution, she gave her protection to the constitutional bishops. Notwithstanding this she was
imprisoned, under the Terror, in the fortress of Saint-
Jean at Marseilles, where she remained from May,
1793, till the 29th of April, 1795. She then found
refuge at Soria, near Barcelona, in Spain, in a country
house, where she took care of the sick. While there
she entered upon a correspondence that was extensive and sometimes peculiar. She affected one of
the Illuminati, Saint-Martin, who in 1796 wrote a
work for her, entitled *Ecce Homo*. In 1800 she
wrote a letter, demanding that there should be no
distinctions among men except those that should be
based on virtue, intelligence, talents, and education;
that the law should prevent the accumulation of
extremely large properties, and that everybody should
be ashamed to be too rich. "Whatever," she added,

"may have been the consequences of the Revolution, I can never quarrel with the object it had in view, but only with the means that it employed."

When she returned to France at the commencement of the Restoration, the Duchess did not go to the Palais Bourbon, but took up her residence in the rue de Varennes, at the Hôtel Monaco, now the home of the Duchess of Galliera. Being very charitable, she received a host of poor people at her house, which she sometimes called the Hospital d'Enghien. Strange as it was, the mother of the victim of the trenches of Vincennes did not have a reputation for hostility to Napoleon, the murderer of her son. It is certain that she remained in France all through the Hundred Days, and that she received, as also did the Duchess Dowager of Orleans, a pension from the Emperor. It was owing to the request of Queen Hortense that this pension was given to the two princesses. How strange a time, when the mother of the Duke of Enghien was the pensionary of Napoleon! But the sight of Queen Hortense receiving from Louis XVIII. the title of Duchess of Saint-Leu, at the instance of the Emperor of Russia, was not, perhaps, less surprising.

The Duke of Bourbon had a sister, Louise Adélaïde de Bourbon-Condé, who was worthy of the highest esteem. Born on the 5th of October, 1757, this pious Princess first shone at the court of Versailles and the château of Chantilly. At that epoch she was called Mademoiselle de Condé, and it seems that for a time there was some thought of making her the wife of the Count of Artois. The Baroness of Oberkirch thus speaks of this matter in her *Souvenirs:* "She is one of those people so far above others that their high rank adds nothing to their personal importance. Mademoiselle de Condé, if born in a farmhouse, would have been the chief personage in it, and yet have resembled no other peasant, merely through her superior intelligence and innate distinction. She is, indeed, beautiful, but in the manner of queens; majesty and power are in her smile. Nevertheless she has a very tender heart; she has a forehead fitted to wear either a crown or a nun's veil." She preferred the veil of religion. In 1786, she became the Abbess of Remiremont. During the emigration she entered the nunnery of Sainte-Vallée-de-Dieu, in Valais, under the name of Sister Marie-Joseph. Driven from this asylum by the republican invasion, she drove in a carriage to Constance; thence to Lintz; from there to Orcha in Russia; and then to Warsaw, where she entered the convent of the Benedictines of the Perpetual Adoration, under the name of Sister Marie Louise de la Miséricorde. There she learned of the death of her unfortunate nephew, the Duke of Enghien. Thence she proceeded to England to take the most tender care of the grandfather and the father of that Prince. When she returned to France at the beginning of the Restoration, she received from the King the mansion of the Temple, and became the prioress of the convent of the Benedictines of Perpetual

Adoration, which she established near the site of the tower where Louis XVI. and his family underwent their dolorous captivity.

The Duchess of Angoulême was delighted to see her pious relative so devoted to religion. The orphan of the Temple had, besides, very lively sympathy for the Condés, and especially for the aged Prince. In January, 1815, at Twelfth-Night, Louis XVIII. gave a family dinner at the Tuileries. The traditional cake was cut. The bean fell to the Duchess of Angoulême, who took pains to choose the Prince of Condé for king.

XIV

THE FÊTE AT THE HÔTEL DE VILLE

WE have endeavored to describe the society in which the Duchess of Angoulême lived, and to portray the persons who composed her family. We shall now take up once more the thread of our story with the month of August, 1814. During the early part of the month the Duchess assisted at the fêtes given in her honor by the city of Lyons. After her return to Paris on the 13th, she went, on the 15th, to divine service at the metropolitan church, where the traditional procession of the vow of Louis XIII. was under way.

"After vespers," said the *Journal des Débats*, "the procession left the cathedral. It advanced in perfect order through a great multitude of people, who looked affectionately upon the princes and Madame, who, in pious meditation, followed on foot the image of the great patroness of France. The day deserves to be memorable. It has restored one of our ancient customs to us. Religion is the mother of all the virtues, and virtue alone can bring prosperity to a nation."

On the 17th of August, the Duchess of Angoulême went to visit the rooms and gardens of the château of Versailles and the Trianons. She desired to see it all once more, — the chapel in which, when a child, she had prayed, alas! in vain, for the safety of the monarchy; the foliage that had thrown its shadow on her earliest footsteps; the Petit Trianon, where her mother's happy days had glided by; the grotto in which the Queen learned, on the 5th of October, 1789, of the arrival of the invaders; the balcony of the château, where the heroic Princess, holding her son and daughter by the hand, had majestically confronted the furious mob, which, in order to guard against involuntary compassion, cried in its rage: "No children! No children!" The orphan mused in the chamber where she and her two unfortunate brothers, the dauphins, were born. Then she returned to the Tuileries, recalling the journey she once made from Versailles to that palace, preceded by demoniacs who bore on pikes the livid heads of massacred body-guards as bloody trophies. Thus it was that, even in the midst of a fleeting prosperity, the daughter of Louis XVI. and Marie Antoinette was oppressed by sorrowful memories.

The 25th of August was Louis XVIII.'s saint's day, and in honor of it he held a reception in the throne-room of the Tuileries. At six o'clock in the evening the King assisted at a great dinner. The people who had been presented, together with a large number of men and women who had been invited to dine, passed in succession before Louis XVIII., who responded affably to their lively expressions of pleasure at seeing the royal family reunited, while, from all parts of the garden continuous shouts gave expression to the feelings of a large assembly that did not withdraw till long after the usual hour. The whole city was illuminated. Paris appeared joyful. One would have said that the people's old love for its Kings had returned. But the Duchess of Angoulême, whom cruel experience had rendered mistrustful, put but little faith in the fidelity of the French nation.

On the 29th of August, the Princess assisted at the great fête given to Louis XVIII. by the city of Paris. This fête is a very curious study; for it makes one understand the prejudices and passions of an epoch when two régimes, the old and the new, were perpetually at strife with each other, and when happenings, to all appearance trifling, disclosed all the anomalies of the situation, the conflict of interests, the violence of pride, and the fierceness of intrigue.

Madame de Staël says: "Among the difficulties that had to be overcome by the ministry in 1814, the influence exerted by the salons was the greatest. Bonaparte had revived the old court customs, but had added to them all the faults of the least refined classes. The result of this was that the love of power, and the pride that it inspires, were stronger and more violent in the Bonapartists than in the *émigrés.* The Bonapartists had been fawned upon by Parisian society during their reign, just as the royalist party which succeeded them was, and nothing hurt their feelings more than to hold only a subordinate place in the same salons where once they had been masters. Besides this, the men of the old régime possessed those advantages which graciousness and the habitual good manners of a former time gave them; consequently there was constant jealousy between the old and the new titles, and in the new men fierce passions were aroused by every little event that arose from rival claims to respect."

The fête of the Hôtel de Ville gave an opportunity for the old and the new nobility to study each other, and that beautiful fête which its originators intended as a celebration of conciliation and concord had its outcome in puerile rivalries, at which one may smile to-day, but which, in 1814, had in public life, and especially at court, nearly as much importance as the gravest political occurrences. Then, as in the days of the Duke of Saint-Simon, aristocrats and bourgeois flew into a passion over the merest questions of etiquette.

In the first place, there was a very lively quarrel between the body-guards and the national guards. The body-guards claimed the right to occupy the interior of the Hôtel de Ville, and wished to relegate the national guards to the outside. From this a fierce discussion arose. "The privilege of watching

MME. DE STAËL

over the person of the King," cried the body-guards, "is ours, as is indicated by our name. It is a right, a duty, which we can share with nobody whomsoever." — "At the Hôtel de Ville," replied the officers of the national guard, "we are in our own house, and nobody can dispute our claim to superiority in the right to entertain the King in our own palace."

As the debate was growing violent, the King made himself umpire, and decided that half of the body-guard and half of the national guard should be distributed through the apartments.

Another question was presented which was yet more perplexing: It had been decided that thirty-six women should be admitted to the royal table. But in what proportion should they be selected for the municipal banquet from the new nobility, which held their titles by the terms of the Charter, and the old nobility, which had regained theirs? This was the problem to be solved. The new nobility was confounded when it saw that only five places were reserved for it. The common citizens considered themselves still more humiliated, since, among all the thirty-six ladies, there were only two who did not belong to the nobility, and because at a fête given by the city the municipal body was not represented by any woman.

Following is the list of the thirty-six ladies, as it appeared in the *Moniteur:* The Duchess of Fleury, the Duchess of Duras, the Countess of Blacas, the Marchioness of Avaray, the Marchioness of Boisgelin, the Countess of Escars, the Marchioness of Brézé, the Duchess of Sérent, the Countess of Damas, Madame de Choisy, the Duchess of Vauguyon, the Princess of Beaufremont, the Countess of Narbonne, the Viscountess of Narbonne, the Duchess of Maillé, the Countess of Durfort, the Countess of Nansouty, the Marchioness of Lagrange, the Marchioness of La Rochejacquelein, the Duchess of Rohan-Montbazon, the Princess of Chalais, the Duchess of Coigny, the Duchess of Mouchy, the Duchess of Rohan, the Princess of Solre, the Princess of Wagram, the Countess of Bournonville, Madame Ferrand, Countess Maison, Maréchale Suchet, the Duchess of Albuféra, Maréchale Oudinot (Duchess of Reggio), the Princess of Laval, the Duchess of Harcourt, the Marchioness of Tourzel, and the Baroness of Montboissier.

Resignation is the salve for wounded self-love. Difficulties of etiquette are arranged according to inexorable laws. The fête takes place on the 27th of August. It is very fine. The King leaves the Tuileries at five in the afternoon. He is in a gala coach, with his brother, the Duke and Duchess of Angoulême, and the Duke of Berry. The troops form in double line. A large escort precedes and follows the royal carriage. The whole distance that the train must go is strewn with gravel. Most of the houses of the quay are adorned with flags, inscriptions, and emblems. At every window there are spectators who join in the cheers of the crowd. On his arrival at the Hôtel de Ville, the first thing that meets Louis XVIII.'s eyes when he enters the great hall is the portrait of Henri IV. placed above the throne. "I shall be fortunate indeed," says he, "if my subjects think that I have taken for my model the good king whose features are here delineated."

Baron de Chabrol, prefect of the Seine, then delivers an address, of which the following is a part: "In one moment France frees itself from its shackles and reassumes its noble position. . . . All hearts are cheered at the sight of a princess who is the very model of virtue, whom heaven has so long tried, and whom its eternal justice must at last restore to happiness." The King replies: "I am most deeply moved at being reunited with my large family, but I have had to wait in order to be surrounded by it" (here the King pointed to the princes about him). "They were my consolation in adversity, and to-day they are my chief blessing. They have given me proofs that they share in all my designs for your happiness. I can hereafter close my eyes in peace, since I am sure that they will inherit my sentiments in regard to France." Baroness de Chabrol, the prefect's wife, then addressed the Duchess of Angoulême in these words: "Memory still recalls to us the tears we shed in our infancy at the story of your noble constancy and your long continued misfortunes. We can truly say that it is in the hearts of women that the sacred flame of love for our kings burns brightest and most purely."

The royal family enters the magnificent hall

where the great banquet which has been the cause
of so many rivalries and jealousies is to be given.
The arms of the chief cities of the realm are among
the decorations. At the foot of the dais on which
the King is to sit, natural lilies are grouped artis-
tically and reflected in the mirrors. On his way
to the dais, the King observes in the centre of the
table a design in sable, representing Henri IV. at
supper. At the King's right sits Monsieur his
brother, at his left Madame, the Duchess of Angoulême, while his nephews, the Duke of Angoulême
and the Duke of Berry are seated, the former beside Monsieur, and the second beside Madame. The
thirty-six ladies admitted to the much-coveted honor
of sitting at the royal table take their places. None
others are at the banquet. The King is served by
Baron de Chabrol, prefect of the Seine; the Duchess
of Angoulême, by the Baroness de Chabrol; Monsieur,
by the eldest of the mayors and the president of
the municipal council; the Duke of Berry and
the Duke of Angoulême, by members of the same
council; and the thirty-six ladies, by persons designated by the council.

As soon as the banquet is ended, the concert begins.
A cantata, of which the words are by the poet Mille-
voie and the music by Cherubini, is rendered.
After the concert, the King goes to the ball-room,
which he leaves at half-past nine in the evening
with the same ceremonies that took place when he
came. Before entering his carriage, he says to the

THE FÊTE AT THE HÔTEL DE VILLE 159

prefect: "I have nowhere seen a fête so beautiful, and, above all, so touching to my heart. I shall count this day, on which I have received so many evidences of affection, among the happiest of my life."

On the day after the fête the courtiers went into ecstasies over its magnificence and the salutary impression which, as they imagined, it had produced. They asseverated that all who had had the honor and happiness of being present would never forget it, that never under the rule of the usurper had anything so beautiful been seen, and that legitimate royalty alone could offer such a spectacle. Nevertheless, the very fête which they admired so much had discontented and affronted many people. The wives of the members of the municipal council were inconsolable for having been excluded from that privileged banquet. The nobility of the Empire lamented the fact that so few of their class had received invitations. The prerogative of serving the King and Princes at table was but slightly flattering to those to whom it had been given. It is true that these high domestic functions were formerly exercised on formal occasions by the greatest personages in the kingdom, but after the Revolution such an antique ceremonial seemed slightly out of place. In conclusion, it should be noted that a liberal journal, the *Censeur*, contented itself with saying, as its sole criticism of this fête of the old régime, that some days previously, when a banquet had been given by the city of Berlin to the officers of the Prussian royal guard and the Russian imperial guard, the King of Prussia and his ministers had sat down with the chief burgomaster of the city.

XV

THE DISTRIBUTION OF FLAGS

FROM this time royalty deemed itself invulnerable and invincible. The ceremony of distributing and blessing the flags of the Paris national guard, which took place on the 7th of September, 1814, on the Champ-de-Mars, confirmed it still further in this robust faith in itself. A platform for the royal throne was erected before the Military School, and in the middle of the Champ-de-Mars stood an altar. At half-past nine o'clock in the morning the whole national guard was under arms and in order of battle. At half after eleven the firing of cannon announced the sovereign's arrival. Upon entering the field, the King took a carriage drawn by eight horses, and, accompanied only by the Duchess of Angoulême, he reviewed the troops. Monsieur, the King's brother, in his capacity as commander of the national guard of the kingdom, stationed himself at the carriage-door and pointed out the different corps to the King.

After the review His Majesty left the carriage, in front of the Military School, ascended the platform, and seated himself on the throne. Surrounded by the principal officers of the crown and marshals and generals of France, he had his brother on his right and his niece, the Duchess of Angoulême, on his left hand. Mgr. Talleyrand-Périgord, Archbishop of Rheims and Grand Almoner of France, was at the altar. The King received the flag of the first legion from Monsieur's hands and lowered the head of the lance towards the Duchess of Angoulême, who attached the tassel to it. He then gave it to the chief of the first legion, who, coming down from the platform, saluted with it and went to rejoin the detachment to which he belonged. The flags of eleven other legions and that of the national horse guards were returned in the same way. The officers then advanced to the altar, where the Grand Almoner blessed the flags. Then the whole guard defiled before the throne.

After it had passed, the King said: "This is a very fine day for me, gentlemen; it binds me anew to my brave national guard. What may not one hope from the French when he sees such troops, which zeal alone has called into existence? Let the enemy come against us when he will. But no such event will happen. We look only for friends." The King's brother then said: "Sire, the national guard is profoundly sensible of the great honor that Your Majesty has done it, by personally presenting it with its flags. I can assure you, Sire, that the guard is worthy of that honor. All are ready to die for Your Majesty's person, and among so many faithful subjects none is more devoted than their commander." The national guards then cried: "Yes, yes; we swear it. Long live the King!" The King then stretched his arms out to his brother, drew him to his breast and embraced him, and, as the *Moniteur* says, tears of sympathy fell from all eyes.

Prayers of the Church, acclamations, an altar in the middle of the Champ-de-Mars, decorations on the Military School, salvos of artillery, hyperbole in the *Moniteur*, official enthusiasm, touching phrases, — 'tis all the same thing under the Empire or under the Kingship. Fraternization, the distribution of eagles and white flags, — it is all the same spectacle, the same pomp. The crowd is gathered on the same slopes; the world of officials is present in the same dress, on the same balcony. The sovereign changes. The flags are not of the same color. Now there are lilies, and now there are bees. But etiquette endures. Solemnities are got up on demand. In conducting them, the same masters-of-ceremonies may be used, and the same editors may be employed to report them in the official journal. Why not keep this throne, this platform, this altar, among the ordinary appurtenances of the monarchy, whatever it may be? The tapestry will only have to be changed a little, and all these trappings will do duty next year for Napoleon's Field of May. Some sincere persons, some men of convictions, have deep and genuine political feelings. But, in general, the bulk of the people is indifferent enough. It looks with a certain curiosity at the scenery and decorations. It follows the action attentively. Occasionally it is moved. It even weeps. But, the play once over, it thinks only of its own affairs. It forgets both play and actors.

As to princes, they nearly always look upon ovations to them as serious matters, and this in spite of experience. Who would not believe in a political religion in which one's self is the idol? Incense is more intoxicating than wine. Deceived from morning till night and from night till morning by their courtiers, men in power, no matter who they may be, princes or republicans, live in a factitious atmosphere and believe more firmly in their own stability, the nearer they draw to their downfall. In France infatuation is the ruin of all governments, — royalty, empire, or republic. There is the rock on which even the greatest men are broken.

At the close of 1814, the throne was already undermined, although no one near the King dreamed of the impending peril. Royalist writers redoubled their confidence and enthusiasm. In his *Réflexions politiques*, published in December, Chateaubriand said: "Each day sees a diminution of the small number of our opponents; absurd tales and popular fears are dying out, and commerce is reviving. Who can lay his hand on his breast and explain what he has to complain of? Never was there a more settled calm after a storm. The government, which has endured for eight months, is so firmly established that if to-day it should make mistake after mistake, it would continue to exist in spite of its errors." And, exulting over the wisdom of the King, the author of the *Génie du Christianisme* adds: "Immovable on his throne, the King has calmed the waves around him; he has yielded to no influence and to no party. His patience confounds; his goodness subjugates and enchains, and his serenity is communicated to all. . . . When anybody comes nigh him, he always seems to say: 'Where could you find a better father? Let me heal your wounds. I forget my own that I may remember only those of others. At my age and after my misfortunes can I love the throne on account of myself? It is for you that I am on it; I would make you as happy as you have been unfortunate.' Any man who observes himself and the course of events and fails to heap blessings on the prince whom heaven has restored to us, is unworthy to be ruled by such a prince."

The Bourbons thought they could depend on the army. At the beginning of December, Marshal Soult had been made Minister of War. He was then the favorite of the most outspoken royalists. When he was commandant of the 13th Military Division and governor of Brittany, he formed, in October, a Breton society for erecting a monument in memory of Duguesclin, Constable of France. In the following month he started a subscription to erect a monument on the island of Quiberon, and a mortuary chapel at La Chartreuse, near Auray, on the field where the defenders of the royal cause had fallen, and which had been consecrated under the name of the "Field of Martyrs." In the salons of the Faubourg Saint-Germain the marshal then passed for an exceedingly circumspect man. He added greatly to his reputation by establishing a chapel in the mansion of the Ministry of War, and having Mass celebrated in it, which he attended with edifying regularity. He promised to maintain the strictest discipline in the army, and to show no pity to officers who were suspected of Bonapartist tendencies. One of his first ministerial acts was to nominate for Grand Chancellor of the Legion of Honor an old *émigré*, Count de Bruges, who was one of the men most respected at the Pavilion of Marsan. The royalists said that, with a commander of the character, energy, and loyalty of Marshal Soult, the army would be as obedient as a child under the rod. They never suspected that, six months afterwards, the marshal would be in the field as the major-general of Napoleon.

XVI

SAINT-DENIS

THE day of the aniversary of the murder of Louis XVI. was drawing near. While Louis XVIII. was exulting in the Tuileries, no one knew what had become of the remains of the martyred King and Queen. On the 21st of January, 1793, the dead body of Louis XVI., and on the 16th of October, in the same year, that of Queen Marie Antoinette, had been dragged in a cart from the Place de la Révolution, the place of execution, to the cemetery of the Madeleine, adjoining the street of Anjou-Saint-Honoré. No tombs marked the spot where either the decapitated King or Queen was buried. There was nothing to indicate their graves, — no inscription, no stone, no cross, — nothing; absolutely nothing. The very cemetery itself had ceased to exist. At that time, as little respect had been paid to cemeteries as to churches. The graveyard had been sold to private persons like common soil, and without care for the dead. Nevertheless, the man who had bought that part of it where the King and Queen lay, was a royalist with a taste for souvenirs. His name was M. Descloseaux. He planted some trees to serve as data. But under the Revolution and the Empire, nobody but himself went to meditate in the sacred enclosure. There were no pilgrimages, no prayers; and it was only approximately known where the bodies of Louis XVI. and Marie Antoinette were interred.

The government of Louis XVIII. ordered that research be made. Four witnesses of the burials were interrogated. These were a priest, a judge, a registrar, and a lawyer. The body first found was the Queen's. The lime had not entirely consumed it. The expression of the face was recognized, and some fragments of dress aided in the identification. King Louis XVI.'s body was found near by. The severed head had been placed between the legs, which now, by the action of time and lime, had dwindled to mere bones. A *procès-verbal*, signed by the principal personages of the realm, verified this double discovery.

The bodies were exhumed on the 18th of January, 1815. On the next day the *Journal des Débats* contained an article by Chateaubriand which began as follows: "The 21st of January is at hand, and for a long time the question has been asked: 'What shall we do? What shall France do? Shall that mournful day be allowed to pass without any mark of regret? Where are the ashes of Louis XVI.? Who has them in keeping?' Had it not been for the piety of an obscure citizen it would scarcely be known to-day where lies the sacred body of that King who should repose in Saint-Denis beside Louis XII. and Charles the Wise. For several years they sought to turn the day of the death of this just man into a day of rejoicing; but how blind were the factions! While they were attempting to remove the pall of mourning that covered our country, and while they were ordaining derisory pomps, citizens were multiplying the marks of their grief; each wept in solitude, or caused the expiatory sacrifice celebrated in secret.

"In vain," continued Chateaubriand, "did a few men summon the masses to abominable spectacles; public sorrow seemed to say to them: 'No, France is not guilty along with you; she has no share in your crimes and festivals.' What an abyss of reflections! How great is the resemblance between the occurrences, the times, the places, and the funereal pomps of Saint Louis and Louis the Martyr!"

This eloquent writer then recalls the fact that Napoleon restored the vaults of the Church of Saint-Denis, in the hope that they would be his imperial sepulchre. "Why," adds the author of the *Génie du Christianisme*, "is Saint-Denis vacant? Rather let us ask why its roof has been restored; why is its altar rebuilt? What hand reconstructed the vault of those crypts and made ready those once empty tombs? The hand of the very man who sat on the throne of the Bourbons. O Providence! He imagined that he was preparing the sepulchres of his own race, and he was but building the tomb of Louis

XVI. Injustice reigns but for an instant; wisdom alone has regard for ancestors and leaves a posterity. Behold at the same time, the Master of the Earth meet his downfall, Louis XVIII. grasp his sceptre once more, and Louis XVI. restored to the sepulchre of his fathers! The kingship of the legitimate monarchs has slumbered for twenty years; but their rights, founded on their virtues, were, like their nobleness, indestructible. At one blow, God ends that terrible revolution, and at the same time the Kings of France regain their throne and their tombs."

It was also announced that while the mortal remains of Louis XVI. and Marie Antoinette were being taken to Saint-Denis, the first stone of the monument which France was about to erect on the Place Louis XV., where the King and Queen were guillotined, would be laid. This monument was intended to represent Louis XVI. about to mount the scaffold. An angel was to support him, and seem to repeat the celebrated phrase: "Son of Saint Louis, ascend to heaven!" On one face of the pedestal was to be a medallion portrait of Marie Antoinette, having as its legend those magnanimous words of the Queen: "I have seen all, understood all, and forgotten all." On another face of the pedestal, there was to be a bas-relief portrait of Madame Elisabeth, surrounded by these words: "Do not undeceive them," — that heroic and sublime expression uttered by the saintly Princess on the 20th of June, 1792, when the Tuileries was invaded by men who, mistaking her for the Queen, threatened to murder her. On the third side of the pedestal was to be inscribed the will of Louis XVI.; that beautiful line: "I pardon with my whole soul all who have made themselves my enemies," was to appear in very large letters. The fourth face would bear the escutcheon of France with the following inscription: "Louis XVIII. to Louis XVI."

After having given the details of the project, Chateaubriand added: "The King, who hitherto has not ventured to go to that bloody field, may some day pass it, if not without sorrow, at least without horror, whilst the judge of Louis XVI., in the shelter of this monument of pity, may himself visit the spot, if not without remorse, at least without fear. In fine, this monument will be a source of consolation to all Frenchmen."

Exactly twenty-two years after the execution of Louis XVI., — that is to say, on the 21st of January, 1814, — the ashes of the King and Queen were borne to the abbey church of Saint-Denis, and their solemn obsequies were celebrated at that necropolis of Kings. About eight o'clock in the morning, the King's brother, the Count of Artois, and his two sons, the Dukes of Angoulême and of Berry, went to the rue d'Anjou-Saint-Honoré, to the enclosure in which now stands the expiatory chapel, built by the architects Fontaine and Percier, and modelled after a mortuary church of Rimini. Both coffins were deposited under a tent, "an image," says M. Alfred Nettement, "of the instability of everything in this land of France, to which all things come and where nothing remains."

The three princes, one a brother and the other two nephews of the martyred King, kneel and pray for a long time, beside the coffins. At nine o'clock, the funeral procession moves through the rue Saint-Honoré, and then along the boulevards. The mortal remains of the King and Queen were carried on a car, by twelve members of the Scotch company of the body-guards. Notwithstanding the extreme coldness of the day, there was a vast crowd all along the route. The procession moved in the following order: a detachment of gendarmes, a squadron of hussars, companies of grenadiers and light infantry, marching in close rank and carrying their guns reversed on the left arm; General Maison, governor of Paris, with his staff, a mounted detachment of the national guards, and a battalion of foot of the national guard preceding General Dessoles; a half-squadron of mounted grenadiers of the King's body-guard, in advance of three coaches, each drawn by eight horses, and in which were the chief officers of the princes; a half-squadron of light-horse; eight eight-horse carriages in which were the principal officers of the crown; the carriage of the King's brother and the Dukes of Angoulême and Berry; four heralds-of-arms and the king-of-arms, all mounted; the Grand Master of Ceremonies, with masters and aides, all mounted also; the funeral car, with the captains of the red companies, one at each wheel. Troops and a great number of the King's coaches closed the procession. The regiments of the Paris garrison lined the rue d'Anjou as far as the barrier of Saint-Denis. Everything wore an aspect of sorrow. The flags were draped. It was remembered that some of the men who took part in the ceremonies had followed Louis XVI. when he was removed from the Temple to the place of execution. The muffled drums which at intervals gave forth their deep tones did not preclude the thought of other drums, those of Santerre, which drowned the voice of Louis XVI. when the Martyr-King wished to speak words of pardon from the scaffold. The procession moved slowly in the midst of a crowd of spectators. Survivors of the Revolution told their children about the 21st of January, 1793. They said that on that day all Paris, with the exception of a few madmen, was deeply grieved and that remorse already hovered over the great capital.

The Duchess of Angoulême was not present at the ceremony, as it was not then customary for daughters to appear at the funerals of their fathers and mothers. But everybody thought of the orphan of the Temple. She remained at the Tuileries locked in her oratory, praying and weeping. There she listened to the far-off echo of salvos of artillery discharged every minute at the barrier Saint-Denis, by a battery from the provinces, while the funeral procession, which did not reach the ancient necropolis till noon, moved along.

The sight of the abbey stirred sinister thoughts. It was to that place that the regicides had pursued even death, to rummage, mutilate, and violate the tombs of the kings. At length the hour of purification had sounded, the blessed hour which the daughter of Louis XVI. and Marie Antoinette had so longed for during the long anguish of captivity and exile. The multitude that thronged the church was deeply moved. Beside the cenotaph were the Duke of Orleans, his sister, his wife, the Prince of Condé, and the Duke and Duchess of Bourbon. Four hundred daughters of the Legion of Honor were assembled in the nave. The Abbé de Boulogne, Bishop of Troyes, and the most renowned preacher of his day, ascended the pulpit. "Peoples and kings!" he exclaimed, "by your battered and encompassed capitals, you recognize at last the terrible truth, that regicide is the greatest calamity that God can draw from the treasure-house of His justice!" And the audience trembled when, in a burning apostrophe to the revolutionists, the priest said: "Insensates! you thought you debased your King, and you have enhanced his glory! You trampled under foot his earthly crown, and you have circled his brow with a crown of immortality. When you bound his anointed hands, you showed that they alone were worthy to bear the sceptre! In irons, Saint Louis was a king. Louis XVI. was a king on the scaffold! . . . Next to the deicide committed by a reprobate people, the greatest crime that ever sullied the earth is regicide, the outrage whose anniversary we this day deplore." And the priest went on to say: "You have not forgotten these words of a dying king: 'I desire that my blood shall bring happiness to France.' Yes, princes, do not doubt it. That blood will save France, as the blood of Jesus Christ saved the world."

The King's brother and the Dukes of Angoulême and Berry descended into the vault where the remains of Louis XVI. and Marie Antoinette were to repose forever. They prostrated themselves at the tomb of the martyrs, and, in the words of the *Moniteur*: "Their only regret in regard to the duties which called them to this mournful place is that all France could not have witnessed their profound veneration and their pious grief." The office for the dead put the royalists who were present into a sort of holy intoxication. The old Count of Suzannet, who had fought in the armies of Vendée, and was a faithful servant of the throne, was so affected by it that he had to be carried out of the church, and died a short time afterwards.

"I will tell you," says Chateaubriand, "about the nightmare with which I was oppressed when, on the evening of the ceremony, I wandered through the half-deserted basilica. It may readily be understood that among these crumbling tombs I reflected on the vanity of human greatness,— such moralizing is common enough and would have arisen from the spectacle itself,— but my mind did not stop there. I penetrated into the nature of mankind. Is all empty and forsaken in the place of the dead? Is there nothing in this nothingness? Does nothing exist where nothing is, and are there no thoughts in dust? Have bones no modes of life of which we are ignorant? Who can tell the passions, the pleasures, the tender thoughts of the dead? All that they have dreamed, believed, hoped — have all things become but phantoms like them and, like them, been swallowed up in the abyss? Dreams, hope, joy, sorrow, freedom, and slavery, strength and weakness, crime and virtue, honor and shame, wealth and penury, talents, genius, intelligence, glory, illusions, loves, — are you but for a moment? Are you but fleeting sensations that are destroyed with the skulls in which they were engendered, with the lifeless breast where once beat a heart? . . . Let us close our eyes and fill the maddening abyss of life with these grand and mysterious words of the martyr: 'I am a Christian.'"

And yet, despite its majesty, this religious ceremony did not disarm all regicidal hate. A sinister incident is mentioned as having taken place during the procession at a point on the way from the rue d'Anjou to Saint-Denis.

The decorations of the funeral car having caught on a street lamp, several persons set up the regicidal cry, the cry of the most terrible days of the Revolution: "To the lamp-post!" "While Louis XVIII.," says M. Alfred Nettement, "was paying to the memory of Louis XVI. and Marie Antoinette the tribute of mourning and just regret, and while by far the larger part of the public shared in these manifestations, the revolutionists were filled with indignation by them." Nothing is more sensitive than remorse. Those who had imbued their hands in the blood of the King and Queen looked upon the honors paid to their memory as an insult directed against the regicides. Instead of comparing the moderation of the restoration of the Bourbons with the bloody reprisals of the restoration of the Stuarts, these men were afflicted because regret was felt for those to whom they had shown no pity.

Doubtless there was at that time considerable exaggeration in the zeal of the royalists. The funeral oration by the Abbé de Boulogne contained such violent anathemas against the Revolution that the ministry did not deem it advisable to let it be printed in the *Moniteur*. The newspapers, exulting over the circumstance, were too forgetful of the saintly words of Louis XVI.'s will: "I recommend my son, if he shall have the misfortune to become King, to remember that he ought to devote himself entirely to the happiness of his fellow-citizens; that he should forget all hatred and all resentment, and particularly everything that has any connection with the misfortunes and sorrows that I have endured." But, in spite of all, Madame de Staël was right in saying: "No one could see without emotion the obsequies of Louis XVI. The heart turned wholly to the sufferings of that Princess who went back to palaces, not to enjoy their splendor, but to honor the dead and to seek for their bloody remains. It has been said that that ceremony was impolitic, but it gave rise to so much affection that no blame should attach to it." No, the solemnities of the 21st of January, 1815, were not impolitic. They produced a deep impression on men of every party. For Louis XVIII. they were the accomplishment of an imperative duty, and for the Restoration they were a sacrament of piety and sorrow.

XVII

THE BEGINNING OF 1815

THE lugubrious memories of the 21st of January did not prevent that month from being brilliant at court and in the salons of the Faubourg Saint-Germain. Receptions, fêtes, and gala plays at the royal theatres were given both before and after that mournful anniversary. On the 10th of January, the King and royal family went to the Opera, where *Castor et Pollux* was rendered. In its report of the proceedings of that evening the *Journal des Débats* said: "People waited impatiently for some happy allusion in the play, and were beginning to despair; but at the end of the fourth act, in the only fine scene in the opera, Lays, in a deep and sonorous voice, pronounced these two lines: —

> "'The universe demanded thy return;
> Reign o'er a faithful people.'

Never did electricity produce a swifter effect. The entire audience instantly sprang to its feet, turned to the King's box, and seemed to repeat affectionately the truth contained in the first line, and the sentiment expressed in the second."

Society was very animated in the Faubourg Saint-Germain. The salons of the aristocracy regained their brilliancy. One would have thought that the days of the old régime had returned. Whoever, among persons of good standing at court, should have expressed the least doubt as to the stability of the royal edifice would have been treated as an alarmist and poltroon. Perhaps he might even have been called a fool. All conversations in the fashionable world were about trifles. Only balls and theatres were talked about. The Duke of Berry, with a surrounding of brilliant young people, received in his apartments at the Tuileries. The highest boon that could be received was an invitation to his parties. The Prince's first ball was given on the 12th of January, and to it only four hundred and fifty guests were invited.

On the 26th of January, there was a reception at the Tuileries. Next day the *Débats* said: "At yesterday's reception the King, with infinite grace, thanked Madame de Staël for having sent him M. Necker's defence of Louis XVI. He talked a long time with the lady, which proves that Louis XVIII. is not afraid of intellectual women, and that, in his reign, —

"'One may be pure, although she be renowned.'"

On the 30th of January, the King, his brother, and the Duchess of Angoulême were in their box at a play at the Théâtre Français. The pieces were the *Homme du Jour* and the *Partie de chasse de Henri IV*. The galleries and balconies were occupied by elegantly dressed ladies. Everybody rose when the royal family entered. In the supper scene of the third act the health of King Henri is drunk, and when it was reached, the enthusiasm knew no bounds. The audience sang in chorus the refrain of the famous song: —

"Vive Henri IV. Vive ce roi vaillant!"

The King and his family returned to the Tuileries by torch-light in a large open carriage.

On the 2d of February, another ball was given by the Duke of Berry. The whole royal family was present. The King came at ten o'clock and did not withdraw till shortly before supper. As soon as the princes and princesses of the blood took their places at the banquet table, where also sat a hundred and fifty court ladies, the curtain, which concealed a small theatre prepared among the pillars, was raised; artists from the Opéra-Comique were seen behind a gauze veil, which produced a charming effect; and the actors rendered a divertissement, the words of which were by Dupaty and the music by Boïeldieu. Its title was the *Troubadours voyageurs*. Mademoiselle Regnault, Madame Boulanger, and Madame Gavaudan took the parts of the damsels, and Baptiste played the troubadour. On the following day, the 3d of February, the entire royal family attended a representation at the Théâtre-Comique.

The Duchess of Angoulême was seen at theatres, but still oftener at the hospitals, where her beneficence was edifying. She visited the Salpêtrière on the 7th of January, the Orphans' Hospital of the Faubourg Saint-Antoine on the 13th, and the Hôtel-Dieu on the 28th.

On the 7th of February, there was a family supper at court, and afterwards a dramatic representation in the Gallery of Diana. Actors from the Théâtre des Variétés played before the sovereign.

Everybody about the King was filled with optimism. Intelligence from abroad was completely satisfactory. At the Congress of Vienna, France secured an amount of moral force which it would have been hard to expect a few weeks before. Marshal Soult, who was steadily growing in favor, said that he could rely on the army. Besides this, the body-guards and the officers of the King's military household never ceased to repeat that with nothing but their fencing-foils they could easily parley with Bonapartist sabres and bayonets. No one regarded as serious the opposition of the *Nain Jaune*, a satirical journal that was published every five days, and with which the King himself was the first to be amused. This little sheet, moreover, never spoke of Louis XVIII. save with the utmost respect. It called him only Louis the Desired, and never was weary of praising the Charter. The *Nain Jaune* was, therefore, permitted to create its imaginary order of the "Extinguisher," in which it made merry with a certain M. de la Jobardière, the type of an incorrigible old *émigré*, whom it maliciously invented. The whole court laughed at this and quoted the words of Beaumarchais: "It is only little men who are suspicious of little writers." Begone, dull care! There is nothing to worry about! What object is there in bothering over the little King of Elba? Is not the Anglo-French fleet that keeps watch over that rock a guarantee more than sufficient? Isn't it better worth while to be interested in the Italian troupe which will presently appear at the Hall Favart under the direction and with the assistance of Madame Catalani?

Nevertheless, the calm was a deceptive one. Passions that seemed to have died out were more alive than ever. The disquietude of those who had seized the national property increased every day. So great was the confidence of many old *émigrés* in an approaching restitution of what belonged to them, that, though some accepted offers of compromise that were made to them through fear, others utterly refused to do so in any shape or form. The story of a priest is told, who said from the pulpit that those who held national property and refused to restore it, would suffer the fate of Jezebel and be devoured by dogs. The *Journal royal* said that an old chevalier of Saint Louis, who had had the bad luck to purchase some landed property once owned by *émigrés*, returned it to its rightful owners before replacing on his breast a mark of honor that could not be reconciled with the seizure of Naboth's field. Alexandre de Puymaigre, a contemporary witness, said: "The more the royal machine went ahead, the more it went astray in the labyrinth of pretensions put forward by the two régimes and the embarrassments occasioned them by exasperated enemies and imprudent friends. So far from the parties becoming reconciled to each other, they turned the theatres, restaurants, promenades, and all public places into arenas where they showed their mutual antipathy in acts, sarcasm, and base caricatures."

The parlors of Queen Hortense became a hotbed of the Bonapartist opposition. True, the former Queen of Holland permitted herself to show no hostility to Louis XVIII., who had made her Duchess of Saint-Leu. She had audience of the King and was received most graciously. Encouraged by the quiet attitude of the Tuileries toward them, the old partisans of Napoleon began to raise their heads once more. As yet their hopes were only vague, but they hoped. All intelligent observers saw that the Bourbons had everything to fear from the army. "Most of the regiments," says M. de Puymaigre, "retained their love for the Emperor and their hatred of the Bourbons. I recollect that once while I was staying at the Hôtel de l'Ecu, at Montluçon, I found the host much scandalized at the conduct of a colonel of hussars whose regiment had spent the previous day in the village. "Your dinner is dear," said the colonel to him. "Is it because meat costs a great deal here? It is cheap in Paris; you have a big pig for a napoleon." All these symptoms of what was coming, and which could not escape the least observant eye, were despised by an incapable ministry, and all Paris knew that a return of the violet was expected (the violet was already the Bonapartist emblem, and the soldiers called Napoleon, Father Violet), and yet these sorry depositaries of power did not take the slightest precautions.

A proof that the court felt perfectly secure is that at the close of February, five days before the Emperor landed, the Duchess of Angoulême, who certainly would not have quitted Paris had she thought that the throne of her uncle there was in the least danger, went to Bordeaux to celebrate the anniversary of the 12th of March, 1814, the day on which the Duke made his formal entrance into the city, and inaugurated the reign of Louis XVIII. The journey of the Duke and Duchess was one long ovation. General Decaen, commander of the 11th Military Division, — the same man who was to unfurl the tricolor a few days afterwards, — announced their coming arrival in an order of the day in which he told his troops: "It will be very pleasant for the garrison of Bordeaux to mingle in the expression of public joy on that occasion, the expression of the love and devotion it feels for the worthy scions of the best kings of whom France can boast." The Duke and Duchess left Paris on the 27th of February, 1815. They slept at Orleans on the 27th, at Bourges on the 28th, at Issoudun on the 1st of March, and at Limoges on the 3d. Everywhere they passed under triumphal arches and amid applause.

All Bordeaux was stirring on the 5th of March. It flocked to the banks of the Gironde, at which the Princess and her husband were to land. Louis XVI.'s daughter had never visited this royalist city, and she was awaited with mingled feelings of curiosity and veneration. At one o'clock in the afternoon the beautiful gondola of the Duke and Duchess appeared. It was preceded and followed by a great number of boats handsomely decorated with white flags. At the moment when the daughter and the nephew of Louis XVI. left their craft to take carriage, twenty young men and the same number of young girls dressed in white attached themselves to the carriage and proceeded to draw it. The streets were strewn with verdure, and the houses hung with tapestry, while flowers were scattered profusely along the path of the triumphal procession. When it paused for an instant at the Place de la Comédie, a band of musicians, placed in the gallery surmounting the peristyle of the Grand Théâtre, rendered the famous chorus from the *Iphigénie:* —

"Let us sing and celebrate our queen," —

a chorus of which Marie Antoinette was very fond and which had very often been sung in her honor.

The 5th, 6th, 7th, and 8th of March were devoted to fêtes, spectacles, and public rejoicings. The multitude could not tire of the pleasure of looking upon the face of the orphan of the Temple. On the 9th of March, the Princess and her husband attended a ball given to them by the local merchants. The whole city was in the midst of rejoicings when, in the afternoon, a courier arrived from Paris with despatches for the Duke of Angoulême. These despatches announced the landing of Napoleon, and ordered the Duke to go to Nîmes at once, and there, as lieutenant-general of the kingdom for the department of the south, take command of the five southern military divisions.

The first words spoken by the Duchess of Angoulême when her husband told her the purport of the despatches were: "O, that this strife may not cost rivers of French blood!" However, the inhabitants of Bordeaux did not at once hear the startling news. In order not to disturb the festivities of the evening, the Prince and Princess decided to divulge nothing till the next day. In the evening they went to the ball, which was splendid, and betrayed in their affable and calm faces no trace of the thoughts that occupied their minds. At five o'clock in the morning, when the ball was hardly over, the Duke of Angoulême left his wife at Bordeaux, entered a postchaise with an aide-de-camp, and set out for Nîmes in all haste.

XVIII

THE RETURN OF NAPOLEON

FOR several weeks there had been, as the saying is, "something in the air" at Paris. The attitude of the troops was disquieting. There were deep mutterings in their ranks. Cries of "Long live the Emperor!" had more than once been heard, and on parade when the soldiers cried " Long live the King!" they added under their breath, "of Rome." Caricatures, the clandestine sale of which constantly increased, represented the eagles flying in through the windows of the Tuileries, while flocks of geese went out through the doors. A few far-seeing royalists had vague presentiments of evil. "A constant dread," says Madame de Staël, "held possession of my mind for some weeks before the landing of Bonaparte. In the evening, when the fine buildings of the city were lighted by the moon's rays, it seemed as though my happiness and that of France were like a sick friend whose smile is sweeter as the time of separation draws near." The ministers were in that state of optimistic tranquillity which always precedes the downfall of a government. "It is well known," says Count de Puymaigre in his *Souvenirs*, that "the Abbé de Montesquiou, Minister of the Interior, left unopened on his table despatches from M. de Bouthilier, prefect of Var, in which, fifteen days before the event, intelligence of the projects of the man from Elba was contained, and that the minister treated with similar indifference despatches which had been sent to him on the same subject by General Bruslart, commandant in Corsica."

No one at the Tuileries even dreamed of the danger when, about two in the afternoon of the 5th of March, M. de Vitrolles, Minister of State, who had the control of the telegraph system, sent Louis XVIII. a sealed envelope addressed to the sovereign. This envelope contained a copy of a telegraphic despatch received at Lyons, and which M. de Vitrolles had not yet read. The King opened the envelope and, after glancing at its contents, said: "Do you know what this is?"—"No, Sire!" "It says that Bonaparte has landed on the coast of Provence." Then he added calmly: "This must be taken to the Minister of War, who will see what is to be done about it." At this time the southern telegraph line did not extend beyond Lyons. Napoleon landed near Cannes, on the Gulf of Juan, on the 1st of March, and it was not till the 5th that General Brayer, commandant of the military division of Lyons, telegraphed to the government the important news which he had received by courier from Marshal Masséna, governor of Marseilles.

General Brayer's despatch read as follows: "On

the 1st of March, Bonaparte landed near Cannes, in the department of Var, with twelve hundred men and four cannon, and went on towards Digne and Gap, apparently on the way to Grenoble. Every means has been taken to arrest and thwart this mad undertaking. All things show the best disposition in the southern departments. Public tranquillity is assured." Louis XVIII. decided to keep the news secret for some time, and the Parisians learned it first from the *Moniteur* of the 7th of March.

Nevertheless some indiscreet acts were committed, and by the 6th the news began to circulate, to the great joy of some and the consternation of others.

Let us hear what Madame de Staël says: "Never shall I forget the moment when, on the 6th of March, 1815, I learned from one of my friends that Bonaparte had landed on the coast of France. I at once foresaw with sorrow the consequences of that event just as they afterwards turned out to be, and I felt as if the earth was opening to swallow me up. . . . I said to M. de Lavelette, whom I met shortly after hearing the news: 'Liberty is over if Bonaparte triumphs, and national independence is ended if he is defeated.'"

Louis XVIII. decided that his brother should go at once to Lyons and take command of the troops intended to stop the march of the invader. The King summoned the Duke of Orleans, and directed him to follow the heir apparent to Lyons and place himself under his orders. This rôle was by no means pleasing to the Duke, but Louis XVIII. dryly gave him to understand that he must obey. In announcing the departure of Monsieur the *Moniteur* of the 7th of March published a decree, in which the King called for an immediate session of the Chambers, together with a royal proclamation, declaring Bonaparte a rebel and a traitor.

Although intelligent royalists comprehended the extreme gravity of the situation, inconsiderate royalists felt or pretended to feel quite joyous. "So much the better!" they exclaimed. "The bandit has laid a trap for himself, into which he will fall. He will be hounded like a deer. He will be shot like a dog. He will be harried." To harry (*courir sus*) was an expression used in the royal proclamation. Chateaubriand himself grows merry over this archaic phrase. He says: "The chief measure employed against Bonaparte was an order that he be harried. Louis XVIII., the legless, running down and harrying the conqueror who bestrode the earth! The revival of this antique legal formula on such an occasion is enough to show the perspicacity of the statesmen at that epoch. Harrying in 1815! Harry whom? Harry a wolf? Harry the captain of a band of brigands? Harry a robber baron? No; harry Napoleon, who had harried, caught them, and branded them forever on the shoulder with his ineradicable N."

However, Louis XVIII. affected an imperturbable calmness. In spite of an attack of the gout, he received all the ambassadors on the 7th of March.

"Gentlemen," said he, "you see me in pain; but do not deceive yourselves; its cause is not anxiety but the gout. Reassure your sovereigns about what is going on in France. The peace of Europe will be disturbed no more than that of my kingdom."

On the 8th of March the *Journal des Débats* said: "Certain shady practices, and certain manœuvres in Italy, which were incited by his stupid brother-in-law, have puffed up the pride of the cowardly warrior of Fontainebleau. He runs a chance of dying the death of a hero, but God will let him die the death of a traitor. The land of France has cast him out; he returns to it, and the land of France will be his grave. On what friends can he rely? On the fathers and brothers of the thousands whom he drove before him on his distant and barbarous expeditions? On the magistrates whom he outraged, the judges whom he insulted in their own courts? On which of his old partisans? On the generals, whose glory he labored so hard to obscure, in order that all of which he had robbed them might make his own glory shine more brightly, the generals whom he released from their vows, and who will so much the better keep those which they have taken since then?"

On the same day, the 8th of March, 1815, Marshal Soult, the Minister of War, addressed an order of the day to the army, in which he — he who a few weeks afterwards was to be the Emperor's major-general at Waterloo, said: "Soldiers, the man who but recently and before the eyes of all Europe abdicated the power he had usurped, and of which he made such desperate use, Bonaparte, has landed on French soil, which he had no claims to see again. What does he want? Civil war. Where does he look for it? Among traitors. Where does he expect to find it? Among those soldiers whom he has so often deceived by practising on their bravery. Will it be made in the name of those families which his name alone still fills with dread? Bonaparte has contempt enough for us to think that we will abandon a legitimate and well-loved sovereign to share the fate of a mere adventurer. He believes this, the insensate man, and his latest mad act shows that he believes it. Soldiers, the French army is the bravest army in Europe! It will prove itself the most faithful."

On the 9th of March, Louis XVIII., seated on one of the balconies of the Tuileries, saw the Paris garrison and the national guard defile in the courtyard. They cheered lustily. Of their own accord the regiments of the line waved their shakos from the points of their bayonets, and cried: "Long live the King!" "To see the enthusiasm," says Count de Puymaigre, who was present at the review, "one would have believed that Bonaparte, with his twelve hundred men, could not fail to be crushed at once; but some of the soldiers were traitors at heart, others were bewildered, and most were awaiting events.

"On leaving the Tuileries, where all were wavering between hope and fear, I went, in order to assure myself of the real disposition of the army, to visit one of my old acquaintances, Lieutenant-General Domon, of the hussars, who was chief equerry to the King, and who is now dead. There were several colonels at his house, and while breakfasting with them I saw that, mistaking me for one of their party on account of my age, bearing, and the simple red ribbon at my buttonhole, they cast off restraint and showed that every one of them had wished for Napoleon's return."

Having explained the situation, M. de Puymaigre goes on to say: "One of them especially, Colonel G——, made me indignant by the irony with which he gave an account of a visit he had paid to the Duke of Berry, and in which he had sworn that his devotion would be found equal to every proof. Upon leaving, I said to General Domon, who had not displayed similar duplicity: 'The business is settled; your army will go over to the enemy.'"

At the same time, the newspapers went into frenzies of rage in their diatribes against Napoleon. They could not find words bad enough to express their feelings. They called him the Brigand of Elba, the Corsican Ogre, the Modern Teutatès. The national guard of the Paris garrison held a review on the 9th of March, and on that day the *Débats* published an article in which the following words were used: "Here we have the poltroon of 1814 entering on the absurdest as well as the rashest enterprise that was ever conceived of. He lands, and the gates of the cities which he supposed would open to him remain closed; the soldiers who were to call him emperor again, respond to the cries of rebels only by shouting, 'Long live the King!' The peasants rush to arms and everywhere assail the bandits who come to ravage their peaceful fields. The great man, who is strong only when borne along by prosperous winds, is doubtless troubled and repentant, but what will he do? He will endeavor to do what he did in Egypt, what he did in Russia, what he did in Saxony: he will abandon the eight hundred unhappy men whom he has dragged to the field of carnage and — to use an expression peculiar to his bulletins of old — he will save himself 'personally,' without regard to the fate of his comrades in arms. May Providence, weary of his crimes, now upset his rascally calculations!"

It is said that on the same day, the 9th of March namely, no one learned anything by the Lyons telegraph, because a thick fog prevented what it announced from being read. The darkness was a presage of evil. In the evening, Madame de Staël went to the Tuileries to pay her respects to Louis XVIII. "It seemed to me," says she, "that an expression showing that he was ill at ease shone through his appearance of courage. While leaving the Tuileries, I saw the still unobliterated eagles on the walls of Napoleon's apartments, and they seemed to me to have become threatening again. At a reception in the evening, a young lady who, with many others, contributed to the spirit of frivolity which they wished to oppose to that of faction, as if the two could contend with each other, approached me and made some pleasantries on the anxiety that I could not conceal. 'What! Madame,' said she, 'can you fear that the French will not fight for their lawful King against a usurper?' How could one reply to so well-turned a phrase without committing one's self? But, after twenty-five years of revolution, had one a right to flatter one's self that a respectable but abstract idea like legitimacy would have more influence with the soldiers than all the memories of their long wars?" Some of the royalists were infatuated enough to rejoice over the return from Elba. "That event," adds Madame de Staël, "must have seemed to them the most fortunate that could have occurred, because Bonaparte would be got rid of, and the two Chambers would see the necessity of giving the King absolute power, — as if that would be tolerated! I am not sure that some of the enemies of any constitution whatever were not glad of disturbances which might bring foreigners into France and impel them to impose an absolute government on the country."

On the 10th of March, the royalists continued to cherish their illusions. The morning's *Moniteur* contained this reassuring paragraph: "A telegraphic despatch announces the arrival of Monsieur at Lyons at ten o'clock on the morning of the 8th, in perfect health. His Royal Highness found the troops and inhabitants united in a common feeling of devotion and fidelity, of which he received the most striking evidences." On the very day when the news of this good reception was circulating in the capital and reviving the hopes of royalists, the King's brother and the Duke of Orleans left Lyons and returned post-haste to Paris, being intimidated by the hostile attitude of the troops.

Nevertheless, it was still imagined that Marshal Ney would arrest the progress of Napoleon. Louis XVIII. issued the following royal proclamation: " Given at the château of the Tuileries, March 11, 1815. — Measures have been taken to stop the enemy between Lyons and Paris. We have ample means of accomplishing this, if the nation will oppose to him the insuperable obstacle of its devotion and courage. France will not be defeated in this struggle between freedom and tyranny, between Louis XVIII. and Bonaparte." Companies of royal volunteers were organized at Paris. In their ranks were M. Odilon Barrot, many students at the Medical School, and all of those at the Law School. Loyal addresses were sent to the King from all parts of the kingdom. Every functionary, military or civil, rushed headlong into adulatory declamation. The only Bonapartist journal of the day, the *Nain Jaune*, which was more and more closely watched by the censorship, said that Napoleon, after having dragged out the last fragments of a dishonored life on the rocks of the island of Elba, would be driven from France with horror. But approaching retractions were already showing themselves under the semblance of enthusiasm and devotion.

Society in the Faubourg Saint-Germain passed from ridiculous infatuation to morbid alarm. The news of the occupation of Lyons by the Emperor and the abrupt return of Monsieur and the Duke of Orleans to Paris put a stop to boastings. A nightmare seemed to oppress all. Every week, every minute, had its new impressions. The women were more over-excited and violent than the men. There was general confusion and disorder. Marshal Ney was no longer expected to keep his alleged promise to the King, and bring the usurper back in an iron cage. On the 14th of March, the Abbé Montesquiou, Minister of the Interior, affirmed in the Chamber of Deputies that, being satisfied with the excellent disposition of the troops, the Marshal had advanced from Franche-Comté on the road to Lyons, there to meet the enemy. It was related on the same day that several foreign ministers had said to the King: "Sire, we will not disguise from Your Majesty that we have informed our courts of what is going on in France, and that if this state of things continues, their answer will be the entry of the troops of our sovereigns into France." The *Journal des Débats* added this comment: "And, Frenchmen! behold in this the benefits bestowed on us by Bonaparte,— a foreign war that may bring the Cossacks once again to the gates of Paris." Alas! this prediction was only too true!

On the next day, the 15th of March, the same journal which had now worked itself up to a paroxysm of fury, said: "What does this man demand? A throne, the throne of France. What is he? We do not speak of his former deeds of madness, — he is a foreigner! And should not that word alone suffice to rally all the sons of France against him? We all rejoiced at the return of the Bourbons, and under them we recovered what we had so long sought, — work and freedom. But even if the Bourbons had betrayed all our hopes, even if the crown were at disposal, by what right and under what pretext could it be snatched by this foreigner? The lowest of our soldiers, the most obscure of our peasants, provided he were a Frenchman, would have a better right to it than this son of a bourgeois of Ajaccio."

And the sheet that was once called the *Journal de l'Empire* added: "Hear the general shouts of confidence and joy inspired among the people by the wisdom of its government and the fidelity of its defenders, 'He shall not return!' It is the burden of all we say, the refrain of all we talk about. . . . And why should he return to Paris? He was driven from it by justice, by force of arms, and, above all, by Providence. He was driven from it by his own remembrances, by a power invisible to all but him, and which acted on him alone. Like the Richard III. of the English poet, and like him tormented on the eve of battle by the shades of his victims, he sees from afar his progress opposed by the ghosts of four millions of men immolated to enhance his fatal glory, and hears them cry in a dreadful voice, 'Scourge of the Generations, thou shalt reign no more!'" And yet this "Scourge of the Generations" had already begun to reign. Within five days he ascended the grand staircase of the Tuileries, and on the next day the *Débats* resumed its old name of the *Journal de l'Empire*.

Listen to an eye-witness, the late Duke of Broglie. In his carefully compiled *Souvenirs* he says: "Both government and society were a sorry sight. False news came in in double quantity, but nobody put the least faith in it. They waxed hot with declamations which were taken at their true value. They made preparations for resistance, in the firm resolve not to withstand the first attack. They swore hatred to the tyrant while they were underhandedly making ready to be well received by him when the right moment came. Forbin trailed his big sword in the parlors of Madame Récamier, Benjamin Constant brandished the article which, unluckily for him, he had inserted in the *Journal des Débats*, and as they did so both these gentlemen were more concerned about the impression they were making on the mistress of the house than on anything else in the world. A few people made their way to the Tuileries and, while shouting 'Long live the King!' were waiting expectantly, to change that cry to 'Long live the Emperor!' The two Chambers felt themselves quite as truly dethroned as royalty was. Their secret committees were unmasked like the councils of the princes, and their halls became cafés to which people came to hear the news." The moment was drawing nigh when Napoleon should say to M. Mollien: " They have let me come as they let the others go." The Duke of Broglie will repeat the famous words of Cromwell, when, hearing the enthusiastic shouts of those around him, the Protector said to Thurloe: " These people would shout still louder and more joyfully if they saw me going to be hanged."

XIX

THE ROYAL ASSEMBLAGE

THE death agony of the first Restoration had begun. Louis XVIII. endeavored at least to fall nobly, and like a king who yet hoped to come back presently to his own. He desired to give royalty a splendid burial; there was real majesty in the solemnities of the 16th of March when the Chambers met at the Palais Bourbon, and the speech from the throne was like a funeral oration of the monarchy pronounced by the King himself in the idea that the monarchy would be restored to life.

At three o'clock Louis XVIII. set out from the Tuileries with a large number of attendants. On the way from the château to the Palais Bourbon the national guard was enthusiastic. The regulars kept silence. But the King paid no attention to this silence. He went over in his mind the discourse that he wished to recite by heart. The floor and galleries were filled with a throng composed entirely of royalists. The Chamber of Peers occupied one half of the semicircle and the Chamber of Deputies the other half. The staff of the 1st Military Division and that of the national guard occupied benches placed beside the throne. The body-guards were stationed in the hall along with the national guard and troops of the line.

When the King appeared, he was greeted with loud and unanimous applause. His face was sorrowful but calm. He wore for the first time the star of the Legion of Honor. After slowly ascending the steps to the throne, at the foot of which stood the princes, the marshals, and the captains of the body-guard, he sat down, and his look, as he bowed majestically to the assembly, showed that he was about to speak. Then, amid a profound and even religious silence, he began his pathetic address in a deep and sonorous voice: "Gentlemen," said he, "at this critical moment when the public enemy occupies part of my kingdom and menaces the liberty of all the rest, I come to you in the desire of strengthening the ties which, by binding you and me, fortify the State. In addressing you, I desire to show all France what are my sentiments and my desires. I have returned to my country; I have reconciled it with foreign powers which will undoubtedly remain faithful to the treaties which have restored us to peace; I have labored for the welfare of my people; I have received, I every day receive, most affecting evidences of their love: how could I, at the age of sixty years, better end my existence than by dying in their defence?"

The King uttered this phrase simply and with emotion. It produced an immense effect. Everybody was moved. The royal orator then continued: "I fear nothing for myself, but I fear for France. He who comes to light the torch of civil war among us brings also the plague of foreign war; he would place our country once more under his iron yoke and will finally destroy that Constitutional Charter that I have given you, — my fairest title to future fame, — the Charter which all Frenchmen hold dear and which I have sworn to maintain." Here the enthusiasm of the liberal royalists knew no bounds. Nothing was more imposing in their eyes than the solemn oath the King had taken to abide by the Charter. "Let us rally around it!" said he in conclusion. "Let it be our blest standard! The descendants of Henri IV. will be the first to stand to it, and all good Frenchmen will come to their side. In conclusion, gentlemen, may the meeting of the two Chambers give to authority the power it requires, and may this truly national war prove by its happy issue what can be done by a great people united through love of its King and the fundamental law of the State."

At the very moment when Louis XVIII. uttered the concluding sentence of his address, a darkness fell upon the hall. All present looked up to discover the cause of this sudden night. The sky was growing black as if in sympathy with the gloom of the situation and in mourning for royalty. One might have imagined himself in a vast and sombre church, and darkness lent yet more solemnity to the ceremony. When the King ceased, the whole assembly, as if electrified, sprang to their feet and, extending their hands towards the throne, cried out: "Long live the King! Let us die for the King! Living or dying, we are the King's!"

Monsieur then approached his brother, and all became respectfully silent as he signified that he was about to speak. "Sire," said the Prince, "I know that I am now violating common rules by addressing Your Majesty, but I implore you to excuse me for expressing at this juncture, on behalf of myself and my family, how thoroughly and from the bottom of our hearts we share the feelings and principles that animate Your Majesty." Then, raising his hand, he added: "We swear by our honor to live and die true to the King and to the Constitutional Charter, which secures the happiness of the French!" Then Louis XVIII. extended his hand to Monsieur, who seized and kissed it in a transport of enthusiasm. The emotion of the audience, which had constantly increased, reached its height when the sovereign, yielding to the general impulse, pressed Monsieur to his heart with all the dignity of a king and all the tenderness of a brother. The *Moniteur* says: "In a single day the destiny of France would be secured and the King, the country, our most inviolable laws, and our dearest rights would be guaranteed forever, if all France could have witnessed that scene. But in effect it was present in its representatives, in its most illustrious military leaders, and a host of citizens impartially admitted to the body of the house, in the soldiers and civilians who were crowded in the hall and outside the walls, and who tumultuously re-echoed the shouts, the vows, and the applause of the Assembly."

This solemnity roused the imaginations of the royalists and deeply stirred their hearts. At the close of the day long files of men of all classes, and carrying white flags, went through the streets lauding Louis XVIII. and heaping maledictions on Napoleon. "Long live the King!" they cried, "Down with the tyrant!"

On the same day the following appeared in the *Débats*: "I swear by France prosperous and happy that the fugitive from the island of Elba shall never again see the walls of Paris. We brave soldiers whom he has insulted by counting on our aid, we soldiers together with our fellow-citizens, will save France, liberty, and the King. Till Lyons, all was unforeseen; after Lyons, all shall be one intrepid defence. What shall we see when we meet the enemy? On the one side will be found the sons of France and the blood royal, all those faithful and illustrious generals at the head of their brave soldiers, fighting for country, freedom, and king; on the other, a fallen emperor invoking oaths which he himself has broken, and a few disheartened bands that hardly deserve to be compared with those companies which appeared in the fourteenth century and were known as 'sons of Belial,'—soldiers from many lands, without title and without name."

The bands which excited the ironical disdain of the royalistic journals approached. They approached, and the terror they inspired was such that the throne crumbled before even their trumpet blasts could be heard. A few hours after the royal séance it became known that Marshal Ney had gone over to the enemy on the 4th of March at Lons-le-Saulnier. Thus vanished royalty's last hope. It might be said that it already heard Napoleon's footsteps from afar.

XX

THE KING'S DEPARTURE

THE situation became more desperate every hour. One man tried to deceive another or endeavored to deceive himself, and people longed for the ability to shut their eyes to evidence. It was known what would be the outcome of all the mouthings of a few days before — of all those pompous and sounding phrases about the fidelity of the army and the stability of the throne. The time for heroic remedies had come.

Marshal Marmont, Duke of Ragusa, said to the King: "I am a man of business and, if full power is given to me, I will pledge myself and with nothing more than the resources now in Paris, to put the Tuileries and the Louvre into such a state of defence that it will require a breaching battery to enter it; and this I will do within five days. Provisions for three thousand men for two months must be placed in the château. The household of the King will be excellent for this purpose, without drawing on the provinces for their services. It is composed of men of courage, each of whom will be solicitors of the honor of taking part in the defence.

The King must shut himself up in a fortress of that sort, together with all that constitutes the imposingness of government, — ministers, both Chambers, and all except his family. A resolution so magnanimous will react most powerfully on the troops. Do you know the state of opinion in three-quarters of France? Except in the eastern departments and a few scattered malecontents, it is everywhere in our favor. In the west, in Normandy, Picardy, and Flanders, the masses are wholly devoted to you. The national guards are for you. Give them time to get in motion; they will not be needed in your behalf for three months yet. . . . Sire, I claim the honor of being shut in with Your Majesty, as commander or common soldier, I care not in what capacity."

M. de Chateaubriand was of Marshal Marmont's opinion: "I said," is his story, "let us barricade ourselves in Paris. National guards from the department are already coming to our aid. While this is going on, our aged monarch, under the protection of Louis XVI.'s will and with the Charter in his hand, will remain peacefully seated on the throne at the Tuileries; the diplomatic corps will be around him, both Chambers will meet in the pavilions of the château, and the King's household will camp on the Carrousel and in the gardens of the Tuileries. We will line the quays and the terrace overlooking the water with cannon. Let Bonaparte attack us in such a position; let him carry our barricades one after another; let him bombard Paris if he chooses and if he has any mortars; let him make himself detested by the whole population, and we shall soon see what will be the result of his undertaking. If we hold out for only three days, the victory is ours. The King defending himself in his castle will cause universal enthusiasm. In a word, if he is to die, let him die worthy of his blood, and let Napoleon's last exploit be the butchery of an aged man. By sacrificing his life, Louis XVIII. will win the only battle he will have fought, and he will win it to the gain of the freedom of the human race."

For one moment the monarch was wise enough to take or seem to take the advice of persons who begged him not to run away. He said in the council of his ministers on the 18th of March: "I shall remain at the Tuileries; I will face the pretender who would seat himself on my throne. . . . I will always count on my people after the reception they gave me." But reflection soon threw cold water on this fine fire. It must be acknowledged that the heroic counsel of those who favored resistance was not very practical, and it is more than likely that if Louis XVIII. had followed it he would shortly have become Napoleon's prisoner. That exceptionally bold man, the almost foolhardy Baron de Vitrolles himself, told his ministerial colleagues: "Bonaparte will capture the rest of Paris and then capture the King shut up in the Tuileries; once master of the whole capital and the whole of France, he will wait for the King to surrender at discretion when the château's provisions give out." The notion of falling alive into the hands of the murderer of the Duke of Enghien was not very pleasing to the sagacious monarch, who had no wish to enter upon the captivity to which his unfortunate brother Louis XVI. had been subjected. Besides this, the scheme of the man who caused the defection at Essonnes probably made him cautious. Fifteen years later it would hardly do to employ the marshal in the defence of the Louvre and the Tuileries.

Louis XVIII. refused to adopt the project of turning the château into a fortress. To judge from the *Mémoires d'Outre-Tombe*, Chateaubriand was inconsolable at this refusal. "What could have been finer," says he, "than for an aged son of Saint Louis to overthrow, in a few moments, a man whom it had taken the combined kings of Europe so many years to put down? If my plan had been adopted, foreigners would not have ravaged France over again; our princes would not have returned through the aid of armed foreigners; legitimacy would have been saved by itself. After success there would have been only one thing to fear, — an overweening confidence in its own power on the part of royalty, and consequent attempts against the rights of the nation."

And this really singular royalist, who was always contented with himself and discontented with others, and who, in his Memoirs always seems to be vindicating his opinions to posterity, adds bitterly: "Why was I born at an epoch so unfit for me? Why was I a royalist against my own instinct at a time when a wretched set at court could neither hear nor understand me? Why was I thrown into that herd of commonplace men who took me for a rattlepate when I spoke courage, and for a revolutionist when I preached freedom?" Then he goes on to describe the confusion at the Tuileries, the two processions that went up and down the stairs of the Pavilion of Flora, asking each other what was to be done; the frightened people who questioned the captain of the guards, the chaplains, the precentors, the almoners; he draws pictures of the tumults, the fruitless consultations, the vain search for news; of young men who wept with rage when their demands for orders and arms proved unavailing; and women who swooned with rage and scorn.

Nevertheless, writers in the royalist journals assumed the tone heroic. Leonidas at Thermopylæ was not more dignified. The *Débats* said on the 18th of March: "Bonaparte needs mercy from all his contemporaries; he needs mercy from the future; but no man worthy of the name of man needs the mercy of Bonaparte. As for ourselves, we have sworn not to receive at his hands the humiliating boon of life, and will show that a patriotic press has, too, its courage, its devotion, and its love of glory. Fame has palms for Lucan as well as for

Thraseas. All services are honorable, all deaths are illustrious, when one labors for freedom and country! King, country, and freedom! These are the price of death, — death in the curule chair of the Senate, on the field of battle, or on the martyr's scaffold — everywhere death is beautiful and to be desired. There is no agony, no torment, that cannot be repaid by sentiments so noble and so tender. But what compassion shall ever compensate for the infamy of living under a tyrant? Long live the King! Long live the country! Long live Freedom!"

And this was not the last oration made in the manner of the ancients. It was said in the *Débats* of the following day, March 19th, when the King took flight: "Under Bonaparte we would have a goverment of Mamelukes. . . . He is an Attila, a Gengis Khan, but more terrible and hateful than they because the resources of civilization are at his command, and it is apparent that he uses them to organize massacre and administer pillage; he does not disguise his intentions; he despises us too much to condescend to deceive us. And, indeed, what people would better deserve contempt, if we should reach out our arms to receive his shackles? And, as the heart of the profound objection to such a course, what should we dare to say to the King whom we could not recall, since the Powers would respect the independence of the national preferences, — what, I repeat, should we dare to say to that King whom we voluntarily brought back to the land where his family had suffered so much already? We should say to him: You trusted the French; we surrounded you with homage, and, believing our oaths, you left your asylum and came among us alone and unarmed. So long as there was no danger, so long as you had the favors of power to dispose of, a great people deafened you with their noisy applause. You did not abuse its enthusiasm. One year of your reign did not cause as many tears to flow as one single day of Bonaparte's rule. But he appeared on our frontiers, — he, the man stained with our blood and but recently driven out with the curses of us all. He came, he menaced, and neither oaths nor manhood restrained us, nor did your trust in us keep us to our duty, nor did we respect old age. You thought you had found a nation, but you found only a horde of perjured slaves.

"No, such shall not be our language. Such, at least, shall not be mine. I say to-day, without fear of misconception, that I have sought for liberty under many shapes. I have seen that it was possible under monarchy; I have seen the King fraternize with the nation, and I will not, like a contemptible time-server, go from one side to the other, cover infamy with sophistry, and cringe with debasing words in order to purchase a shameful existence."

Contrary to the custom of the journal, this was a signed article. It bore the signature of Benjamin de Constant. Why did that eminent political writer, contrary to his custom, now put his name at the end of his article? Because he wished to protect himself against himself, to forearm himself against future changes by making these solemn declarations? Ah, well! that precaution was not of much avail. Two days afterwards, the *Débats* appeared under its former title of the *Journal de l'Empire*, and, within a short time, M. Benjamin de Constant, who, on the 19th of March, had played the part of Cicero against Catiline, was made councillor of state by Napoleon.

The last hour of the first Restoration had struck. Louis XVIII. decided to set out in the evening, but on the 19th of March he wished to play the King once more. He went at noon to review his military household in the Champ-de-Mars. "It was then only by miracle that royalty could be saved," says the Count de Puymaigre, an eye-witness, "and yet on seeing that huge national guard, the newly created household troops of the King and the rich uniforms that glittered in the courtyard of the Tuileries, who would not have believed that the throne was established on unshakable foundations? I put myself under the protection of a subaltern attached to the service of the château, and we went as far as the Horloge Pavilion at the foot of the grand stairway, and there, at a time mournful and sombre as the future of France, I saw Louis XVIII. painfully get into his carriage to proceed to the accomplishment of a last duty of royalty. This then, said I to myself, is one of the last days of monarchy, which dies amid all the semblances of formidable strength and all the deceitful appearances of power."

The review was very fine. The King's military household greeted him with great warmth. The sovereign's intention to leave the country was not yet known. The morning's *Moniteur* had characterized the rumor on that subject as an absurd lie which only evil-disposed men believed. But the King knew perfectly well that he was to leave in the evening. At nine o'clock in the morning he had summoned Marshal Marmont, who had general control of the military household, and had given him a slip of paper designating the time of departure to a minute, and saying that the King would go to Saint-Denis where he would remain to give further orders.

When the review was over, the King went back to the Tuileries in all the calmness of despair. These words are used by Baron de Vitrolles, who continues: "The rest of the day was passed in conferences, personal arrangements, and discussing the intelligence that we constantly received of the Emperor's approach, and which did not come fast enough for us if we got it every fifteen minutes. One would have had to be present during those last moments in order to understand the singularity of that situation in which, though still alive, one knows that one will be dead to-morrow. While passing a room on the ground-floor of the Tuileries, I was struck at seeing a magnificent dinner prepared in honor of the Spanish Ambassador. It was what is called in the language of etiquette an 'entertainment,' that is to say, a repast of twenty-five or thirty covers, and given in the King's name by his maître d'hôtel. The dinner was ended four or five hours before the King's departure! We were, forsooth, the masters as yet, and everybody obeyed us as if we were still in full sway. People even came to ask for decorations."

At half-after eleven in the evening, M. de Vitrolles went to Louis XVIII., whom he found calm and acting as usual. The King said to him: "Go to Bordeaux and Toulouse, and do there whatever you think necessary on my account. Send this letter to my niece, whom you will direct to stay at Bordeaux as long as she can, and then counsel to do as I am doing." Taking the letter from the King's hand, M. de Vitrolles then said: "Sire, I greatly regret that I could not have foreseen Your Majesty's orders: I wish I could have been with the ministers while receiving your instructions. They would have enlightened me about them." — "*Mitte sapientem et nihil dicas,*" replied the King. The Baron made a profound bow on receiving this Latin compliment, and assured His Majesty that he was happy to have another opportunity to prove his unbounded devotion. He merely observed that the important trust confided to him required powers from the King. "Powers?" replied Louis XVIII.

"You do not need any; you are my minister and have full powers. Besides, the presence of my nephew and niece will give you all the authority you require." After these words he extended his hand to the Baron, who kissed it and withdrew, more moved certainly than the King was himself.

Let us hear M. de Vitrolles further: "I cast a last look at the Tuileries, but now so brilliant with lights, so joyous, so full of men and motion, — at that palace which but a short time ago was surrounded with all that seems great and powerful, but now dark, lonely, abandoned by its masters, and ready to be given over to a Corsican who had no other right to it than his audacity and the servility of a horde of fanatics. And it was before such a man that the royal family and a whole monarchy was taking flight, driven for a second time along the highroad to exile!

"I went home full of sorrowful thoughts. There I found a few friends, among whom was the *Moniteur Officiel*, in the person of Sauvo, who had come to submit the articles to me, as if for us there would be a morrow to that fatal day. I smiled at the thought that we would still throw this last word to the public after having gone away."

That last word was the proclamation which appeared in the *Moniteur* on the following morning, — the 20th of March, and in which the fugitive monarch said: "Divine Providence, which called us to the throne of our fathers, now permits that throne to fall through the treason of an armed force that had sworn to defend it. We might take advantage of the faithful and patriotic sentiments of the immense majority of the inhabitants of Paris, and dispute the entrance of the rebels into the capital, but we shudder at the thought of all the evils of every sort that would be brought upon the inhabitants by a battle under their walls. We retire with a few brave men whom intrigue and perfidy have not succeeded in seducing from their duty, and, since we are unable to defend our capital, we will go away to collect forces and seek in another part of the kingdom, not subjects more loving and faithful than our good Parisians, but Frenchmen in a better position to declare for the good cause."

It would soon be midnight. In a few minutes the hour fixed for the King's departure would strike. Travelling-carriages stood before the Pavilion of Flora. A few persons at the château were informed of the sovereign's determination. In an instant everybody knows it, and there is general consternation. Body-guards, employees of the palace, and national guards on duty hasten from all parts to await Louis XVIII. in the vestibule. Under the light of torches which an hussar carries before him, the King, supported by M. de Blacas and the Duke of Duras, slowly descends the staircase of the Pavilion of Flora. Men kneel before him, kiss his hands, beg him to remain and swear to defend him. Unusually moved, the royal fugitive says to the weeping crowd: "My children, your attachment touches my heart; I do not say adieu, but *au revoir*." The weather is dreadful; rain falls in torrents. It is a night filled with anguish and mourning. The King slowly enters the carriage, and the wind blowing in violent gusts extinguishes the torches that cast a dismal glare over the scene, the prelude of exile.

The late Duke of Broglie, who was as ill-disposed towards the elder branch of the Bourbons as towards the Emperor, exclaims in his *Souvenirs:* "On seeing that little man, made so great by a hundred victories, at the head of a handful of old mustaches, tumble down a card castle with one fillip of his fingers, and kick over the whole scenery of the play, I could not help recalling an incident in the romance of Cervantes, where the hero of La Mancha goes into a booth of marionettes, and, seeing a puppet dressed like a captive princess and in thrall to a huge painted giant, draws his big sword, and cuts down dungeon and prisoners, mountebank and stall."

The Duke describes also the 20th day of March: "The day following the departure of him who had been permitted to depart was still more mournful than that which preceded it. Paris was sad; the public squares were deserted, and the cafés, where men used to meet, were for the most part closed; passers-by avoided them, and in the streets hardly anybody was met but belated military men, officers in merry mood, and drunken soldiers singing the

Marseillaise Hymn — the everlasting refrain of roisterers, offering tricolor cockades to everybody in jest and almost at the sabre's point." Then he shows us, like the little piece before the main play, how at nightfall Saint-Didier, formerly prefect of the palace, placed himself at the head of the imperial domestics, stewards, cooks, and scullions, each having doffed his livery, triumphantly took possession of the disordered apartments, beds still unmade and chafing-dishes still steaming, and made a clean sweep of all that was left of the royal housekeeping.

"The master came," continues the Duke de Broglie, "in the words of the New Testament, which were never more appropriate, 'like a thief in the night.' He ascended the great staircase of the Tuileries, supported by his generals, and all the followers of his fortunes, past and present, whose faces, nevertheless, were fully as anxious as they were expectant." There is to be a complete change of scenery. The *Débats*, once more the *Journal de l'Empire*, is about to say: "Paris, March 20. — The Bourbon family left Paris last night. It is not yet known what road they took. To-day Paris puts on a look of security and joy. The boulevards are filled with an immense crowd, impatient to see the army and its heroic leader who has already returned. The small number of troops who were foolishly expected to oppose him have rallied to the eagles, and the whole French militia, become national again, is marching under the banners of glory and the fatherland. The Emperor has sped like lightning across two hundred leagues, in the midst of a people transported with admiration and respect, filled with present happiness and the assurance of happiness for the future." What! Is this the language of the *Débats!* The journal is still published at the old stand, No. 17 Prêtres-Saint-Germain l'Auxerrois. 'Tis the same printing-house, — that of Le Normant; the sheet is as large as ever and its look is the same; nothing about it has changed except its opinions.

And now hear what the *Débats*, which is Bonapartist again, says in its issue of March 22d: "Paris, March 21. — Yesterday His Majesty the Emperor entered Paris at the head of the same troops that went out in the morning to oppose his march. The army which has sprung into existence since he landed, was unable to come further than Fontainebleau. During his journey His Majesty reviewed several bodies of troops. Wherever he went he was preceded and surrounded by an immense number of people. This morning and all through the day a vast concourse covered the terrace of the château of the Tuileries, making the air resound with the liveliest acclaims of love and joy. His Majesty appeared several times at the windows of his apartments, and was welcomed with endlessly repeated shouts of 'Long live the Emperor!'" And when Napoleon shall go to the theatre and be received with the boisterous applause by the same claqueurs who once welcomed Louis XVIII., the journal will exclaim: "Last evening the Emperor was present at a representation of *Hector*. The audience was very large. His Majesty was greeted with hearty applause, which was repeated all through the play with inexpressible enthusiasm. Among the lines that brought forth universal plaudits were the following: .

> " ' Like some Colossus vast, a warrior comes
> To the unshaken army. 'Tis he! Achilles 'twas.
> He came at last.'

At these words, cries of 'Long live the Emperor!' filled the air. The stalls and the parterre mingled their shouts, which were renewed every moment, since every scene of the drama afforded striking allusions to the memorable events which we have just witnessed."

How strange the epoch! How melancholy the shifting of scenery! The bravest soldiers and the best citizens asked themselves what they ought to do, and their consciences thus questioned knew not what to reply. Never was seen such a confusion in facts and opinions. It resembled the eclipse of right and duty. France was like a puzzled actress who, having been assigned to two different parts in the same scene, confounds the one with the other. For one single nation there were two sovereigns, two flags, and, it may even be said, two countries.

XXI

BORDEAUX

WE left the Duchess of Angoulême at Bordeaux on the morning of the 10th of March, 1815, at the hour when her husband, having passed the night at the ball given in their honor by the city merchants, set out post-haste for Nîmes, where he was to take command of the troops opposed to the progress of Napoleon.

The news of the Emperor's landing on the coast of the Gulf of Juan did not change the sentiments of the Bordeaux royalists. The fête which the city gave to celebrate the anniversary of the 12th of March, when Bordeaux was the first French city to proclaim the restoration of the Bourbons, was signalized by a fresh outburst of enthusiasm. The Duchess of Angoulême could have wished to return to Paris immediately after the festivities, there to share the perils of the King. But Louis XVIII. sent orders that she was to remain at Bordeaux to organize resistance in the city. Thereafter the Princess displayed indefatigable activity; she made the troops take the oath of loyalty over again, held reviews, created corps of volunteers, received subscriptions, and presided over a government council with as much presence of mind as firmness.

On the morning of the 23d of March Baron de Vitrolles arrived at Bordeaux. He was driven at once to the palace of the Princess. The doors were immediately opened, and he saw at the end of several parlors the daughter of Louis XVI. on her knees before her prie-dieu. At the noise made by the Baron on entering with the hussar who announced him, the Princess rose with a disturbed contenance. M. de Vitrolles at once and without preamble presented the King's letter; then he told her the sad news from Paris and spoke of the impossibility of getting any one there to defend the capital, and also of the abrupt departure of the sovereign. The Princess courageously fortified herself to hear without pallor the recital of these events, which Louis XVIII.'s letter did not explain. The Baron tried to console her by laying down a plan of resistance for the western and southern provinces: the occupation of the left bank of the Loire by troops drawn from the corps of Marshal Gouvion Saint-Cyr and the Duke of Bourbon; the establishment of a central administration at Toulouse; a levy of volunteers from Marseilles to Nantes; the disbanding of those regiments which were uncertain; and the concentration of all the royalist forces in the strongest possible way. The face of the Duchess of Angoulême cleared, and hope seemed to take the place of anxiety. "That, Madame," said the Baron in conclusion, "is what we are going to do, or rather what we shall try to do as soon as possible and with all the energy that the noble cause we defend can give us; that is what we shall endeavor to accomplish, though probably too late." — "Why do you say that?" asked the Princess. "Because it is too late, Madame; because Paris is no longer ours, and its influence will paralyze all our efforts. Because . . ." — "Don't tell me that," interrupted the Princess; "what is so well conceived is already successfully executed."

The Princess then said to M. de Vitrolles that as yet she had seen no sign of defection among the troops of the Bordeaux garrison; that the officers, without being consumed with zeal, seemed disposed to do their duty. That General Decaen, who commanded the division, was suspected of incapacity by some people, and of still worse things by others, but that nothing seemed to her to justify these suspicions. She then accompanied M. de Vitrolles to the great hall of the palace, where three or four hundred civil and military officers were assembled. She introduced the Baron to the assemblage and announced the powers with which he had been invested by the King to complete the administrative organization of the loyal provinces, and then she withdrew.

M. de Vitrolles remained and addressed the functionaries. His enticing words roused enthusiasm in his auditors. Then he had a private conversation with General Decaen. "I congratulate you," said he, "on the confidence with which you have inspired Madame. In our coming relations, my confidence in you will be boundless." He then gave the general to understand that faithful servants would merit the greatest recompense from the crown for their assistance amid such dangers.

A courtier employed by the Spanish embassy was going through Bordeaux. A letter was given to him, in which the Duchess of Angoulême asked the Duke of Montmorency-Laval, Louis XVIII.'s ambassador at Madrid, to beg the King of Spain to send a body of troops into France. "General Decaen," says M. de Vitrolles, "was the first to speak to me of the coming of Spanish troops, and he proposed that I should go on and prepare for their reception. . . . The Duchess of Angoulême instructed me to send the King's letter to the Duke of Bourbon, in which the purport of my mission and my approaching residence at Toulouse were made known to him. . . . Madame's expectations in regard to the outcome of the projects we had in mind at that time and the part she was disposed to take in all of them that were glorious, though dangerous, inspired admiration for her person and character and gave unspeakable energy to all who were called into her service. One could have wished to realize the most extravagant of them, if only so as not to be put to the pain of destroying such noble illusions. I left Bordeaux, at which I had stayed for thirty hours, loaded with evidences of her goodness, and proud of the boundless trust she reposed in my zeal in defence of the royal cause and for the safety of the Duke of Angoulême, — thoughts with which she was constantly busied."

Nevertheless, the situation was hourly growing more gloomy for the Princess. It became evident that she could not count on the fidelity of the garrison. On the 26th of March, they went to review without wearing the royal arms on their shakos. It was learned at the same time that General Clausel, whom the Emperor had placed in command of the 11th Military Division on the removal of General Decaen, was approaching to take possession of Bordeaux.

On the 29th of March, the Duchess of Angoulême wrote to Count de La Châtre, Louis XVIII.'s representative in London, a letter which the Marquis of Thury has obligingly permitted us to see, and which shows the extremities to which the Princess was reduced: "I readily avail myself, sir, of the offer of the Duke of Lorges to return to England, to inform you in regard to my position and that of the south. All the ports of Rochefort, La Rochelle, and Nantes are in insurrection. Bordeaux still remains faithful, but God only knows how long it will stay so. It must be saved for the King, and to that end I have directed the English consul here, whom I cannot too much praise, to ask his government to send English vessels up the river and bring money, arms, and troops, as it is absolutely necessary to save the region to the King. I have succeeded in making the authorities see the necessity of summoning foreigners to their aid and receiving them amicably. The consul has promised me that they will come as friends, as they did last year, and will commit no hostilities where they see the white flag. He mentioned Blaye, and asked if the English might go into garrison there. I refused and told him that there ought to be national guards in the fortress; but I now learn that the troops refused to obey the governor's order to return, and that they, like the city, are in open revolt. . . . I shall remain here as long as possible. One cannot say what will happen from one day to another, or even in a few hours. The fires of rebellion are spreading through the whole neighborhood. As yet we are untouched and have courage and the best wishes of the good and faithful, but timid citizens. Some bad subjects have acted foolishly, and one of the regiments is at least doubtful. I am very well satisfied with the authorities. I believe that if I have to leave this good city to which I came under such happy circumstances, and without foreseeing all these new misfortunes, I shall go to Spain. This is what I am advised to do. I have already written twice to Ferdinand VII.; the first time to ask for assistance, protection, and brief asylum in his dominions if I should be forced to seek it, and the second time, after I had received powers from the King, to ask him to send troops to France. This is very important. I trust that they will be well received by the inhabitants, coming, as they will, as friends and allies of the King, and that they will give support to our volunteers and national guards, the only troops on which we can still count. I do not want to cede Bayonne to the Spanish so long as it can be defended against Bonaparte.

"According to the latest advices, the Duke of Angoulême is still at Nîmes. He has assembled a number of troops of all classes and will march against Lyons. He is satisfied with the disposition of the country, but his position is very perilous. I avow that I am not without grave anxiety about him. Thrust as he is into a district from which he has no certain means of escape, if escape should become necessary, he certainly has much to fear. This makes it requisite that the Spaniards should come promptly to his assistance. May God watch over and make him victorious! The position of the Duke of Bourbon also seems very difficult. Yesterday evening a courier came to me from him; he is still in Vendée and hopes to bring the people to his support; there are very few of them, and they are without weapons; some of the cities are in revolt, and all the ports, which fact deprives him of means of escape. This is why I write, asking you to urge the English ministry, if it wishes to rescue the Duke of Bourbon, to send troops at once to the river-front of Bordeaux with sufficient money and arms to support the well-affected volunteers."

The Duchess of Angoulême, whose heart was thoroughly French, must have suffered cruelly to implore foreign aid. Her letter ends thus: "There you have, sir, all the news I can give you from here. The news is not pleasant, but as yet there is no cause for despair. I keep up my courage and am hopeful. But the position of the King afflicts me greatly, and I am very sorry about the journey that separated me from him while such things were going on. My only consolation is the thought that perhaps my presence here may be of service to him; my sole desire, my one object, is to work in his behalf."

The chief characters in the drama we are about to describe are the Duchess of Angoulême, General Decaen, and General Clausel. We say drama, because in the eyes of the daughter of Louis XVI. it was one of the saddest episodes in her history, and one replete with catastrophes. The assistants in the drama are the city population, the national guard, and the volunteers.

The Duchess of Angoulême, a woman devoted to duty, and one of deep convictions and indomitable heart, and who closely resembled her grandmother the great Empress, Maria Theresa, understood how to set an example of courage and energy to everybody. The idea of flight was revolting to her pride. Being unable to get used to the thought that all the enthusiastic demonstrations of which she had for a month been the object would prove to be shams, she was willing till the end to put confidence in sworn fidelity. The soldiers of the garrison greeted her with the same applause as the inhabitants of the city. Did not the officers continually tell her that though she ran risks, they would be happy to shed their last drop of blood for her? Did they not weary her with their protestations of devotion? Was not the odor of the incense burned before her extremely encouraging? Ah, well! The time to keep all these fine promises has come. What! would all this splendid talk turn out to be a mere lie? The daughter of the martyred King and Queen, the orphan of the Temple whose legendary woes had been remembered with such piety and tenderness, — was she not to remain even one year in her native land before once more being driven into exile? How cruel the thought! How unspeakable her anguish! The Duchess sometimes says to herself: "No; not flight, — rather death!" It is not alone as a princess of the House of Bourbon that she suffers, but as a Frenchwoman. Convinced that the brief triumph of Bonaparte will be the cause of terrible disasters, bloody catastrophes, and hecatombs of victims if foreigners invade the country, she acts neither from selfishness nor from ambition. She will not deign to bow her head before the tempest, however rude it may be, for she is firmly convinced that the Bourbon cause is the cause of her fatherland.

This is why that woman who would willingly have sacrificed herself if she had acted on her own impulse, is so furious, so impassioned, in defence of the King. To her it is a question of conscience; it is a question of honor.

General Decaen was preyed upon by the greatest perplexities. Filled with admiration for Napoleon and for the Duchess of Angoulême, he wanted to serve both the Emperor and the Princess at the same time. The oaths he had taken in succession were mutually contradictory in the court of conscience. At the outset he did not think that his former master would be successful. While living in an atmosphere of the most pure and exalted royalism he had issued a proclamation to his command, on the 11th of March, and in it were the following expressions: "A man who betrayed the dearest interests of France and was ready to sacrifice them to his personal ambition, — a man who left the country defenceless and at the mercy of foreigners; who voluntarily abdicated a crown which he was not intelligent enough to keep although a million brave soldiers had died in its defence, has now proved false to his oaths and come, at the head of a horde of insensate men, to violate our territory." The general took part in the royalist fête of the 12th of March, and was connected with all the manifestations of devotion to the daughter of Louis XVI. Since then he had been incessantly at the side of the Princess, who gave him distinguished proofs of confidence and treated him in the most flattering way. At banquets — for the troops still fraternized with the national guard — it was he who proposed the toast to duty and fidelity. It was hard for him to forsake a man who was his sovereign. But a woman! To betray a woman; to deliver up a woman to her enemies was repugnant to the heart of a Frenchman. Besides this, General Decaen had a horror of civil war. He believed that the Bourbon cause was irrecoverably lost, since he knew that the Emperor had triumphantly entered the Tuileries. His opinion thereafter was that Napoleon could only have returned with the consent of the Powers, and especially of Austria, and that Louis XVIII. could rely on foreigners no more than he could on France. And then, — what would be the use of a fratricidal struggle with his old comrades in arms? How unhappy is a time when men of courage are exposed to such uncertainty as to what is duty and right!

As regards General Clausel, it was but a few days since he had entertained no animosity whatever against the Restoration. Very well placed at court, given the grand cross of the Legion of Honor, and made inspector-general of infantry by Louis XVIII., he had every reason to be satisfied with the King. He had received the Duke of Angoulême at Toulouse the previous year, and given him the most loyal and respectful welcome. He had the highest esteem for the character of Louis XVI.'s daughter, and would have grieved to see any misfortune happen to that noble and courageous Princess. But, like all the rest of the army, General Clausel was carried away by the prestige of Napoleon's coming to conquer France with a handful of men. After the King's hasty flight, he could not believe that a woman could entertain the idea of defending Bordeaux. Already sure of the imperialist sentiments of the garrison, he started with only two aides-de-camp, and without concerning himself about the currents of the Dordogne and the Garonne, which he must cross before reaching his post. A few pieces of cannon suffice to arrest considerable bodies of troops. On his way, General Clausel picked up several gendarmes and about two hundred foot soldiers. With this little band he proposed to conquer his own command, the 11th Military Division, whose headquarters were at Bordeaux. It was a sort of miniature edition of the return from Elba. The general advanced tranquilly, feeling convinced that the National Guard of Bordeaux would oppose no serious resistance, and hoping that the Duchess of Angoulême would understand the situation, and fly as her uncle, the King, had done.

The population is very well disposed towards the royal cause, but it would not be wise to demand great sacrifices from them. Bordeaux, that amiable, intelligent, and lettered city, proud of its fine theatre and its vast commerce, would not willingly undergo a siege like that of Saragossa. Bordeaux it was which, on the 12th of March, 1814, had been the first French city to unfurl the white flag. But—thanks to British troops—that exploit was very easily accomplished. The people of Bordeaux will burst into tears, talk, and cheers, but a battery of imperial artillery pointed at their walls will very soon set them to thinking.

The national guard is still enthusiastic over the Duchess of Angoulême. Accompanied by troops of the line, it may even fight bravely, but to struggle alone against imperialist regiments will be a task absolutely beyond its powers. When it shall be advised by some one to make a sortie *en masse* to meet the little army of General Clausel it will reply, perhaps rightly: "It is impossible; we should be between two fires. As soon as we had left Bordeaux, the garrison would declare against us and pursue us."

Nevertheless, some volunteers are found among the more decided, the men who are under orders to march against General Clausel. There are about five hundred of them, and, with several cannon, they are placed on the left bank of the Dordogne — General Clausel takes up a position on the right bank, at the castle of Saint-André de Cubzac. He asks the royal volunteers to send him somebody with whom he can confer. M. de Martignac is sent. The general tells him that resistance will be useless; that, had it been his wish, he could already have been master of Bordeaux, where the entire garrison is impatiently expecting him; that out of respect for the Duchess of Angoulême, of whom he had the most pleasant recollections, he had postponed for a day his entrance into the city in order to give the Princess time to make her escape; but that a second postponement was out of the question, and that he thought it a proof of his deference for Madame that he begged her to go away. He then gives the messenger a despatch for the authorities of Bordeaux; it is a demand that the gates of the city be opened to the imperial troops on the next day, the 31st of March. M. de Martignac withdraws and takes the despatch to the Duchess of Angoulême.

The Princess convokes the general council of the department, the council of the arrondissement, and the city council, in order to discuss the situation. General Decaen assists at the deliberation. He does not conceal the truth. The garrison at the citadel of Blaye, at the mouth of the Gironde, has already been won over by emissaries of General Clausel. It has unfurled the tricolor, and the Bordeaux garrison awaits only a signal to follow the example. If the national guard leaves the city, the troops will at once pronounce for the Emperor. It is learned also that General Clausel has just crossed the Dordogne, where the royal forces have been repulsed.

M. de Martignac returns, in his quality as go-between, to the general to ask of him a further delay of twenty-four hours, during which perhaps the Princess will decide to take her departure.

This delay is granted. But the daughter of Louis XVI. does not want to abandon her post. She is informed that the tricolor already floats on the right bank of the Garonne. Nothing either intimidates or discourages her. On the morning of the 1st of April she says to General Decaen: "I wish the troops to assemble at once in their barracks; I will go and see them." — "Madame," replies the general, "I ask Your Highness's permission to disobey you. You do not dream of the possible consequences of such a visit at such a moment." "General, I wish it. If it has bad results, it is I who take the responsibility." Somebody said: "But, Madame, doubtless, does not understand that there has been a fresh distribution of cartridges this morning, one made by the orders of government." — "I will compel nobody to follow me," says the Princess. "'Tis enough; I have given an order; I wish to be obeyed."

It is two o'clock in the afternoon. The Duchess of Angoulême sets out in an open carriage, to go to the Saint-Raphael barracks. General Decaen, on horseback, is at her right hand. Surrounded by a comparatively large staff, she is followed by an escort of officers, volunteers, and national guards. When she reaches the barracks, she alights and enters them. The soldiers are placed in two ranks that face each other. The officers come forward and surround the Princess. "Gentlemen," she says, "I am not ignorant of what has been going on. A usurper has taken the crown from your King. Bordeaux is threatened by a factious crowd. The national guard is determined to defend the city. Are you willing to assist the national guard? I want you to answer me frankly. Let there be no equivocation. Yes or no — will you fight for the King?"

There is no response. An icy silence prevails. "You do not then remember the oath you renewed but a short time ago, between these hands of mine? If there still remain among you some men who do remember them and who are faithful to the cause of the King, let them come out from the ranks; let them show themselves!" A few officers step out. "There are very few of you. It does not matter. I know at least who are to be counted on!" A chief of battalion says: "Your Highness may count on us to look after you personally." — "The matter," says she, "does not concern me; it concerns the King. Yes or no — will you serve him?" "We have no desire for civil war. We will not fight against our brothers!" — "Your brothers? You forget that they are rebels!" — and the Princess withdraws, calm and haughty.

Still less does her visit to the second barracks reassure her. This time, the Duchess of Angoulême is received not with silence, but with actual hostility. She wishes to speak, and her voice is drowned with cries of "Long live the Emperor!" She looks at the soldiers with dignity, and leaves them with laggard footsteps.

"Now," she says, "I will go to the third barracks, those of the Château-Trompette." In vain do they try to dissuade her. Despising all pusillanimous advice, she goes her own way. When she reaches the very entrance of the fortress Château-Trompette, she is notified that she will not be permitted to enter with her generals and her equerry, M. de Lur-Saluces. "No matter," she says, "I will go in alone." In the barracks she finds a regiment of the sixty-second line. She asks the commander: "Do you intend to fight in the King's cause."— "No, Madame," replies the commander; "circumstances are changed, and, besides, our soldiers will not fight against Frenchmen." "If that is the reason that prevents you from doing your duty," replies the Princess, "promise me at least to remain neutrals, and allow the national guards and the royal volunteers to defend themselves."— "No, Madame," cries the captain of the battalion; "if the national guard attacks us, we will throw ourselves on it in turn." These final words draw tears from the daughter of Louis XVI. She dejectedly says: "Then you no longer regard as Frenchmen those who remain faithful to the calls of honor," and, turning to the officers, she says: "Do you all think as your commander does?" They answer, "Yes." One alone, Captain Cosseron de Villenoisy, opposes the general defection. Stepping from the ranks and advancing toward the Princess, he says: "I will not increase the number of traitors. Rather will I die for the King than be false to my oath." The Duchess of Angoulême replies: "I cannot consent to your sacrifice, Captain." At this moment some of the soldiers become menacing. The officer cries out: "If you would only reflect for a moment, you would follow my example." Quiet is then restored, but the Princess, despairing of being able to recall the battalion to its duty to the King's cause, finds it necessary to withdraw. She goes back again under the batteries of the fort. Captain Cosseron de Villenoisy accompanies her. In the dignity of her mien, and in her imperturbable calmness, she shows herself worthy of her mother. Marie Antoinette, looking down from the balcony of the château at Versailles on the afternoon of the 6th of October, 1789, and surveying the crowd that swarmed in the courtyard, displayed no greater firmness and pride. Her daughter withdrew with dignity, and as she left the fortress she was saluted with the roll of drums.

It is finished; the end at last is at hand. The Princess summons M. de Martignac. "You will cross the river," she tells him, "and say to General Clausel that in happier times I recognized his services, and that then he often assured me of his devotion. I ask of him only one thing more, and that is that he will defer his entry into Bordeaux till to-morrow. I shall be most grateful for what he will have done for me."

A review of the national guard and the volunteers took place in the afternoon on the quay of the

Garonne. The Duchess of Angoulême attended it. General Clausel's troops could be seen on the opposite bank. The two flags were face to face, — the white on one shore, the tricolor on the other. The soldiers of the two rival causes were separated from each other only by half a cannon-shot. As soon as the Princess appeared she was received with unanimous shouts by the militia of Bordeaux. Rising in her carriage so as to be heard more distinctly, she cries: "Citizens of Bordeaux, I am about to ask of you a new sacrifice, a new oath. Do you swear to obey me in everything?"— "We swear it." "Alas! after what I have seen we can no longer reckon on the help of the garrison. It is useless to attempt to defend ourselves. You have done enough for honor. Keep some faithful subjects for the King when better times shall come. I take everything on myself. I command you to resist no longer."— "No, no! we will die for the King and for you." "I have heard your oath. Surely, my good people of Bordeaux, you will not condescend to perjury. Your King's niece commands you. Obey. You must stop fighting. I am about to leave you. Receive my adieus." Hereupon a great tumult arises. Some are willing to obey, and others wish to struggle as long as possible. General Clausel, who, on the other bank of the river, hears the hubbub, trains some pieces of artillery on the spot where the Princess is reviewing the troops. Within a few days he will say to M. de Saint-

Girgues, one of the royal volunteers: "It was Madame, the Duchess of Angoulême, who saved you all. I could never consent to fire on the Princess, while she was writing the finest page in her history. It was the first duty of a soldier to respect such courage."

During the review of the national guards on the quay of the Garonne, M. de Martignac, who has been sent as commissioner, is on the opposite side of the river with General Clausel. He is very anxious to defer the general's entry into Bordeaux till the next morning, the 2d of April. "What is the use of all this disturbance?" says the general, as he hears the shouts of the national guards in the distance. "Am I not already master of the city? Do you want proof of it? I have but to give a signal, and immediately you will see the tricolor floating from the top of the Château-Trompette." No sooner said than done. The three colors appear there. On seeing them, the national guard send up a howl of rage. "We are betrayed!" they cry, and fire upon several of their officers whom they regard with suspicion. Unspeakable disorder prevails. The garrison is already leaving its barracks.

Nevertheless, the Duchess of Angoulême goes back to the Château-Royal, accompanied still by General Decaen. Suddenly angry shouts are heard before the gate: "Let us shoot General Decaen! He is a traitor!" The Princess had to appear on the balcony in order to appease the crowd and keep it from crime.

M. de Martignac has just returned, bringing General Clausel's last word that, when the proper time comes, he will enter Bordeaux. Not wishing to be taken prisoner, the Duchess of Angoulême decides at last to leave the city. "Gentlemen," says she to the officers by whom she is still surrounded, "you answer to me for the safety of the town. Keep your troops and preserve Bordeaux from all disorder. From this moment it is in your hands." — "We swear it!" they cry. "Ah!" she replies, "more oaths! I have heard enough of them. I want to hear no more. The niece of your King gives you her last command. Obey it!" It is eight o'clock in the evening. The city is in gloom. The weather is as bad as it was when Louis XVIII. left Paris. Rain falls in torrents; the storm rages, and the daughter of Louis XVI. departs in despair.

XXII

LONDON

THE Duchess of Angoulême sets out from Bordeaux as a princess, with an escort of volunteers and mounted national guards, who do not leave her till she embarks. On the day after her departure, a few minutes before General Clausel's entrance, people read the following proclamation dictated by the Princess and posted on the city walls on the 1st of April: "People of Bordeaux, your fidelity is known to me. Your boundless devotion prevents you from seeing any danger, but my attachment to you and to all Frenchmen demands that I shall be on the watch. My longer residence in your city would only make your position graver and visit you with heavy vengeance. I have not the courage to see Frenchmen unhappy and to be the cause of their misfortunes. I leave you, my brave citizens, deeply affected by the sentiments you have expressed in regard to me, and I assure you they will be faithfully transmitted to the King. By the blessing of God I shall soon be in better circumstances, and then I will show you how both the Prince whom you love and myself appreciate your attachment."

On the morning of the 2d of April, in a cold rain accompanied by gusts of wind that had been blowing all night, the fugitive reached Pauillac, the little county-seat of a canton on the Gironde, in the arrondissement of Lesparre. There she heard Mass, and embarked on the English vessel *Wanderer*. In taking leave of the Frenchmen who composed her escort, she gave them some white and green ribbons that she wore in her hair. "Bring them back to me in better days," she said, "and Marie Thérèse will show you that she has a good memory and that she has not forgotten her friends at Bordeaux."

The bad weather that had begun on the 1st of April lasted a whole week. The waves of the sea were as tumultuous as the destinies of the unhappy Princess. The ship that bore her skirted the coasts of Spain, but could not effect a landing there, and it was not till the 8th of April that the port of Passages was entered.

Hardly had she landed when she received a letter from the King of Spain, offering her an asylum in his dominions. She interrogated the Spanish officers, and, finding that she could not effect anything to her purpose, she set sail for England on the 11th of April. The sea was rough and the wind contrary, and it was not till the 19th that she reached Plymouth, whence she proceeded to London. On the same day of the foregoing year she had left Hartwell Castle, where she had spent most of her exile, and, with her uncle the King she had made a

triumphal entrance into the English capital. On
that day she had been welcomed with the greatest
enthusiasm. The crowd unhitched the horses and
drew the carriage of Louis XVI.'s brother and
daughter. The London streets were draped with
white flags and the windows were thronged with
elegantly dressed women who waved their handkerchiefs in delight. To Louis XVIII., at whose side
his niece sat, the Prince Regent had said: "The
triumph and transports of joy with which Your
Majesty was greeted on your entrance to your own
capital can hardly surpass the delight elicited by
Your Majesty's restoration to the throne of your
ancestors in the breasts of the inhabitants of the
capital of the British Empire."

How great the difference between the Duchess of
Angoulême's departure from London in April, 1814,
and her return to London in April, 1815! She
came not now as a victorious Princess, but as a
fugitive, a woman proscribed, but a proscribed
woman who would not bow her head under the
blows of fate — a proscribed woman full of intelligence and pride, who, instead of succumbing to so
cruel a series of disasters, showed in misfortunes
only increased firmness, energy, and courage.

Since leaving Bordeaux the Duchess of Angoulême had known absolutely nothing of what had
become of her husband, and this uncertainty plunged
her into the gravest apprehensions. When she
reached London, where she became the guest of

Count de La Châtre, Louis XVIII.'s ambassador, she learned that the Duke was Napoleon's prisoner. On the 21st of April, M. de La Châtre wrote to Count de Blacas: "The Princess displayed the greatest courage on the receipt of this dreadful intelligence, but tears filled her eyes when she was alone with me."

At first the Duke of Angoulême had met with some success. After having added to his troops of the line some volunteers from Aix, Marseilles, and Nîmes, he took Pont-Saint-Esprit on the 28th of March. At the head of six thousand men he led the white flag against the tricolor and entered Valence on the 3d of April. But his success was short-lived. Abandoned by most of his officers, menaced by a force superior to his own, attacked in front by the troops and national guards of Lyons and his retreat cut off by General Gilly, who had aroused the regiment left at Nîmes, he knew that all was lost. Then, intent only on saving those who were devoted to him, he capitulated on the 8th of April at Palud, a town near Pont-Saint-Esprit. The royal volunteers were to be disbanded, lay down their arms and return to their homes without molestation. The troops of the line were to give in their submission to the new government, and their officers were not to be molested because of their fidelity to the royal cause. As to the Duke of Angoulême, he was to betake himself to Cette, where he should embark for Spain. These were the terms of the capitulation concluded by Baron de Damas with General Gilly, and ratified by the Prince. On the following day he set out, and on reaching Pont-Saint-Esprit, he was arrested by the orders of General de Grouchy, who for some hours had been commander-in-chief of the imperialist forces. Without regard to the capitulation, the general asked orders from the Emperor.

In attendance on the captive Prince were the Duke of Guiche, Baron de Damas, Viscount des Cars, and Count Gaston de Lévis. What was to become of him? Should he dread the vengeance of Napoleon, outlawed by the Vienna Congress? Was he to be held as a hostage, or was something worse in store for him? The royalists mentioned with terror the name of the Duke of Enghien. The Bonapartists raised threatening outcries around the house where he was held prisoner. But the Prince was perfectly untroubled: "I am resigned to everything and worried only about those whom I hold dear," he wrote to Louis XVIII.; "but I ask and even exact that the King shall give up nothing in order to secure my release. I fear neither death nor imprisonment, and shall willingly accept at the hands of God whatever may come."

Such was the news received by the Duchess of Angoulême upon reaching London. Her apprehensions, grave at first, will subside when she learns, a short time afterwards, that her husband has been set at liberty after six days of captivity, and that — the Emperor, having finished by accepting the capitulation at La Palud — the Duke has embarked at Cette and arrived safely at Barcelona, whence he proceeded to Madrid.

In short, the Duke of Angoulême acted the part of a brave man. Once while he was making a reconnaissance of Pont-Saint-Esprit, somebody warned him that he was going too near. "I am somewhat short-sighted," he replied; "I like to see the enemy close by." The following passage occurs in Baron Louis de Viel-Castel's *Histoire de la Restoration:* " The simple and courageous conduct of the Duchess of Angoulême excited great enthusiasm in the royalist party. And even outside of that party, profound admiration and respect were felt for a Princess who, condemned from childhood to so many misfortunes, still displayed a bravery equal to the most varied tests. Napoleon was fond of saying that she was the only man in her family. The expression was much quoted by the enemies of the Bourbons. In the guise of a just compliment to the daughter of Louis XVI. it branded all her relatives as ridiculous and despicable. And besides, at that very moment the Duke of Angoulême was showing in another portion of the south that he was not unworthy of his noble companion."

The energy displayed by her husband was a great consolation to the Princess. While in London she resided at the house of Louis XVIII.'s ambassador. "Madame the Duchess of Angoulême," wrote Count de La Châtre, "is much pleased to be with us. She sees little of society. Nearly all the English ministers have visited her, as also have their wives. The diplomatic corps came also, but each embassy separately, in accordance with Madame's wishes."

The Princess was actively engaged in politics. She was, in reality, the emissary of Louis XVIII. With the assistance of Count de La Châtre and the Prince of Castelcicala, who was ambassador of the King of the Two Sicilies at London, she carefully watched over the interests of the royal cause.

The attitude of the Duke of Orleans, who with his family was then in London, caused Louis XVIII. some misgivings. The Duke was vaguely suspected of cherishing ambitious designs. On the 30th of March, the Prince of Castelcicala wrote to Count de Blacas: "As to the Duke of Orleans, without saying too much in regard to him — for I would like with all my heart to see him render service to the King and to be able to be serviceable to him myself, since he is the husband of my master's daughter, who is a truly good and virtuous Princess — it must be said that his way of blaming and censuring the government of the King attracts to him all people of like mind, which is not coming to the support of the government at all." And on the 1st of April, Count de Blacas wrote from Ghent to the Prince of Castelcicala: "The visit of the Duke of Orleans to London without asking the King's consent, and contrary to the way in which matters were evidently tending, disturbed me very much. An English journal, the *Morning Chronicle*, spoke of the Duke as 'the only prince able to unite public opinion in France.'"

Under these circumstances Louis XVIII. summoned the Duke of Orleans to Ghent. He refused to go. He wrote to Prince de Talleyrand: "It is reported and, I trust, truly reported, that the King has made you his prime minister. If this is the case, I trust you will not permit anybody to summon the first Prince of the blood in such haste and without giving the slightest indication as to what awaits him or what he is expected to do. It is better for him to remain in retreat if he is wanted only to figure in a procession or a drawing-room." It could not be asserted positively that the Duke of Orleans exerted an influence antagonistic to Louis XVIII., but it is certain that at London he did not share in the opinions of the Duchess of Angoulême, who perfectly represented the politics of the court of Ghent.

The daughters of two sisters, Queen Marie Antoinette and Queen Marie Caroline, the Duchess of Angoulême and the Duchess of Orleans, granddaughters of the great Empress Maria Theresa, were cousins-german. They were equally pious, and in 1814 and 1815 had entertained for each other in Paris a mutual regard founded on esteem and sympathy. The two Princesses were grieved at not finding themselves at harmony in ideas and politics at London. One of the objects of the Duchess of Angoulême in her mission to England was to keep track of the plans which the Duke of Orleans was vaguely accused of laying while under the protection of the British government. She was called to Ghent towards the end of May, and eagerly responded to the appeal. Louis XVIII. wished to thank her for and congratulate her upon her fine conduct at Bordeaux and her attitude in London.

XXIII

GHENT

THE Duchess of Angoulême was very well received at Ghent. Some days before her arrival she was mentioned in some dithyrambs by M. de Chateaubriand, who in his capacity as Minister of the Interior, made on the 12th of May a report to the King on the condition of France, in which he spoke of the courage of the Princess: "What shall I say of the defence of Bordeaux by Madame? No; they were no longer Frenchmen — those men who could find it in their hearts to turn their arms against the daughter of Louis XVI. What! is it the orphan of the Temple, is it she who has suffered so much by us and because of us, she to whom we can never offer sufficient atonement, love, and respect, — is it she whom we have just now driven from her native land with cannon! And to install in her stead the murderer of the Duke of Enghien, the tyrant of France, and the devastator of Europe! Bullets have hissed around a woman, and that woman the daughter of Louis XVI. If she returns to France, the decrees against the Bourbons will be applied to her; in other words, she will mount the scaffold, as her father and mother did. Amid her new perils she is the same as she showed herself to be in her youth, amid assassins and executioners. A true daughter of France, the descendant of Henri IV. and Maria Theresa, reared among troubles and tears, tested by prison, persecution, and danger, what reason has she not to hold life in contempt!'"

The literary minister was not less eloquent over the Princess's husband. "The heroic enterprise of Monseigneur the Duke of Angoulême," he adds, "takes rank among the most illustrious deeds of arms in our history. Wisdom and boldness in plan and courage in execution — all was there. How many misfortunes would Monseigneur the Duke of Angoulême have averted from our country if he could have got as far as Lyons! One of the rebel soldiers who saw this Prince under fire, said in admiration of his valor: 'One half-hour more, and we would have cried: "Long live the King!"'"

Notwithstanding this somewhat declamatory flattery, the Duchess of Angoulême was in great distress. The events that were taking place about her did not raise her spirits. Louis XVIII. had been unable to remain in the north of France, and since the end of March had been a refugee at Ghent, a residence assigned to him by the King of the Low Countries. This place became the seat of a phantom government, a gathering place for *émigrés*, a new Coblentz, but not so pleasant as the old one. Louis XVIII., who would always have looked upon himself as King, even in a barn or a stable, was as calm and majestic in the little Belgian city as in the capital of France. The sovereign, who seemed like a monarch summering in the country, bore his troubles like a prince habituated to exile. Every day after dinner he went out in a coach-and-six, with his first gentleman of the bedchamber and his guards, merely to drive about Ghent. If he met the Duke of Wellington on his way, he gave him a condescending nod as he passed. He did not alter his habits in the least, and etiquette at Ghent was the same as at the Tuileries.

M. Guizot, who spent several days at this court in exile, said of it: "Two things remain strongly impressed on my memory, — the powerlessness and the dignity of the King. In the attitude and look of that old man, motionless and confined to his chair, there was a proud serenity in the midst of his feebleness, a tranquil confidence in the power of his name and the justice of his cause, that struck and touched me. . . . He gave me the impression of a rational, liberal-minded man, elegantly superficial, courteous to everybody and careful about appearances, not over-occupied in probing to the bottom of things, and about equally incapable of the mistakes that lose and those that secure the future of royal houses."

There was the semblance of a ministry in which were Chancellor Dambray as Minister of Justice; General Clarke, Duke of Feltre, as Minister of

War; Baron Louis as Minister of Finance; Count Beugnot, Minister of the Navy; Count Blacas, director of the King's household; and in the absence of Prince de Talleyrand, who was still at Vienna, Count de Jaucourt acted as Minister of Foreign Affairs. Twice a week at Ghent the official journal of royalty in exile was published. But this phantom of government could not conceal the melancholy truth that the Bourbons would be unable to return to France without foreign aid.

The habitual quiet of the city of Ghent was already disturbed by the noise of military preparations. English and Belgian recruits were drilled on the squares and streets. The Duke of Wellington came from time to time to review the troops. "Cannoneers, contractors, and dragoons," says Chateaubriand, "brought in trains of artillery, droves of beeves, and steeds pawing the air, throwing their riders or leaving them hanging by the saddle girths; vivandières came with sacks and children, carrying their husbands' guns. All this went on, without anybody knowing why, or taking the slightest interest in it, at the great rendezvous of destruction that Bonaparte had prepared for them. As to us *émigrés*, we grew like the women of the city of Charles V., who, seated at windows, watched by means of little inclined mirrors the soldiers who passed by in the street."

Some French troops were under arms at the camp of Alost, very near Ghent. They were under the command of General Maison. It appears that at one time there had been some idea of having them join in the military operations which the Allies were preparing against France, but fortunately this project was soon abandoned. General Maison issued an order of the day to the effect that the soldiers who had arrived or should thereafter arrive with legitimist flags, should form a reserve corps, as the King did not wish to see them shedding the blood of their brothers. But they were to have the honor of bringing their sovereign back to his capital. On the plain of Walden, near Alost, the Duchess of Angoulême assisted at a review of two or three thousand French body-guards, volunteers, and students: "Ah!" said she, "I feel as if I were in a small France."

What would these two or three thousand Frenchmen have been able to do if foreigners had not taken into their own hands the task of conquering Bonaparte? This is the heavy thought that weighs on the patriotic heart of the Princess like humiliation, not to say remorse. She suffers equally because of the dissensions, intrigues, and pitiful jealousies, of which the little court at Ghent is the theatre. Her frank and lofty spirit groans when she sees the way in which people are abandoning her for Napoleon. In the words of Chateaubriand: "That epoch when frankness is everywhere lacking is like a weight on the heart. Everybody threw out a profession of faith like a foot bridge on which to cross the difficulty of the day, content to change his direction the difficulty once over. Infancy alone was sincere, for it was in its cradle. Bonaparte solemnly announces that he renounces the crown; he departs and comes back again within nine months. Benjamin Constant prints his energetic protest against the tyrant, and in twenty-four hours he recants. Marshal Soult stirs up the troops against their former captain, and, after a few days in Napoleon's cabinet at the Tuileries, he laughs at the pomposity of his proclamation and becomes a major-general at Waterloo; Marshal Ney kisses the King's hands, vows to bring Bonaparte to Paris in an iron cage, and then turns his entire command over to him. Alas! And how stand matters with the King of France? He declares that at the age of sixty he can die in no better way than in defence of his people, — and then he takes flight for Ghent. At this impossibility of truth in sentiments, and at this discord between words and actions, one feels disgust for the human race." In the words of the author of the *Génie du Christianisme*, the Duchess of Angoulême might have been tempted to say: "At Ghent I remained as far as possible unengaged in intrigues, which were repugnant to my nature and contemptible in my eyes, because I perceived under our own ruin, the ruin of society. My refuge from idle and credulous people was the enclosure of the Béguinage. I used to go to that little universe of women, veiled or wearing gimp-edged caps, and consecrated to various

Christian works, — a region of calm that lay, like an oasis in a desert, in the track of tempests."

The Princess remained only a few days at Ghent. She left on the 4th of June, charged with an important mission to London. Its chief object was to negotiate with the English government for the sending of such arms and munitions as the western and southern provinces might require. If a favorable opportunity offered, the Princess was to go in person to the southern French coasts. While at London she learned the result of the battle of Waterloo and the second Restoration. She remained some time longer in England, and did not go to Paris till the 27th of July, 1815; that is to say, not till nineteen days after the return of her uncle, Louis XVIII.

She left London with much more regret than she had left it fifteen months previously. 1815 was more gloomy than 1814. The second Restoration opened under circumstances much more unfavorable than those of the first. Political animosities reached an enormous pitch, and the foreign yoke pressed on the necks of the conquered in a way that, in some respects, was far more galling than it had been in the preceding year. In 1814, the Duchess of Angoulême was under illusions that no longer existed in 1815. She understood that her return to France had been possible only because the great nation had passed under the yoke. At that time party spirit was silent in the noble woman's heart.

The termination of her exile seemed to her not less grievous than its beginning. Far from being joyous and elated with success, the daughter of Louis XVI. said to herself: "Of what good is it to live in the palace of the Tuileries, if my country is unhappy?" In her fate all was doomed to be melancholy and affliction.

PART SECOND

THE SECOND RESTORATION

I

LOUIS XVIII.'S RETURN

THE second Restoration had just begun. People were far from being in the tender mood of the preceding year, — far from those royalist idylls and eclogues with which the return of the Bourbons was welcomed in 1814. With the exception of a few partisans of the egoistic sort that can be happy even among ruins if so be they may rebuild their fortunes there, all Frenchmen were plunged in gloom. As the imperialists suffered because of Waterloo, so the royalists groaned at seeing in the King's councils a regicide who had been Bonaparte's minister of police during the Hundred Days. Nowhere could good reason for exultation be found.

Count Beugnot thus expresses himself in his Memoirs: "It is not without compassion that I read and hear it said on all sides that twice in succession, namely in 1814 and in 1815, the House of Bourbon has been restored to us by foreigners. On the first occasion the sovereigns of Europe were not opposed to the Restoration, but they did not set it on foot, and, far from wishing it, they rather had doubts of its success. The second time, namely in 1815, the King left the city of Ghent without consulting them, and went straight to Paris and entered it, to the great astonishment of the foreign troops who took possession of the capital and its neighborhood, and understood very well how to profit from the recollection of their stupid indulgence during the foregoing year." The assertion of Count Beugnot is, perhaps, correct. Perhaps it is true that royalty was not brought back by foreigners. But what is at least as true is, that without the foreigners there would have been no Restoration whatever. It was the very coincidence between the defeat of the French and the return of the Bourbons that so fatally handicapped a government that would, under so many other circumstances have been respected, and reparative. It is for this reason that the Duchess of Angoulême wished so much that Napoleon should be repulsed by the French themselves instead of succumbing under the blows of foreign armies.

Chateaubriand says: "The whole outlook was threatening for the second Restoration. Bonaparte came back at the head of four hundred Frenchmen. Louis XVIII. returned behind four hundred thousand foreigners; he went from the sea of blood at

Waterloo to Saint-Denis, as if going to his grave. . . .
At the close of the Empire, Bonaparte went to Malmaison, whereas, when the monarchy is beginning, we leave Ghent. Pozzo, who knew how little weight legitimacy had in high places, hastened to write Louis XVIII. a letter, urging him to leave and come quickly if he wished to be King before the place was taken; it is to this letter that Louis XVIII. owed his crown in 1815."

Before returning to his capital, the King paid a brief visit to Saint-Denis, where he lodged in the abbey buildings. Chateaubriand says that it was with the greatest difficulty that the little girls whose fathers had belonged to the Legion of Honor could be kept from crying, "Long live Napoleon!" The author of the *Génie du Christianisme* entered the church at the side. Part of a wall in the cloister had fallen, and the ancient abbey was lighted by a single lamp. "I prayed," he adds, "at the entrance to the vault into which I had seen Louis XVI. lowered. I was filled with misgivings about the future, and I do not think that my heart was ever stirred with a profounder or a more sacred religious grief. Then I rejoined His Majesty. On being shown into one of the chambers preceding that of the King, I found nobody present. Seated in a corner I waited. Suddenly a door opened. Into the stillness of the chamber came vice leaning on the arm of crime, M. de Talleyrand supported by M. Fouché; the infernal apparition passed slowly before me, entered the

King's apartment, and disappeared. Fouché came to swear fealty and homage to his lord; the feal regicide knelt before the King and placed the hands that caused the head of Louis XVI. to fall between those of the brother of the martyred King; the apostate bishop administered the oath."

In his *Souvenirs* the late Duke of Broglie expresses himself not less bitterly: "The worthy rival of Barrère, Fouché, the ex-Oratorian (of Nantes), otherwise known as His Excellency the Duke of Otranto, was, like Barrère, a disgusting monster, but still more bloody, malicious, and filthy than Barrère himself — if that were possible — and committed his last treason, which was certainly one of the least of his sins, by taking his oath between the hands of the son of Saint-Louis and Louis XVI.'s brother, amid the applause of silly royalists. His patron in this exploit was the former bishop of Autun, — the man who in succession doffed his frock on the downfall of the monarchy, his toga at the overthrow of the Directory, and his coronet of Bénévent at the close of the Empire, had kindly condescended to become the Prince de Talleyrand, Prime Minister of this most Christian King.

"How did this most Christian King look between these two unfrocked priests? I have not the slightest idea. I have heard that on seeing them take carriage together, Pozzo di Borgo said smilingly to his neighbor: 'I would much like to hear what those lambs are saying.'"

Louis XVIII. was deeply impressed by a situation so painful to the dignity of his person and the majesty of his throne. He did not desire that his return should be like a triumph, and that people should have it in their power to say that the King of France regarded Waterloo as a royal victory. When he re-entered Paris at three o'clock on the afternoon of the 8th of July, 1815, his niece was not in the carriage with him as on the 3d of May, 1814. It is possible that the daughter of Louis XVI. may not have desired to be seen associated with a policy the result of which was the selection, as a king's minister, of a man who had voted for the death of her father. We incline to the belief that this choice, which the austere Princess looked upon as humiliating, was one cause of her decision to put off for some days her return to Paris.

British and Prussian troops bivouacked with their wagons and caissons in the public gardens and squares, and before the porch of Notre-Dame; loaded cannons were seen at the extremities of the bridges. An effort was made, through fear of revolutionary manifestations, to persuade the King that he ought to enter not by the populous quarter of the Faubourg Saint-Denis, but by the Clichy gate or the Champs-Elysées. He refused to take this prudent advice, and the event showed him to be right, since no hostile demonstration took place during his entrance. He was not, as on the 3d of May, 1814, in an open coach, but in a closed carriage. The Count of

Artois and the Duke of Berry, each in the saddle, rode, one at the right and the other at the left of the carriage. Then followed a less numerous group of marshals and generals, among whom were Marshals Macdonald, Victor, Oudinot, Marmont, Clarke, Gouvion Saint-Cyr, and Generals Maison and Dessoles. The escort was made up of body-guards, musketeers, light-horse, gendarmes of the royal household, mounted grenadiers, the Hundred Switzers, and some royal volunteers. No regiment was present from the regular army. The national guard formed the double line. The King was received at the barrier Saint-Denis by the City Council. Count de Chabrol, prefect of the Seine till the 20th of March, and who had been reinstated in his office, delivered an address in which he said: "A hundred days have passed since that on which Your Majesty, forced to stifle your dearest affections, left your capital amid tears and public consternation." This was the first use of the expression "Hundred Days," which was destined to be adopted by history to designate the second reign of Napoleon.

Louis XVIII. answered: "I left Paris only with liveliest sorrow and the deepest emotion. Evidences reached me of the attachment of my good city. I return with deep affection; I foresaw the ills with which it was threatened; I wish to prevent and cure them." The procession moved forward and reached the Tuileries by way of the Faubourg Saint-Denis and the boulevards.

In the words of Baron de Vitrolles, the King was received by an immense concourse of people and with universal satisfaction. If the procession of the foregoing year had seemed less enthusiastic, it was because the appearance of the sovereign was less expected. Louis XVIII. was perfectly satisfied with it and did not see the coming cloud. "On the same evening," adds M. de Vitrolles, "I had an audience with Sauvo, the intelligent, and even imperturbably intelligent, editor-in-chief of the *Moniteur*. But this time the changes had worn out his endurance to such a degree that it had become transformed into pleasantry. He came, very deferential to me, but revolted by the recantations he had been obliged to make without having an opportunity to pass by easy stages from one fashion to another. He told me that he could no longer hold his position, and asked that he should be retired. I raised him in his own eyes, and encouraged him by saying that his work was necessarily subject to the rapid course of events, and that, in submitting to official requirements, his personality would be left intact. He picked up again the chain and harness, and wore them for many years more."

On the next morning the *Moniteur* was exceedingly spirited. It reported in the same old style the enthusiasm of the populace, the cheers, the refrain of Henri IV.; the whole city spontaneously illuminated, the union of all parties in sentiments that thereafter were to be unalterable; the devotion and fidelity to the monarch, the united vows of all, and all the efforts to restore liberty to France under a paternal government, and the happiness that would result from a peace that all Europe longed for.

Notwithstanding all this verbiage, Louis XVIII. was ill at ease. How could he forget that an English army was encamped in the Bois-de-Boulogne, at La Vallette, and the Chapelle-Saint-Denis, and that Paris was at the mercy of Prussians? Did he not know that an order of the day signed by the Duke of Wellington and Prince Blücher had make General Muffling, a Prussian, governor of the capital by placing the national guards and the police under his authority? Could he forget that the disappointment occasioned by his return to the Tuileries was so great at General Blücher's headquarters, that it had been decided to pay no attention to his royal person and to act as if he were still at Ghent? When he looked from the palace windows, what did he see? Cannon planted at the Pont Royal, and directed even against the Tuileries, while cannoneers stood ready to touch them off; Prussian soldiers washing their soiled linen and coats in the courtyard of the château, and making the finials of the fences do duty for drying-rooms. "You yourself have seen it," said the King to Count Beugnot. "They have bivouacked in my courtyard of the Tuileries and planted cannon on the Pont Royal. What do they mean? I can never bring myself to believe that the sovereigns have authorized any such proceedings." After these words he leaned his elbows on a chest of drawers and buried his face in his hands. When recalling these melancholy memories, M. Beugnot exclaimed: "Old Brennus was right! *Væ Victis!*" And in the present instant no distinction of the parties was made; for in the eyes of the foreigners every Frenchman, beginning with the King, was a conquered man.

Nevertheless, since the allied sovereigns had come to Paris, dissatisfied this time at not entering it before the King of France, it was necessary to receive them with extreme courtesy. The *Moniteur* said: "Paris, July 11, 1815. — Their Royal and Imperial Majesties, the Emperor of Russia, the Emperor of Austria, and King of Prussia, arrived at Paris yesterday evening. An hour after the arrival of Their Majesties, the King visited them. To-day the three monarchs went to the Tuileries, and, after an interview with His Majesty, they did Monsieur and Monseigneur the Duke of Berry, the honor of returning the visit which Their Highnesses had paid to Their Imperial and Royal Majesties. The capital heard with the most lively satisfaction of the presence of these august sovereigns, for which all had prayed. Paris has not forgotten what in 1814 it owed to the powerful protection and magnanimous accord that existed among them and the outcome of which was the happy Restoration. The capital earnestly hopes that the coming together of these monarchs, in the existing state of affairs, will soon lay the foundation of an unalterable peace, and perpetually strengthen the bands which should unite France with Europe under a stable and legitimate government, to the end that Europe may at last see the accomplishment of the great purpose for which she took up arms."

A nation is to be pitied when it has to use such language to its conquerors. Beyond question Louis XVIII. helped to soften the rigor of the conditions imposed on his subjects, and, had he not been in the Tuileries, France would have been still more unfortunate. But he had too much good sense not to understand all that the former conquerors of Europe were to be forced to endure.

The royalist journals praised the King beyond measure. In reporting the fact that he had shown himself at one of the windows of the Tuileries to the people assembled in the garden, the *Journal des Débats* said: "If it were possible to compare heaven and hell with each other, and if such a comparison were not in its very self an odious blasphemy, who could remember without a chill of horror, that at the same place where the celestial face of our father was then beaming with love for his people and with all the sincerity of a virtue not less than sublime, but lately had been seen, half-concealed behind his hateful satellites, that leaden-hued and tiger-eyed Corsican who never smiled save when he looked on carnage." The same journal — once the *Journal de l'Empire* — said of the vanquished Napoleon:

"Bonaparte, whom but lately so many arms encircled, could not to-day find the hand even of a slave to do him the service of killing him. Baser than the effeminate Otho, more evil-starred than Nero, he could not yield himself to death, and is not now certain of receiving even that poor boon. All those kings, all those princes like himself, whom we have seen figure with him in costumes and poses more or less theatrical and grotesque, have scattered like a troop of masqueraders on the day after the Carnival, throwing aside their crowns, their sceptres, and their dominoes."

The way in which the French recanted made foreigners smile. What a revenge they had for the occupation of their capitals, Berlin, Madrid, Naples, Vienna, Moscow! How they gloried in the sight of that long-threatening nation now bleeding and humiliated! Louis XVIII. owed his throne entirely to the victorious Allies and could not avoid thinking with regret of that glorious epoch when Louis XIV. grappled with combined Europe. He was proud of his high lineage, and it pained him to be dependent on sovereigns whose houses were of more recent origin than his own.

This justice, also, should be done to Louis XVIII. He wished to moderate the passions of the ultra-royalists, who had completely forgotten the clemency shown in the words of Louis XVI.'s will. Blinded by hatred and party spirit, these reactionaries longed to wreak vengeance on the men who had terrorized them. Forgetting that they themselves were French, they greatly preferred Englishmen, Russians, and Prussians to Bonapartists. The King had wisely reflected on the battle-field where so many Frenchmen met heroic deaths and, when afterwards, he went to Notre Dame he forbade the singing of the *Te Deum*. But, instead of following this noble example, many people exulted blatantly while the country mourned. The ministry, whom the royalists distrusted, did not dare to repress this effervescence of glee. Every evening crowds of people stationed themselves under the King's windows at the Tuileries, and struck up songs of victory and joy. All sorts and conditions of women danced with men whom they did not know, and even with the foreign soldiers. If anybody dared to object to these demonstrations, which were certainly exceedingly strange, he rendered himself liable to rough usage. The dancing, which disturbed the sleep of Louis XVIII., lasted into the night, and it was hard to clear the garden even after eleven o'clock. The theatres became hotbeds of agitation and disorder. Actors who had shown Bonapartist tendencies during the Hundred Days were insulted on the stage. Fleury and Mademoiselle Mars were jeered at and forced to cry: "Long live the King!" before being permitted to go on with their parts. France was divided against itself at a time when the invading armies numbered one million two hundred thousand men, without counting two hundred and fifty thousand who were stationed on the opposite banks of the Rhine. Some Frenchmen looked on Waterloo as a victory for the French, and others considered it a defeat. Already were seen the beginnings of an obstinate struggle between the two rival nations that one and the same country contained. Such was the lamentable spectacle offered to the Duchess of Angoulême when she came to the Tuileries. We have said that the daughter of Louis XVI. would nevermore know joy on earth. At the very time when, as a princess, she should have been happy, she, as a Frenchwoman, was most deeply wounded in her patriotism and her pride.

II

THE RETURN OF THE DUCHESS

THE Duchess of Angoulême arrived at Paris on the 27th of July, 1815, escorted by the Duke of Berry and a number of generals. After receiving the respects of the court, she showed herself at one of the windows of the Tuileries and was heartily applauded by the crowd. On the 1st of August, the *Journal des Débats* spoke as follows: " Yesterday the people of Paris gave Madame the Duchess of Angoulême the same evidences of their devotion, respect, and heartfelt joy, that they had given the King five days before. An innumerable multitude went to the Tuileries and gathered under the windows of the palace. There, to cries of 'Long live the King,' 'Long live the Bourbons!' and 'Long live the Duchess of Angoulême,' were united transports of admiration for the Antigone of Courland, the heroine of Bordeaux, the woman strong and great in all kinds of adversity. Then followed all varieties of dancing, and the festivities lasted till evening. Meantime bands of young people, most of whom were royal volunteers who had come together in the morning, paraded the boulevards under the royal ensign, and filled the air with shouts of joy and victory. Some evil-disposed persons who tried to lessen the effect of this enthusiasm by getting up a counter-demonstration, came very near suffering at the hands of an indignant public."

The enthusiastic flattery lavished upon her hardly moved the Princess at all, for she continually reflected: "All these things were said to me before the Hundred Days." When disaster left her for a time some rest, she recalled her past exiles, and was filled with apprehensions of others still in store for her. She seldom smiled. In the palace she felt as in an inn which she soon must leave. She had no illusions about either men or things, and distrusted many people. And in this she was right; for the ministers apparently most devoted to Louis XVIII. were soon to become the most obsequious courtiers of Louis-Philippe.

The Princess thought it undignified that Talleyrand and Fouché should be in the ministry. She was obliged to keep her feelings to herself, and suffered on account of the compromises that royalty thought it necessary to make. Thus her attitude was constrained, and her face, which was almost always sombre, bore painful evidence of her feelings.

The situation was dolorous even for royalists. All people of sense and probity deplored the reactionary movements, entitled the White Terror, which had been made at Nîmes, Uzès, Avignon, and Marseilles. The straight-forward and upright Duke of Angoulême, on his return from Spain, had remained for a time in the south of France, where he earnestly tried to establish a policy of moderation. But the passions of people about him impeded him in his pacificatory labors. His intentions were misunderstood, and an attempt was made to get him to abandon the service of Louis XVIII. According to some slanderers, the Duke aimed at nothing short of separating the south from the kingdom and making a distinct state of it. Later on, some even went so far as to say that the appearance of white and green cockades was the first sign of the projected rebellion. These absurd rumors even reached the Duchess of Angoulême and justly irritated her.

In some respects the ministerial policy met with the approbation of the Princess. She looked upon acts of severity as necessary, but it seemed more than strange to her that the list of proscribed men should be drawn up and signed by Fouché, who had been minister of the imperial police during the Hundred Days. The list of the 24th of July ordered the arrest and production before the councils of war of nineteen persons, namely: Ney, Labédoyère, the elder and younger Lallemands, Drouet d'Erlon, Lefebvre Desnouettes, Ameil, Brayer, Gilly, Mouton-Duvernet, Grouchy, Clausel, Laborde, Debelle, Bertrand, Drouet, Cambronne, Lavalette, and Rovigo. Then followed a list of men to be exiled, including Marshal Soult, General Exelmans, the Duke of Bassano, Carnot, General Lamarque, Count Regnault de Saint-Jean d'Angély, Baron Lelorgne d'Ideville, and others. M. de Viel-Castel says in his *Histoire de la Restauration:* "As to the terms used in this order to designate these proscribed men, everything in them was offensive. There was a studied design to treat them with contempt. Some, like Marshals Ney and Soult, were designated merely by their family names; others, like the Dukes of Bassano and Rovigo, by ostentatiously omitting their titles; and sometimes the names were incorrectly spelled. In a a word, information as to the personal position of the proscribed was so defective that M. de Lavalette, who had not been in military service for fifteen years, was among those who were produced before the councils of war. Probably never before was there seen in a similar act such an accumulation of blunders, confusions, and reckless neglect of equity and the merest decency. It seemed as if, in drawing up that order, Fouché thought that he was still at work for the Committee of Public Safety. . . . From one end of it to the other, it bore the impress of the truculent levity and revolutionist ways of its author."

The era of vengeance was inaugurated. It began with the execution of General de Labédoyère. The Duchess of Angoulême, who thought it impossible to secure pardon for the unfortunate general, withdrew without regret from Paris, where residence at the Tuileries — that vestibule of the scaffold to her parents — had become ever-increasingly painful.

On the 13th of August, 1815, after having been present at the votive procession of Louis XIII. at Notre Dame, she went to Bordeaux by way of Versailles and Chartres. She reached the city on the 19th, having rejoined her husband on the road.

The royal pair had a magnificent reception. A small and very choice pavilion which had been erected on the shore of the Gironde, served the Princess as a resting-place after her journey, and there she was visited by the ladies of Bordeaux, who gave her a splendid dress in exchange for which they asked her own, to be divided into small pieces that should be kept as relics. At two o'clock in the afternoon the Duke and Duchess arrived at the Bastide, and crossed the water in a gondola decorated with flags, amid the roar of artillery from all the ships in the roadstead, the ringing of bells, and the acclaims of the vast multitude that had assembled on the quays and crowded the boats with which the river was covered.

All the houses were decorated with white flags and hung with verdure. The cortège proceeded along the quay as far as the gate Chapeau-Rouge. At the head of the procession was a detachment of the legion of Maria Theresa, followed by a number of men and women bearing banners on which were portraits of the King, the Princes, and the Duchess of Angoulême, the heroine of the fête. Then one saw a troop of children dressed in Henri IV. costume, and maidens in white, carrying bouquets of lilies. After these was the carriage so impatiently expected. Drawn by men, it came slowly along in the midst of enthusiastic shouts, and was followed by the Duke of Angoulême on horseback. Having descended the Place Dauphine and passed through the allées d'Albret, the procession entered the château grounds through the larger garden gate. It was a triumph.

In the evening the Prince and Princess went to the Grand Théâtre, where the *Héritiers Michaud*, and a vaudeville composed for the occasion by a young Bordelais named M. Bouglé, were rendered. The title of the vaudeville was *Enfin les Voila!* and it was encored by the audience three times.

III

GENERAL DE LABÉDOYÈRE

ON the day when the Duchess of Angouleme entered Bordeaux in triumph amid the tumultuous applause of the royalists, the Bonapartists in Paris were in consternation because of the execution of General Labédoyère, a man for whom they had the greatest admiration. His trial, symbolically summed up, as one may say, the dissensions which were at once the weakness and shame of France. In that act were reviewed all changes of opinion, all political cruelty, and all the irony of fortune.

What pictures must have passed before the mental vision of the accused as he lay in prison! What a drama had been played within a few weeks! What incidents! What unaccountable changes! All was like the scenes of a tragedy now dazzling and now lugubrious. In imagination the prisoner recalled that 7th of March when, at the head of his regiment, the Seventh of the line, he was on the road to Grenoble, shouting, "Long live the Emperor!" and then: "Soldiers, who loves me follows me!" — that day on which Napoleon threw himself into his arms and cried with emotion: "Colonel, 'tis you who reseat me on the throne!" and the army hailed the colonel of the Seventh as liberator and saviour. He recalled the honors rained upon him during the Hundred Days: the rank of a general of brigade, promotion to the grade of general of division, and then a seat in the Chamber of Peers. Would that Napoleon had established himself firmly on the throne, and then, who could tell how high the fortunes of that general at twenty-nine might not have soared! But even in full glory he had a presentiment of his fate. During the Hundred Days he told his friends more than once that he was to fall victim to his devotion to the Emperor; he said the same thing to his mother; he had left his wife in dread of what might happen.

Then came before him the awful day of Waterloo, on which he was one of the last to leave the battlefield; and then that stormy session in the Chamber of Peers on the 22d of June at which he had spoken those prophetic words: "If the Chambers desert the Emperor, all is lost. In a few days the enemy will be in Paris. Then what will become of our liberties, what will become of those who have embraced the cause of the nation? As to myself, my fate is not doubtful; I shall be shot." He knew well that, accordingly as affairs turned out, he would be deemed a hero or a traitor.

After the overthrow of all his hopes, Labédoyère still retained some illusions. He imagined that his life would be spared. He believed that Article 12 of the capitulation of Paris on the 3d of July would be lived up to, and this article covered those who had taken part in the acts of the Hundred Days. Before the re-entrance of the King, he had received from Fouché offers of money to leave France. He refused them, without comprehending his position, and with inexplicable imprudence he had remained at Clermont, and, though attainted by the ordinance of the 24th of July, he had set out for Paris, there to say farewell to his family. On the 2d of August he was arrested by a police officer who recognized him in the diligence on the road from Clermont to Paris.

A great outcry was raised in legitimist salons against a man who seemed to those who frequented them all the more criminal in that he belonged to one of the most ancient of French aristocratic families. It was said that his fate was decided out of his own mouth. Was it not he who told the Chamber of Peers on the 22d of June: "I ask that traitors shall be judged and punished in such a way as to terrify those who would imitate them; that their names be made infamous; that their houses be razed, their families proscribed and never again permitted to set foot on French soil." Charles de Labédoyère was a count; he had as brothers-in-law MM. de Damas and de Chastellux; his family were entirely of royalist stock. His descent, it was said, ought to be looked upon as an aggravation and not as an excuse. If mercy should be shown to him, no one could be condemned. The great ladies of the Faubourg Saint-Germain were, for the most part, furiously enraged. A young woman of high society who, in order to calm her ire a little, had been informed that there was no manner of doubt that the accused would be convicted and executed, replied: "It really seems so, but you will see that he will be spared for some reason or other."

Meantime there was a woman who was deeply interested in the prisoner's fate, and who, since she despaired of saving his life, made prodigious efforts to save at least his soul. This woman was a foreigner, a Russian, who because of her excessive mysticism suggested the project of the Holy Alliance to the Emperor Alexander, whose conscience and policy she directed. This was the Baroness de Krudener. She was a very odd woman who, while yet in her first youth, had distinguished herself by a sort of fanaticism for Garat, the singer, before whom she knelt in public, — she, the same feminine author who execrated Napoleon, perhaps because he laughed at her romance *Valêrie*, and who, by assuming Biblical modes of speech and Biblical allusions, as if she were a prophetess, exercised a mysterious influence over the Czar. Struck by a prophecy in which she had predicted to him the chief political events of the last three years, the Czar gave her a valuable bracelet, the medallion of which represented an open eye; it was his own left eye, which he had caused to be painted after nature, according to an old Russian notion that the way in which an absent person is thinking is reflected in the image of his eye. She wore this bracelet as a talisman so long as she was on good terms with him whom she called the White Angel sometimes, and sometimes the Saviour of All.

In the salon of Madame de Staël, Madame de Krudener had met Charles de Labédoyère when he was hardly more than a youth, and had been inspired by him with a sentiment which he did not at all return, and which, possibly, may have been nothing more than mystical love. This handsome young man of nineteen had strongly affected her, and when, ten years afterwards, he was about to die so tragic a death, she spoke admiringly of him to the Emperor Alexander. "My brother in Christ," said she to the Czar, "they will not spare poor Labédoyère. Ah! could you but have seen him in his beauty ten years ago, how you would have admired him! How admirable he was! His noble head; his expressive features; his fiery mien; his splendid hair; his sensitive heart; his brilliant wit! And this, all this, will soon be nothing but a dim memory! Let us pray, let us pray that Divine mercy will receive him to bliss eternal!"

The bibliophile Jacob, "Paul Lacroix," that much-lamented writer, gives in his painstaking work on Madame de Krudener, details, not previously published, of the part played by that extraordinary woman in the pathetic drama which ended in the execution of the young general. Thanks to her, the general secured an interview with his wife in prison. At the close of this first interview Madame de Labédoyère wrote to the Czar's Egeria: "Ah, Madame, how sad I was when I saw my unhappy husband once more. Nevertheless, his calmness and his noble tranquillity gave me heart again. It is impossible for anybody to be more resigned to any fate that may await him. To me he seemed sublime. Ah! Madame, how happy should I be if my prayers should be blessed by heaven and it should deign to restore to me the father of my child! This will be the last day of the investigation. The council meets on Monday. Judge, Madame, of my affliction! I cannot breathe. . . . For twenty-four hours my babe has not taken the breast. It hurts me cruelly to look at him. . . . I cannot restrain my grief. I seek in vain to interest the allied sovereigns in my woes. I cannot even reach them. Their protection, however, would give me so much hope! I have done my best to send a letter to His Majesty, the Emperor of Russia, whose generosity is so well known and inspires confidence in the heart of every Frenchman, but I do not know whether it has reached him and whether His Majesty has condescended to read it."

Madame de Krudener's answer, which bears date of the 11th of August, 1815, is a sort of sermon. It opens as follows: "Would that I could console you, you dear and unhappy woman! But this work is not for man. I point you to the only means by which you can be released from this deep sorrow. It is God and God alone, Madame; Christ the Saviour, the Mediator, the Restorer; Christ, the Infinite Love, the Ocean of Charity. . . . Implore the living God! Cast yourself on His breast, and seek no aid from human support forbidden by His Holy Law, since He says: 'Accursed be he who leans on the arm of flesh.'"

The whole letter was nothing but one long preachment. Madame de Krudener spoke perpetually about the eternal salvation of the accused, but said not a word about his temporal salvation. She added: "I have pointed out your great duties. Woman on earth has but tears; the true woman is the spouse of eternity to which she should be bound with ties sublime. There is the marriage the Church affords us; every other is naught but adultery." The letter — or rather the sermon — ended as follows: "Be truly great by weeping at the foot of the cross, by giving your whole heart to God, and by saying to yourself: 'My business is to instruct my husband, not to deceive him; to show him the bitter fruits of a life given over to worldliness.'. . . I have spoken the truth to you. I do not know what words I have used. Charity is my duty. It is by turns tender and severe. I am a Christian and, while humbling my nothingness at the feet of Christ, I have the boldness of loftiest hopes, for I know His profound compassion, and I trust that your husband may be saved if he will but cast himself on the breast of the Saviour who rejects no one."

Madame de Krudener's letter plunged Madame de Labédoyère into deep dejection. She read and re-read it, pondering over those words: "I trust that your husband may be saved." She could not believe that it referred only to the salvation of his soul. She longed to have his body rescued also.

Meantime, Madame de Krudener had appeared in mourning garb at the prison wicket, and, laying down a Bible, insisted that the book should be given to Labédoyère on her behalf. Then the general wrote her the following letter: "Madame, I cannot refuse myself the happiness of thanking you for the interest you have taken in my unhappy wife. You have appreciated her goodness and her virtues, and you certainly wished to comfort her. Do not take it amiss, Madame, that I thank you for it. I appreciate the book you sent me. There are times in life when one specially loves to be absorbed in the great and sublime thoughts that religion affords. I trust I shall profitably employ the brief moments still at my disposal."

Charmed with such pious talk, Madame de Krudener replied in the tone of a parson: "I thank you, sir, for that letter, which turns my bitter tears to tears of sweetness. . . . How lofty a thing is the death of the Christian praying to Christ! It allies him to all the great men, who have been the splendor of the ages; the Augustines, the Jeromes, the Tertullians, the Fénelons, the Saint Francises, all those who hold names most dear to humanity, are associated with him. And what made the Bayards, what made men like Gustavus Adolphus, the greatest captains of their times? . . . Would that I could see you and that my accents could express the compassion I have found at the foot of the Cross! I do not leave you. . . . My hopes are immortal. In death the Christian begins life, while the unbeliever begins only a round of frightful torments. May the Saviour in whom is all my hope, may Christ, may the living God, bless you."

The accused was produced before the council of war on the 14th of August. The number of spectators was very large. Among them were the Prince of Orange, the Prince Royal of Wurtemberg, Prince William of Prussia, the foreign ambassadors, and many great ladies who were drawn to the trial by morbid curiosity. The attitude of Labédoyère was calm and full of dignity. "If my life alone were at stake," said he, "I, who before now have led brave men to death, would meet it myself like a brave man, nor would I seek to delay your sentence; but my honor is assailed along with my life, and that honor does not belong to me alone. A woman, a model of all the virtues, a son in his cradle, have the right to demand that I consider it, and I would that they should hereafter be able to say that, despite the blow that befell me, my honor was unsullied. I was deceived myself as to the true interests of France; glorious memories, ardent love of country, illusions, misled me, but the very greatness of the sacrifices I made in breaking the dearest of ties, shows that no self-interest entered into my conduct."

The accused then gave some explanation of the state of opinion at the time of the return from Elba: "If my voice may have the solemnity of the feeble accents of the dying," said he, "what I am about to submit to your consideration will, perhaps, not be without service to my country. In 1814 the nation and the army left Napoleon to his fate; the family of the Bourbons was received back with enthusiasm. How did that situation come to be changed? Through the words and actions of faithful servants, of friends blinded by personal interests, by false ideas, by misapprehension of the state of France." At these words the president cried out: "You are accused of a crime; it is not yours to discuss the motives that led you to its commission. The council cannot pronounce on motives. In its eyes there is no such thing as guiltless crime." — "Do you wish me," replied the general, "to deny well-known facts, and actions which I avow? My only defence is in the examination of the political causes that led me to the deeds for which I now answer before you. You do not wish to hear me? I shall not insist upon it." Then he expressed his desire that all the

French should be but a single family around the throne. "Probably," said he, in closing his address, "it will not be for me to witness that grand and touching sight. Already have I shed my blood for my country, and now I shall die resigned and calm, trusting that my death, preceded by the acknowledgment of my error, will not be wholly useless, and that memory of me shall never waken a painful thought; that my son, when old enough to serve his country, shall not blush for his father, and that his native land will not reproach him with his name."

The accused was unanimously condemned to death. "Monsieur Bexon," said he to his counsel, "I did as they wished; they stifled my defence, but none the less do I die defending myself, shot before the eyes of the allied sovereigns who signed the treaty of Paris." On the following day he received from Madame de Krudener a writing entitled *Meditation*, which, after giving a description of the earthly Paradise, ended thus: "O, Splendor of the Primitive Destiny of the King of the Earth, tell us, instruct us; make the captive blush who, though in chains, still thinks of earthly affairs and is puffed up with pride when he has lost all, and all things accuse him; who is proud of having availed himself of liberty to resist God, to betray Him, to forsake Him, to make unto himself shameless idols, or sing praises to his passions and to look with longing upon vanities invented by the Enemy of us all."

Application for an appeal was refused, notwithstanding an eloquent address by the lawyer, Mauguin. "I expected the refusal," said the condemned man. "I have received a letter informing me that Baroness de Krudener has been authorized to visit me. Thank the lady, in my behalf, for all she wished to do, but I do not wish to see her. I will see nobody but my old friend Abbé Delondelle." This ecclesiastic, who was chaplain of the Carmelite ladies of the rue Saint-Jacques, had been the general's early teacher.

The condemned man wrote to his mother: "I send by M. Delondelle, who is good enough to be with me during my last moments, a few words expressive of my affection and respect, and the regret I feel for the sorrow I have caused you and the misfortunes I have made you undergo. He comes to ask your blessing for me, and with it I know I shall die more peacefully. . . . Adieu, dear mother; bless your son once more, and forgive him." He wrote also the following letter to his mother-in-law, the Countess of Chastellux: "Receive, my dear mother, the last farewells of a son who was never quite worthy of your Georgine, but who is dying, and at the moment of his death ventures to speak of his appreciation of all your goodness. Take care of my dear Georgine; she loves me, and her sorrow will be great; but your care and that of my excellent sister Gabrielle and all the family and my little angel, will bring her some consolation. Pardon me all the ill I have done you. Pray for me, and weep for an unfortunate man who, in his early years, loses so many sources of happiness."

What could be more touching than the unhappy general's letter to his dearly loved wife, so soon to be his widow? "Receive, my adorable Georgine, my last adieu! My latest sigh will be for thee. Dear friend, how grieved I am over all the misfortunes I have brought on thee, and thy unhappy family, and on mine! I had hoped, dear friend, to make thee happy. The thought of the sorrow I have caused thee is sadder than the thought of death. I shall die a Christian; that will console thee. Think on thy child, thy mother, thy sisters; console thyself, dear Georgine; 'tis a sacred duty. Adieu!"

Following is the general's will, which we have received from his grandson, Count Jean de Labédoyère: "This is my will. As a testimony of friendship I give my watch-chain and all the seals to Charles de Flahaut. I beg Jules de Sayve to accept my watch as a last token of remembrance; I desire that the picture of my dear Georgine, which I shall wear till the moment of death, be transmitted to my son. I confide it to my excellent second mother, and ask her not to give it to him till he can comprehend all that it means. May the words engraved on the clasp of its chain be ever sacred to him! May he forgive his father for having for a moment forgotten them! I give my brother Henri the ring I wear on the fourth finger of my right hand; it contains some of my little George's hair. May he protect the boy, and sometimes speak to him about his father! I give Henri de Chastellux the large portrait of my good, my too good, Georgine. Let him watch over and console her, and may he sometimes remember his old friendship for me! I beg my brother Henri to select two of the best works in my library, and I ask that he and my sister Ambroisine d'Estampes will each accept one of them. I beg my dear mother to accept the picture of my little angel and to transfer to him the tenderness she had for me. — Paris, the 19th of August, 1815. — CHARLES DE LABÉDOYÈRE."

While making his will, the condemned man was under no delusion in regard to his fate. One alone, his unhappy wife, still was able to hope against hope. Towards three o'clock in the afternoon, when the King was about to enter his carriage in the courtyard of the Tuileries to take his usual airing, a woman dressed in black threw herself on her knees before him, weeping bitterly and crying: "Pardon! pardon!" It was Madame de Labédoyère. — "Madame," said Louis XVIII., "I understand your feelings and those of your family, and never was I more grieved to refuse a request." The poor woman fell in a swoon.

Two hours later, about five o'clock, another woman in deep mourning, stood in the courtyard waiting for the King's return. It was the condemned man's mother. She tried to approach the carriage, but orders were given to prevent her from doing so. Louis XVIII. saw her at a distance and made an impatient gesture, muttering at the same time: "No pardon!"

Half an hour afterwards, in the plain of Grenelle, General de Labédoyère knelt to receive the blessing of his old preceptor, the Abbé Delondelle, and then, rising calmly, stepped toward the gendarmes who were about to shoot him, and, pointing to his breast, said: "My friends, do not miss!" and, refusing to have his eyes bandaged, gave them the order to fire. The day of execution was the 19th of August, 1815.

When Madame de Krudener learned the end of the drama, she shed abundant tears. "O my God, how I thank Thee!" she cried; "Thou hast saved a soul while men were wreaking vengeance on a miserable body! Thine be the glory! Thine the glory, God of love and mercy!"

IV

FOUCHÉ

THE Duchess of Angoulême left Paris on the 15th of August, — that is to say, four days before the execution of the unhappy Labédoyère, — and returned on the 11th of September. Her journey was a continuous ovation. It might almost be said that the daughter of Louis XVI. advanced under triumphal arches. On the 5th of September the *Moniteur* quoted the following notice from the *Indicateur de Bordeaux:* "September 2. — Her Royal Highness, Madame, the Duchess of Angoulême, set out at six o'clock yesterday morning. Never shall we forget Madame's too brief sojourn in the faithful city that so ardently desired to see the daughter of kings again, and which nothing but her auspicious promise to live here always could ever console for her recent departure. All Her Royal Highness's time has been spent in wiping away the tears which the new misfortunes that have pursued her have caused us to shed. She knew that her presence was a soothing balm for the wounds of the heart. The reveille at daybreak was not merely for the national guard. Everybody wished to see the object of universal regret once more. The procession slowly proceeded through a crowd, as it did a fortnight ago; but at that time all hearts thrilled with delight, and joy was depicted on every countenance. But yesterday all faces wore another expression, — that of melancholy, of grief. Barely had the population strength enough to breathe unanimous blessings which resembled matin prayers, which are never so fervent as when they are borne upward by hope."

Everywhere the Duchess of Angoulême was worshipped as an idol. At Toulouse, which she entered on the 2d of September, two lines of poplars, plane-trees, and acacias, carefully transplanted, shaded the façades of the houses with foliage and made masses of green. The horses were detached from her carriage, and forty young men disputed the privilege of dragging it. Groups of maidens dressed in white, girdled with green scarfs and crowned with lilies, preceded and surrounded the coach and strewed flowers in its path. At the theatre on the 5th of September, General Ricard announced to the audience that the Spanish army, which had theretofore been in occupation of a part of the department of Basses-Pyrenees, had crossed the frontier and was already on the march. This news produced all the effect of a theatrical situation, and was received with shouts of "Long live the King! Long live the Duke of Angoulême! Long live Madame!" On the next day the Princess visited the Capitol, where she received the respects of the Academy of Floral Games. The Toulousains brought out all their inventive genius and taxed their ingenuity to receive her with the very refinement of flattery. As she passed the church du Taur, two doves, which appeared to descend from the sky, deposited in her lap a crown of lilies.

At the hour when the Duchess of Angoulême was preparing to re-enter Paris, something poisoned the pleasure she would otherwise have felt at being there again, and this was the reflection that she would once more find a regicide among her uncle's ministers. At a time when a gory reaction had been inaugurated by the execution of the unfortunate Labédoyère, it was surely by some irony of fate that the proscription lists should be made up by a terrorist of the Convention. The Princess was a woman of conviction and as strongly attached to her political as to her religious faith, and consequently she could not familiarize herself with this idea.

Meantime the credit of Fouché, like that of Talleyrand, began to receive some heavy shocks. "The Duchess of Angoulême is coming," said the King to Baron de Vitrolles, "and the dismissal of Fouché would be a fine bouquet to give her." — "Where should we be, Sire, if the policy of the State should be reduced to bouquets?" "The King said no more," adds M. de Vitrolles; "but on the next day, His Majesty of his own accord returned to the immediate dismissal of the ministers as if he wished to persuade me. I readily saw what kind of influence was being exerted on the King. The prefect of police, urgent to have done with the minister whom he wished to replace, pushed matters beyond bounds and seriously disturbed the King about his personal safety. Matters even went so far as to make him think that the Duke of Otranto was strongly suspected of a conspiracy to have him and his family murdered in the Tuileries. When I insisted that for every reason of policy and dignity he should not permit himself to be drawn into hasty action, his voice changed. . . . 'But, meanwhile,' said he, 'I must be taken care of.'"

In reality, from the very first day the presence of Fouché in the ministry had weighed like a nightmare on the conscience of the King.

In speaking of the conduct of Fouché while he was in the ministry of the second Restoration, M. Guizot says in his Memoirs: "A little less hurry and a little more steadiness would have spared Louis XVIII. a sad scandal. He had only to wait a few days, and there would have been no need for him to run the risk, not of revolution and disastrous disturbances, but of a prolongation of disorders and alarms. Necessity imposes itself on nations just as it does on individuals. The necessity of which Fouché made use in order to become one of Louis XVIII.'s ministers was in a great degree factitious and temporary; that which brought Louis XVIII. back to the Tuileries was natural,

and became more urgent day by day. He had no
need of taking Fouché into his cabinet at Arnou-
ville; he might have remained there in peace; they
would have soon been obliged to go there after
him."

A noteworthy thing is that it was by the most
enthusiastic royalists that the selection of Fouché,
Duke of Otranto, and Napoleon's minister of police
during the Hundred Days, was imposed on the
King, and that it was through them that he became
Louis XVIII.'s Minister of Police under the second
Restoration. Baron de Vitrolles, Count Beugnot,
and Chateaubriand express, not without surprise,
the singular enthusiasm felt by the defenders of the
throne and altar for a regicide. M. de Vitrolles
says: "The opinion of the royalists and the notables
of the Faubourg Saint-Germain was suddenly and
in an unexpected way given in favor of the Duke of
Otranto. Had he exercised over them those influ-
ences, the art of which he understood better than
anybody else? Or was it that the capricious wind of
opinion had blown upon them? It is certain that
with one voice they called for Fouché as Minister
of Police. He alone, they said, could protect the
throne from the plots of its enemies, and fear came
to their aid. When I objected, my objections had
not the slightest weight. Up to that time I had
thought that such shiftings of opinion were reserved
for the ignorant populace, and I was astounded to
find it easier to carry the people of the Faubourg

Saint-Germain off their feet than the frequenters of the drinking-places of the Faubourg Saint-Antoine."

It greatly surprised Count Beugnot to find the Constable of Crussol, sometime captain of Monsieur's body-guard, and a legitimist *par excellence*, distinguishing himself by his zeal in behalf of Fouché: "I recoiled," says Count Beugnot; "I could not believe it. What! the Constable of Crussol, the last of our chevaliers, the very type of fidelity, — does he propose the selection of such a man to the brother of Louis XVI.! I reproached the worthy man, and my reproaches were pretty severe, but he always replied: 'What would you have? Fouché preserved us all when the King went away; it is owing to him alone that M. de Vitrolles was not shot, and really, who in France are the enemies of the royal family? The Jacobins! Well, Fouché holds them in his hand, and so long as he is for the King, we may sleep in peace. My dear M. Beugnot, families in the Faubourg Saint-Germain are old; we have suffered too much; we need rest.'"

And what is M. de Chateaubriand's opinion? "Was not the Faubourg Saint-Germain right in its belief in M. Fouché? When M. de Saint-Léon went to Vienna he took three letters, one of which was addressed to M. de Talleyrand; the Duke of Otranto desired Louis XVIII.'s ambassador to urge the son of Philippe Égalité to seat himself on the throne if he saw his way clear. What probity in these negotiations! How fortunate we were to have to do with such honorable gentlemen! We admired them, however; burned incense before them and blessed these Cartouches; we paid court to them and called them 'monseigneur.'" And, like M. de Vitrolles, like Count Beugnot, Chateaubriand shows us the entire Faubourg Saint-Germain singing a canticle of gratitude in honor of the notorious regicide. "Everybody," he adds, "had a hand in the nomination of Fouché, when it was once secured, — religion and impiety, virtue and vice, royalist and revolutionist, foreigner and Frenchman, — all exclaimed: 'Without Fouché, no security for the King; without Fouché no safety for France; he alone can do the work.' The old Duchess Dowager of Duras was one of the noble ladies most animated in the hymn. . . . The timorous had been so much afraid of Bonaparte that they took the assassin of Lyons for a Titus."

After these laments, the author of the *Génie du Christianisme* tells the following anecdote. "'Well?' said Louis XVIII. to me, opening the conversation with that expression. — 'Well, Sire, are you going to take the Duke of Otranto?' 'It is necessary to have him; from my brother to the Constable of Crussol (and the latter is not suspected) everybody says that we cannot do otherwise. What do you think?' — 'Sire, the thing is done; I ask Your Majesty's permission to be silent.' 'No, no; speak; you know that I have opposed the measure ever since Ghent.' — 'Sire, I can only obey your orders; pardon my fidelity; I believe the monarchy is at an end.' The King did not reply, and I was beginning to tremble at my hardihood when His Majesty resumed: 'Well, M. de Chateaubriand, I am of your opinion.'"

Notwithstanding her habitual obedience to the King, the Duchess of Angoulême had always declined to receive Fouché. As soon as she perceived his presence at the Tuileries she became anxious and disturbed. But she was not to suffer long from this humiliating sight. It was not necessary for her to secure the removal of the Minister of Police. He fell of himself. At the time when the Princess entered Paris, after her triumphal journey to Bordeaux and Toulouse, a new Chamber of Deputies was opening its sessions. This was the celebrated "Undiscoverable Chamber,"—an assembly more royalist than the King himself.

With a Chamber like this, even Fouché saw that his further presence in the ministry had become impossible. Up to the last moment he was the victim of illusions. He had secured the intervention of the Duke of Wellington in his favor. A domestic event whose importance he much overestimated had just strengthened his chimerical hope of definitively conciliating the Faubourg Saint-Germain. He had for several years been a widower, but he succeeded in persuading a young woman of high family, but without fortune, Mademoiselle de Castellane, to accept his hand. But on his very wedding day he was given to understand that the Duchess of Otranto would never be well received by duchesses of ancient lineage. The daughter of Louis XVI. was installed at the Tuileries on the 11th of September, 1815. On the 19th, Fouché was dismissed. Five days afterwards he dragged the Prince de Talleyrand along with him in his downfall. Thus this Talleyrand-Fouché ministry, the object of so many intrigues, ambitions, and resentments, lasted only three months. On the stage of history do not celebrities resemble the poor marionettes whose thread is pulled by a mysterious and invisible hand?

On leaving the Ministry of Foreign Affairs, Prince de Talleyrand had the address to get himself appointed grand chamberlain, at a salary of a hundred thousand francs. Fouché contented himself with being the French minister at Dresden, which was a court all in the family, inasmuch as Louis XVIII. was the son of a princess of Saxony. Once again was the irony of fate shown in the presence of a regicide, as representative of the Most Christian King at that patriarchal court, where, besides, Napoleon was always held in highest honor.

While Fouché, Duke of Otranto, was making ready to go to his diplomatic post, he received from Louis XVIII. a letter couched in friendly terms. He answered it with an epistle like a Parthian shaft, denouncing to the King, the Princes of his family, and especially the Duke and Duchess of Angoulême, for alleged attempts to overthrow the throne. Then this man who, two months before, had wrested from the Emperor his abdication and driven him from the Elysée to Malmaison, and from Malmaison to the sea, took up in turn his road to the frontier, more like an exile than a diplomat, and disguised, till he should have left France behind him. On the 2d of October, 1815, while on his way, he wrote as follows from Brussels to his chief, the Duke of Richelieu, president of the Council and Minister of Foreign Affairs: "My Lord Duke: I left Paris after receiving my credentials. . . . I congratulate myself on the relations that have come to exist between Your Excellency and myself. They will surely make you appreciate my services. I know that those which I rendered during my ministry have been misconstrued. I must expect that intrigue will continue to depreciate them, if only to show its zeal. I confide in the justice of the King, in public opinion, and in time to be revenged for all outrages. I hope, My Lord Duke, that in the functions which I shall exercise, I shall place in your hand weapons for my defence. In the present condition of Europe, there is no diplomatic mission that may become more important. Questions are about to arise, and the way in which they are dealt with will give more or less lustre to this or that legation."

On the 11th of October, 1815, the Duke of Richelieu replied: "My Lord Duke: I am in receipt of the letter which you did me the honor to write from

Brussels, on the 2d of this month. I shall be delighted to see relations established between us which your information and experience may render of great advantage to the welfare of the State. You may rely on my eagerness to cause the King to appreciate the services you may render in the mission His Majesty has confided to you."

Arrived at his post, the French minister to Saxony thus reported his reception: "Dresden, October 30, 1815.— My Lord Duke: I reached Dresden on Saturday. Yesterday, which was Sunday, I presented my credentials to the King, who received me kindly, and invited me to dine with the royal family. An equal feeling of gratitude and veneration for our august sovereign animates the court of Saxony. It earnestly prays that his good fortune may equal his virtues and his enlightenment."

To this despatch the Duke of Otranto added the following profession of royalist faith accompanied with a bit of flattery to the Duke of Richelieu: "All opinions, parties, and factions must be pretty well convinced by this time that France cannot recover its independence as a nation save by rallying frankly and strongly around the King. To Your Excellency belongs the task of bringing this truth home to every heart. Your noble character, now perfectly well known to the whole nation, inspires entire confidence in your words."

In his correspondence, Fouché thought less of

casting light on the affairs of Saxony than of giving advice about the inside condition of France, and pleading his own cause, for his conscience was his accuser. In a despatch, dated on the 3d of December, 1815, he wrote: "Your ministry will be honored and blessed if you reconcile all the parties around the throne and prevent any one of them from becoming too prominent. I had no other thought during my ministry. My Lord Duke, lofty souls are sincere. I meditated no lie when I swore to the King that I would serve him. My heart was so filled with the necessity of uniting with him that it would willingly have leaped into the midst of France, poured its blood into every breast, and so penetrated all with its sentiments. All Paris appreciated my conduct during the terrible crisis that shook the throne. It required some courage to declare for the Bourbons before the King had entered his capital. I was at the head of the French government. It is well known that no personal dangers chilled my devotion to the King. It is easy now for an orator to cast reproach on any minister from the height of the two Chambers, but it is a somewhat delicate matter to insult an absent minister; and he who, after the subsidence of a storm, attacks the minister who quelled it, shows more passion than good sense. . . . The way in which your predecessors are denounced is sufficient to forewarn you of the way in which unjust men will appreciate the eminent services you are to-day rendering to your country. . . . Any moderation for which you are blamed, the King will be blamed for. Constant efforts will be made to withdraw him from the course which his reason and information have themselves laid down for him. A constitutional king seems to men of limited understanding a king without power and without energy. If the present ministry permits itself to be drawn along by the current, it will end by belonging to the party of exaggeration. Man does not always know the import of the vows he takes."

Forgetful of the fact that he had drawn up and signed the lists of proscribed on the 24th of July, the Duke of Otranto ended his despatch, or rather his apology, with the following words: "It was not disorder alone that we had to repress; order had to be established in a stable manner, and it was necessary to give great moral force and authority to the King. In order to do this, we thought there was nothing better than to pacify France with thoughts of security, pardon, and tolerance, and by instilling the belief that there could not be too large forgetfulness of the past, and that guarantees of security could not be too greatly multiplied."

This justification of his conduct was but pains wasted. Fouché, Duke of Otranto, and minister of France at Dresden, was to be stricken down by the law against regicides. On the 4th of January, 1816, the Duke of Richelieu wrote to him: "My Lord Duke: I have the honor to inform you that the King has decided to terminate the mission with which you have been charged at the court at Dresden. I send herewith the letters of recall which His Majesty has on this occasion sent to His Majesty, the King of Saxony." The other day we said to ourselves on looking at this short and dry letter: "So, this was the end of that noisy and troubled career. A few official lines copied down by an employee of the Minister of Foreign Affairs; thenceforth nothing, nothing but exile and oblivion. He who yesterday proscribed is himself proscribed to-morrow. Why struggle so hard to reach such a goal at last?"

V

MARSHAL NEY

"IDEAS of right and duty," says M. Guizot, "sentiments of respect and of fidelity, were confused and conflicting in many minds. So to speak, there were then two real and natural governments face to face, and many minds might easily, and without perverseness, be perplexed as to which should be chosen. Louis XVIII. and his advisers might, therefore, and in their turn and without weakness, have taken this moral perturbation into consideration. Marshal Ney is the most signal illustration of it. The greater the harm he had done the King, the easier would it have been, without danger, to use clemency as well as justice, and to show towards him, when he was condemned, that magnanimity of head and heart which is so efficacious both in establishing power and commanding fidelity. Even the violence of the royalist reaction, the fierceness of party spirit, and the thirst for chastisement and vengeance, would have given to that act additional brilliancy and effect, for they would have signalized the return of manliness and liberty."

The Restoration did not comprehend that if there was one man that should be pardoned, it was the man who, in a nation justly celebrated for courage, was called "the bravest of the brave."

Notwithstanding the capitulation of the 3d of July, 1815, which gave him legal protection from all prosecution, Marshal Ney withdrew from Paris, at the instance of his family. He took with him but little luggage, but was unwilling to leave behind him the Egyptian sabre that the First Consul had given him in July, 1802. He went to the waters of Saint-Alban, near Roanne, where he remained till the 25th of July. Then he sought refuge in a château near Aurillac, which belonged to one of his wife's relatives. There he lived secluded in an upper chamber from which he did not emerge when there were strangers in the house. But he had the imprudence to leave on a sofa his beautiful Egyptian sabre, the gift of Napoleon. The richness of the weapon excited the attention of a visitor, who, on the next day, gave a description of it at a house in Aurillac. From the details that he gave, another person concluded that the sabre could belong only to Ney or Murat. This was reported to the prefect of Cantal, who sent fourteen gendarmes to the château Bessanis to arrest the marshal. They came on the 5th of July and found the proscribed man walking quietly in a courtyard. It was he to whom they first explained their errand. "I am Marshal Ney," answered the bravest of the brave, and he was taken to Paris as a prisoner. At some leagues' distance from the capital the marshal's wife met them, and when he saw the beloved companion of his glory and his misfortunes, he could not control his emotion. His eyes filled with tears.

"For lion hearts are father hearts."

"Do not be surprised," said he to his captors; "I am not brave when I think of my wife and children."

Upon learning of the marshal's arrest, Louis XVIII. cried with rare good sense: "He does us more injury to-day by permitting himself to be taken than he did on the 14th of March." It was thought desirable to bring him at once before a council of war composed of French marshals. Marshal Moncey, Duke of Conégliano, who held the seniority, refused to take part in the council of war, and for this refusal he was deprived of his rank as marshal by an order of the 29th of August, 1815, and condemned to imprisonment for three months in the fortress of Ham.

Some days afterward Marshal Mortier, Duke of Treviso, received a visit from M. Dupin at his house in the Faubourg Saint-Honoré. There was a portrait of Mortier in the splendid uniform of a marshal of the Empire in all his decorations, and opposite was a picture of his father, a venerable old man with long hair and dressed in farmer's clothes.

"You see there," he said, with emotion to his visitor, "my father's picture and my own. I will undergo every disgrace, — they may render me destitute; it is nothing. I will leave everything; I will assume the garb and take up the occupations and toils of that good man, rather than condemn Marshal Ney. I know I can work."

In the salons there was no pity. M. de Viel-Castel says that women of the sweetest disposition on ordinary occasions became transformed into veritable furies, and without the least scruple gave expression to their impatience for blood. The investigation lasted for more than three months. When it was remarked by somebody that it was rather barbarous to prolong by empty temporizing the life of a man whose fate was no longer in doubt, "Well, then!" cried one of the women, "don't let him languish, nor us either."

The fury of these demoniacs, of whom more than one had been at the feet of Napoleon and both his Empresses, excited horror. "Oh!" as Madame de Rémusat with good reason wrote to her son, who had told her about the "bloodthirsty speeches" of these charming dames, "I am as angry as you at the rage of all those women, whether they have blue eyes or black. When an unfortunate criminal is crushed by justice, one should be silent and leave him to the tribunal whose duty it is to decide his fate, and to God who probably has often overruled the judgment of man. Revolutions surround men with such difficult circumstances that though kings may be pardoned for severity employed to render states secure, the public should be indulgent. But this maxim is out of date, and charity no longer is classed among the Christian duties. I wish that women could be persuaded that these hateful passions mar them much. Surely, my friend, love would be much more becoming to them and, passion for passion, hatred will the more surely drag them to hell." Shame to the Red Terror! Shame to the White Terror! Shame to the great ladies who by their cruelty became imitators of the knitting women of 1793! Both are a disgrace to their sex.

The jurisdiction of a council of war composed of marshals being out of the question, the Duke of Richelieu said in the Chamber of Peers on the 11th of November, 1815: "Not only in the King's name, but in the name of France, so long treated with indignity and now in a stupor, let us fulfil the duties of the administration of public justice. In the name of Europe we come at once to conjure and to require you to decide the question of Marshal Ney." The Duke of Richelieu opened his ministry disadvantageously by speaking as prosecutor, — he whose heart was generous, — and by making against "the bravest of the brave," an address which, it is said, he did not write, and which he subsequently regretted. On the next day people said: "Have you read the ukase of the Duke of Richelieu?" the allusion being to the fact that he had been governor of the Crimea during the emigration.

Debate began in the Chamber of Peers on the 21st of November, 1815. During the foregoing night the accused had been transferred from his prison, the Conciergerie, to the Luxembourg, where the Peers held their sessions. In places reserved for them were the Prince Royal of Wurtemberg, Prince Metternich, the foreign diplomats, and English and Russian generals. When the marshal appeared, in the custody of four grenadiers of the guard, his calm and martial attitude produced a vivid impression even on his bitterest enemies. He came as the incarnation of a defeat terrible but glorious, — the defeat of Waterloo. People remembered that on that day, seven times unhorsed, covered with blood and powder, on foot and sword in hand, he had said, alas! in vain: "My friends, you shall see how a marshal of France dies!" It might be said that all the sufferings, all the griefs, all the disasters, of the beaten-down and vanquished fatherland were concentrated in his person.

There was a second public session on the 23d of November, and a third on the 4th of December. Witnesses were heard on the latter day. The most important of them was General de Bourmont, the same who on the 14th of March, at Lons-le-Saulnier, did not abandon the marshal, and who, after asking the Emperor for a command, went over to the enemy on the 15th of June, — that is to say, three days before Waterloo. Ney could not contain himself when he found his former lieutenant a witness against him. He burst out in a fury of indignation: "The witness has been preparing his thesis for the last eight months, and has had time to make it a good one. When he was getting up his denunciations at Lille he probably imagined that I would be treated like Labédoyère, and that he and I would never meet face to face. But he was wrong. I have no talent for speech-making; I go directly to the point. It is a fact that on the 14th of March I had an interview with the witness in the presence of General Lacourbe. It is hard that Lacourbe should be dead; but I appeal against all this testimony to a higher tribunal, — to God who hears and will judge us, — judge both you and me, Monsieur de Bourmont!"

After this apostrophe, the accused told the history of his defection at Lons-le-Saulnier. According to his account, he had called Lacourbe and Bourmont, his two generals of division, shown them the draught of his imperialist proclamation, and asked them, on their word of honor, what they thought about it. General Lacourbe made a brief and evasive reply, but General Bourmont approved of the draught, induced the marshal to read it to the troops, and engaged to win them over. "He had two hours to reflect," added the accused. "As to myself, did any one say: 'What are you about to do? You are risking your honor and reputation in this desperate course!' No! I found only men who urged me towards the abyss. . . . I did not even know where Bourmont's troops were. If he thought I was doing wrong, he was free to arrest me. With his large command he could have done so, and I was alone, without officers, and without a single saddle-horse to escape on. But he was shrewd, and conducted the affair very ably. I wanted very much that he should lodge at my quarters, but he declined, and took refuge with the prefect, the Marquis of Vaulchier, and together they arranged to watch the progress of events, and, in any case, to leave themselves a door of escape. When the troops were assembled, Bourmont and Lacourbe put me at the head of a body of officers and conducted me to the middle of the square, where I read the proclamation. Soldiers and officers alike ran to us, embraced and almost stifled us with their demonstrations. The troops dispersed in good order. The superior officers came to dine with me. I was dejected, but, if Bourmont means that, the guests were cheerful. That is the truth of the matter."

While General Bourmont and Marshal Ney were face to face before the Chamber, many a judge said to himself: "Why did Bourmont ask the Emperor for a command during the Hundred Days, when he was not obliged to do so? Why did he take General Labédoyère as a pledge of his fidelity to the imperial eagles? Why did he go over to the enemy on the eve of Waterloo? And yet Bourmont is loaded with honors, and Ney is to be shot!"

The chancellor asked the witness why, after disapproving, as he pretended, of the resolution taken by the accused, he accompanied him to Lons-le-Saulnier, where the troops were gathered. Bourmont answered that he wished to see what would be the effect of the reading of the proclamation by the marshal, and thus be able to give the King an exact account of all that took place.

The accused then spoke again, and strenuously denied what the witness had asserted, namely, that to his knowledge the marshal, while reading the proclamation, wore the decoration of the Legion of Honor with the Emperor's picture on it. "General," he cried, "it is infamous to say that I had already the design of becoming a traitor." Then he recalled the fact that when a colonel came to him to offer his resignation rather than join in the defection, he had freely permitted him to go away. Why did not Bourmont act in the same way? "I had no guard," he added, looking the witness in the face. "You yourself might have arrested and killed me; you would have done me a great service by doing so, and perhaps you would have done your duty."

Bourmont having expressed the opinion that the marshal would probably have saved the day for the royalists if he had taken a musket and, at the head of his troops, at once charged Napoleon, Ney replied: "Would you have done so, had you been in my place? No; I do not believe you capable of it; you have not character enough."

M. Berryer, the elder, who, with M. Dupin, was counsel for the accused, asked the witness the following question, which ended the inquisition: "When everybody was shouting 'Long live the Emperor!' did you, M. de Bourmont, cry 'Long live the King?'"

The session of the 5th of December was busied with the capitulation of Paris on the 3d of July, 1815, the twelfth article of which read as follows: "The inhabitants and, in general, all who were within the capital shall continue to enjoy their rights and liberties without being liable to be disturbed or questioned as to anything that they are doing or may have done, or as to their conduct or political opinions." One of the plenipotentiaries who had signed the treaty of the 3d of July, namely, General Guillemont was interrogated by Chancellor Dambray, and answered thus: "As chief of the general staff I was instructed to stipulate for amnesty to all, whatever might be their opinions, functions, or conduct. Amnesty was not accorded without opposition. I was ordered to break off all negotiation if the terms were not accepted; the army was ready to show fight; it was this article that induced it to lay down its arms."

Marshal Davoust, Prince of Eckmühl, declared that he instructed the plenipotentiaries to withdraw from the conferences if the clauses proposed by him to insure the safety of persons and property should not be accepted. M. Berryer, the elder, then asked the witness to say what he would have done in case of refusal. Marshal Davoust answered that he would have given battle as he had a fine and well-disciplined army consisting of sixty-five thousand infantry, twenty-five thousand cavalry, and four or five hundred cannon. "The capitulation," exclaimed Marshal Ney, "was protective to such a degree that I counted on it. Without it can any one suppose that I would not have preferred to die, sword in hand?"

At the close of the hearing on the 5th of December, M. Bellart, the public prosecutor, thus opened his ridiculously declamatory address: "Gentlemen, when in the recesses of deserts once covered with populous cities, the philosophic wanderer who has been led thither by his insatiable curiosity — an attribute, gentlemen, so characteristic of our species — perceives the melancholy remains of those celebrated monuments constructed during remote ages in the fatuous hope of braving the jaws of time, and which now are but formless masses of ruins and dust, he cannot escape being plunged into profound melancholy as he reflects upon what is the end of human pride and its achievements. How much more crushing to the feelings of him who loves his fellow-men is the spectacle of the ruins of a splendid fame fallen into opprobrium through its own fault!"

The last session was held on the following day,

the 6th of December. It lasted five hours, and did not end till three o'clock in the morning of December the 7th. What had been the attitude of more than one great lady for the last few days? Lamartine, who belonged to Louis XVIII.'s body-guard, says: "The life accorded to the hero of Beresina seemed a theft committed against the law of reprisal. In the salons of the aristocracy people clamored around the King's ministers, demanding the hero's blood as if for a personal favor. Women of the highest rank, young, beautiful, rich, laden with gifts, favors, titles, and dignities by the court, forgot their families, their pleasures, their indolence, and their amours, and ran about from morning till night if so be they might prevent a single vote in favor of mercy or secure one in favor of punishment. We ourselves have observed with grief and astonishment, the runnings about, the petitions, and the hands of these women clasped in suppliance for concessions which they implored for the satisfaction of their hate. We blush for them yet. Who need be astounded at the brutal ferocities of the masses, when rank, fortune, and courts become possessed by such reckless inhumanity, such frenzies of rage, and such thirst for blood on the day of vengeance?"

Alas! the cruel passions of these women were to be satisfied. The chancellor did not even permit the defence to argue from the capitulation of Paris. Another treaty covered the marshal, — that of the 20th of November, 1815. The marshal was born in

1769, — in the same year as Napoleon, — at Sarrelouis, and, by the treaty of the 20th of November, 1815, that city was ceded to Prussia. It was stipulated in the documents, that "any person born in the countries ceded or restored should not be annoyed or troubled in his person because of his acts or political opinions." M. Dupin made a point of this. "Marshal Ney," said the lawyer, "is under the protection not only of French law, but under that of the law of nations. He has always been French at heart, but he was born in a country which no longer belongs to the King of France." Then the marshal, much excited, cried out: "I am French and I shall die a Frenchman!" He then read the following protest: "Hitherto my defence has seemed to be unrestricted, but now it is hampered. I thank my generous defenders for what they have done, and what they are ready to do, but I beg them rather to cease entirely from defending me than to defend me imperfectly. I would rather not be defended at all than to have only the simulacrum of a defence. I was brought to trial contrary to the faith of treaties, and I will not invoke them. I appeal to Europe and to posterity."

A hundred and thirty-nine peers voted for death. Among them were many of the marshal's old comrades in arms, such as Marshals Kellermann, Pérignon, Sérurier, Victor, and Marmont, and Generals de Beurnonville, Dessoles, Maison, de La Tour-Maubourg, Lauriston, and still others. Seventeen peers voted for banishment: MM. Porcher de Richebourg, de Maleville, Lenoir-Laroche, Lemercier, Lanjuinais, General Klein, Herwyn, General Gouvion-Saint-Cyr, Calaud, Chollet, General Chasseloup-Laubat, Berthollet, the Duke of Broglie, Lally, General Curial, Fontanes, and the Duke of Montmorency. Five peers who voted for death added a recommendation to the mercy of the King. These were Marshal Marmont, General Dessoles, and MM. de la Tour du Pin, Emmery, and Beaumont. Five peers abstained from voting, — MM. de Choiseul, de Sainte-Suzanne, de Brigode, d'Aligre, and de Nicolaï. "Clement but timid neutrality," says Lamartine, "which neither smites nor spares, but which is never permissible between the sword and the victim."

The conduct of the young Duke of Broglie, who then voted for the first time in the Chamber of Peers, was specially honorable. The chancellors first put the question of fact: "Did the marshal read to the troops the proclamation hereunto adjoined?" Of what effect would it have been to say yes, when the accused himself had admitted the fact? The question of law was then proposed: "In doing so, was the marshal guilty of high treason?" Upon this, the Duke rose and replied: "No." In his *Souvenirs* he writes: "I owe it to the Chambers to testify that the temerity, and, in view of the times and circumstances, I may almost say the scandal, of my vote excited neither exclamation nor murmur and that at the close of the session no one stood aloof from me or was cooler than usual. Meanwhile we must all live, and at that time we lived in an atmosphere of intimidation that was stifling. I cite only one example.

"Among the old senators who still sat in the new Chamber of Peers, was a little general named Gouvion, but who, I think, was not related to the marshal. I had known him at Antwerp, where he was in command at the time M. d'Argenson lived there as prefect, and I often conversed with him. Some time before the opening of the session, I saw the little man fidgeting in his seat as if in pain. At last he came to me and asked what I intended to do, — that is, how I meant to vote. I told him. Unquestionably he did not understand me fully, although he said: 'I shall do the same.' — 'Very well,' said I; 'then sit down here beside me; we will encourage each other.' He sat down, but, when the question of culpability was put, he said 'yes,' like all who had preceded him. And when the time came to vote as to the punishment, he said 'death!' in the same way. Poor man! Precisely the same thing happened to him that had happened to Marshal Ney on the plain of Lons-le-Saulnier."

When the verdict was rendered, Count de Rochechouart, commandant of Paris, to whom the arrangements for the execution of the prisoner were assigned, proceeded to take possession of the Luxembourg, and there keep guard over the doomed man.

VI

THE DEATH OF MARSHAL NEY

IT had been decided that the accused should not be present when sentence was passed. He withdrew before the vote and was taken back to the prison of the Luxembourg, where he was to pass the night. He asked for dinner and ate with good appetite. On seeing that a small knife which he was using put his jailors in fear lest he should commit suicide with it, he threw it aside. After dinner he smoked a cigar and then threw himself down fully dressed, and fell into a deep sleep. At half after three in the morning he was roused by M. Cauchy, secretary of archives to the Chamber of Peers, who had come to read the death warrant. Before beginning, M. Cauchy tried to speak some kind words in order to show his regret at being obliged to come on such a mission. "Sir," said the marshal, "do your duty. Every one must do his duty. Read."

When, as he proceeded to read, the clerk came to the enumeration of the titles and style of the condemned, the marshal interrupted him with these words: "Say Michel Ney, soon to be a pinch of dust." When told that he was at liberty to say farewell to his wife and children, he requested that word should be sent to them to come between six and seven o'clock in the morning. "I trust," he said, "that your note will not tell my wife that her husband is condemned; it is for me to tell her of my fate."

M. Cauchy then withdrew. The marshal lay down again with his clothes on, and went to sleep. In a short time he was again roused by the arrival of his wife, accompanied by his four sons and Madame Gamot, her sister. On entering the room, the unfortunate woman, who was soon to be made a widow, fell rigid to the floor. The marshal raised her with the assistance of his keepers. Tears and sobs succeeded to a long swoon. Madame Gamot was on her knees in a condition not less deplorable than that of her sister. The marshal tenderly embraced his four sons, Napoleon, Michel, Eugene, and Edgar Ney. The eldest (who died in 1857, a general and a senator, and whose sister married the Duke of Persigny) was twelve years old. The youngest (who was a general, senator, and master of the hounds during the reign of Napoleon III., and who married the widow of the son of General Labédoyère) was only three years of age.

The unhappy father who, like all heroic natures, was as tender-hearted as he was energetic and brave, took the four boys on his knee, one after the other, and, speaking in a low voice, gave them the last counsels of paternal love. The last accents of that sweet and strong voice were to remain forever an ineffaceable memory in the hearts of the children.

Meantime the condemned man, who saw that his wife was giving way to despair, was desirous of ending adieux so harrowing, and, that he might lighten the wretched woman's grief, he endeavored to instil into her a hope in which he himself had no share. Leaning towards his sister-in-law, he said so that his wife might hear it, that if that unhappy lady should go to the Tuileries without a moment's loss of time, she might perhaps see the King and secure a pardon. Then came the last embrace, and the wife went away with her sons and her sister, and in all haste sought the palace of Louis XVIII. The condemned man was not under the least illusion in regard to his fate. He had advised his wife's act only in order that she might be willing to withdraw. After she had gone he sat down at a table and made his will.

So great was the apprehension caused by the prestige that the bravest of the brave had among the troops, and so pressing was the fear lest he might yet escape, that his keepers were body-guards disguised in the uniform of grenadiers. Lamartine, who belonged to the body-guard at the beginning of the Restoration, said of these masquerading wardens: "They were young and amiable noblemen, the élite of their companies, and of incorruptible honesty, and utterly incapable of insulting a captive whose fate they deplored and whose glory was their admiration. Although they were officers they were dressed in the uniform of simple mounted grenadiers of the royal guard. In this costume, they went among the gendarmes and other people whose duty it was to keep watch over the prisoner; they guarded him in his room and conversed familiarly with him, not to embitter, but to distract and cheer his loneliness. They encouraged him to hope and flattered themselves that the marshal, condemned and pardoned by the King, would, under better stars, remember them as comforters in his evil days. It is from their own lips that we received these confidences."

When the condemned man had ended his will, one of the guards said to him: "Marshal, in your extremity would it not be well to think of God? It is always a good thing to become reconciled to God." The marshal paused, looked at his interlocutor and said, after a moment's silence: "You are right; yes, you are right. One should die like an honest man and a Christian; I should like to see the curé of Saint-Sulpice." Some minutes afterwards the Abbé Depierre, curé of that parish, entered the condemned man's room and heard his confession. At the end of three-quarters of an hour the venerable priest withdrew, promising to return and assist the marshal in his last moments.

Meanwhile the marshal's wife and her four poor little children had arrived at the Tuileries. Before daybreak the suppliant family contrived to make their way as far as the rooms adjoining the apartments of the King and the Duchess of Angoulême. Would the orphan of the Temple intervene to prevent the four children from becoming orphans? Would she remember that the bravest of the brave and the martyred Queen had occupied the same prison, the Conciergerie? Would the farewells but now spoken by the marshal recall to the Princess those of her father, Louis XVI.? Would she forget the words of clemency and pardon spoken by the victim before mounting the scaffold on the 21st of January? Could she forget, too, that the marshal's wife was the daughter of the unfortunate Madame Auguié, sister of Madame Campan; of that Madame Auguié who was Marie Antoinette's lady of the bedchamber, and who went mad with grief when she learned of the Queen's execution, and so killed herself? And the marshal's wife thought: "No; it is impossible that the Duchess of Angoulême, who is generous and good, can fail to pity me. The first nobleman of the Chamber, the Duke of Duras, allowed me to enter the Tuileries. This permission to enter the château and almost reach the royal apartment can be nothing less than a tacit promise of mercy to my husband and my little ones. Louis XVIII. is still asleep. When he wakes, it will be to pardon."

The shadows of night have passed away. Day is beginning to dawn, a day sombre, chill, wintry.

It is the 7th of December. The marshal's wife is waiting. The Duchess of Angoulême will listen to nothing, will know nothing. Her door remains closed. Closed, too, is the King's door. Hour follows hour, — hours of prostration, of anguish. And what is doing while the poor wife waits there so long?

It is half after eight in the morning. Faithful to his promise, the Abbé Depierre, the curé of Saint-Sulpice, returns to the Luxembourg. A carriage stands waiting for the priest and the marshal. When both are beside it, the priest steps back to allow the illustrious warrior to enter first: "No, no, monsieur, get in before me," says the condemned man, and then, looking towards heaven, he continues, "I shall ascend to yonder sky before you." At the sound of this affectionate dispute, the driver turns his head. At the sight he grows pale and falls from his seat. 'Tis an old soldier who recognizes the bravest of the brave. Vain efforts are made to revive the coachman, and the horses have to be led by the bridle.

The morning is cold and gloomy. An icy mist almost prevents the eye from distinguishing the leafless branches of the mighty trees. The horses move slowly. The condemned man listens respectfully to the consoling words of the priest, his last friend. He believes that he will be taken to the plain of Grenelle, the common place of execution. Suddenly the carriage stops, and enters the gate of the Luxembourg and the Observatory. The marshal is surprised at this halt at half the distance. The gate swings back. The marshal is requested to alight. He sees that he is not to enter the carriage again. The government feared that there would be a crowd at the plain of Grenelle, and therefore during the night it changed the place of execution.

The marshal now gives his gold snuff-box to the curé of Saint-Sulpice in keeping for his wife, and also some louis to be distributed among the parish poor. Then, after embracing the venerable priest, he walks firmly towards the platoon of veterans ranged before him. The officer proposes to bandage his eyes. "Do you not know," says Ney, "that for twenty years I have been accustomed to look straight at bullets and cannon-balls?" Touched by such pride and courage, the officer hesitated before giving the word to fire. "Before God and my country," cried the noble victim, "I protest against the verdict that condemns me. I appeal to mankind, to posterity, to God. Long live France!" General de Rochechouart, whose lot it is to see that the sentence is carried out, orders the commander of the platoon to do his duty. The marshal takes his hat in his left hand as he held it at the last charge at Waterloo, and, placing his right on his breast, cries: "Soldiers, straight at the heart!" Three bullets strike him. It is nine o'clock in the morning. The hero has lived his life.

And still the marshal's wife waits for the King to rise. At last she is told that the audience she seeks cannot be accorded, for now it would be futile. At first the poor widow does not understand the words. They have to be explained to her.

Conformably to the rules of military executions, the body of the marshal remained exposed for a quarter of an hour on the place of punishment. Passers-by asked whose body was thus abandoned as a public spectacle. No one dared to reply: "It is Marshal Ney; it is the Duke of Elchingen; it is the Prince of Moscow." When the fifteen minutes had passed, a few sisters from the neighboring Charity Hospital went to claim the body, and had it borne to their chapel, where they watched over it in prayer.

Three hours afterwards the unhappy widow had an interview with the curé of Saint-Sulpice which is thus described in an unpublished letter that a relative of the marshal's wife was good enough to let us see: "Paris, Abbaye-aux-Bois, December 11, 1815. — Yesterday the marshal's widow saw the curé of Saint-Sulpice. The interview was distracting. She wished to know all. It was on their knees that the unfortunate children heard the last words of their father. I want to tell you some of the details given by the curé. They soothed and softened her poignant grief. When the curé heard of the marshal's sentence, he went to the Luxembourg. As soon as the marshal saw him he said: 'I counted on your coming, monsieur. Your character is known to me. I have often heard you spoken of, and always with praise. I wish to do my duty as a Christian. I was reared by deeply religious parents and have never forgotten what they taught me. I can even say that I have never undertaken anything without commending myself first to God. If you will hear me, I will confess.' At the moment of absolution his emotion was very great. 'I am deeply indebted to you,' said he to the curé; 'I am calm and resigned.' Then he gave the priest what money he had, asking him to distribute it among the poor, and to say some masses for the repose of his soul.

"When the guards came to take him to execution, he was surprised. He had hoped to see his wife and children once more. 'What!' said he to the curé, 'I thought I was to have twenty-four hours.' '*Within twenty-four hours*,' answered the curé. — 'A few hours sooner or later; 'tis all the same; I am prepared.'

"He had dreaded a civil execution. When he saw the troops, his face took on a look of content. He made an exclamation and grasped the curé's arm. On reaching the fatal spot, he handed his snuff-box to the priest, begging him to give it to his wife with his own hands. It is said that he fell, shouting 'Long live France!' I am sure that these details will do you good; they will assuage your grief by bringing tears. It is consoling to think that he died so like a Christian."

M. Guizot says in his Memoirs: "Had Marshal

Ney been pardoned and exiled, after his condemnation, by royal letters drawn up for weighty reasons, royalty would have risen like an embankment above all, whether friends or enemies, to stay the stream of blood, and the reaction of 1815 would have been put down and closed, as well as the Hundred Days."

M. de Lamartine, who had so energetically branded the murder of the Duke of Enghien, censured with no less eloquence the murder of Marshal Ney. In his *Histoire de la Restauration* he wrote: "The Duchess of Angoulême alone might have drawn upon herself the rage of the royalist party and let tears weigh in the balance against the hero's blood. . . . Fatal inspirations of severity prevailed with her over the natural part that Providence had assigned to her. . . . And therefore she carried out in her family, her cause, and herself the most irresistible of policies, — the policy of feeling. This was more than obduracy; it was a mistake that condemned her dynasty to a brief existence." And Lamartine ends with these words: "The court was cruel, the King weak, the ministers complaisant, the Chamber of Deputies implacable, Europe urgent, and the Chamber of Peers as cowardly as a senate in the evil days of Rome. Let each take its share in the blood of a hero; France wants none."

Meantime the government, blinded as it was, rejoiced in this execution as if it had been a triumph. On the 7th of December the *Moniteur* reproduced from the *Débats* an article which gave the most exciting details of the victim's last moments, and without even suspecting that the tears which so imprudent an account would cause to flow would be tears of vengeance. At the close of this article the reader, already softened, saw in a sort of stupor, the proceedings characterized as "noble, generous, *indulgent*." The journalist ended the lucubration, which was reproduced in the official sheet, as follows: "Posterity to which the accused made his appeal will ratify this verdict which is already confirmed by impartial contemporaries and by all who do not sacrifice evidence to impassioned pretensions, and history will apply to the memory of Marshal Ney a justice which it is easy to foresee and which only his still-smoking blood prevents us from forecasting."

Ah! surely the editor of the *Journal des Débats* is not a good prohpet. Could he peer into the future, what would he see? He would see the memory of Marshal Ney avenged successively by the Republic and the Empire, the provisional government decreeing on the 18th of March, 1848, that a monument should be raised to the hero on the very spot where he fell! He would see Rude, who made the bas-relief of the Marseillaise for the Arc-de-Triomphe of the Champs-Elysées, sculpturing the statue of the marshal, sword in hand as when he cried "Forward!" And on the 7th of December, 1853, thirty years to a day after the execution, and on the same spot where the illustrious victim was shot, what will be taking place? The great bodies of State, the marshals of France, the authorities, and detachments of troops of all arms, will be assembled. The Archbishop of Paris will give the absolution. The Minister of War will recall the martial deeds of the gallant warrior. His statue will be unveiled with pomp and ceremony. M. Dupin, his lawyer during the trial, will urge, — and this time victoriously — the plea of 1815. "To-day," he will exclaim, "after a very long interval furrowed with sundry revolutions, I come with the marshal's sons to assist at the great deed of reparation accorded to the memory of their father. It is an honor with which I am grateful to be associated. . . . Marshal Ney, Duke of Elchingen, and Prince de la Moskowa, victorious on so many battle-fields, was the holocaust offered in expiation of the military glories of the Empire. 'Twas the tricolor immolated to the white flag! . . . It was reserved for the nephew of the Emperor to make reparation for that outrage, to raise a monument of honor in place of a funeral monument, and to erect the hero's statue on the very spot that saw the victim fall!

"Honor, gentlemen; honor to the men who are thus recalled from the tomb, and who rise before posterity amid the consoling ceremonies of religion, and the acclaims of their fellow-citizens, and, like Marshal Ney, in the attitude of command!"

Let us, for the rest, do the Duchess of Angoulême the justice to say that it was not long before she came to regret the death of Marshal Ney. She had occasion to see General de Ségur shortly after the publication of his dramatic account of the campaign of 1812, in which he spoke admiringly of the hero of Bérésina. The Princess had an heroic soul like that of her grandmother, Maria Theresa, and her mother Marie Antoinette. "Ah! general," said she, "if we had known all this, Marshal Ney would never have been shot."

VII

COUNT DE LAVALETTE

ON the 7th of December, 1815, a man who had been captured and consigned to the Conciergerie at the same time with Marshal Ney, and who was still in that prison, wondered what had become of the marshal, and anxiously interrogated one of the jailors as to his fate. The jailor hesitated, but finally said that the bravest of the brave had been executed. "At La Grêve, on the scaffold?" cried the captive. "No; shot." "He was very lucky!"

The jailor did not understand what this meant. He thought his charge was going mad.

The prisoner dreaded a harder fate than that of Marshal Ney. A few days previously he had written as follows to his former general, Marshal Marmont: "My head is doomed. I was able to hear without disquietude the fatal decree that proscribed me; but I confess that it is not without horror that I see myself surrounded by executioners, and going to the scaffold. For us old soldiers it is a trifle to die; we have braved death on splendid battle-fields; — but La Grêve! . . . Oh! it is horrible! . . . One must, alas! leave this life so crossed with misfortunes; so brief; but, in the name of our old friendship, in the name of the dangers we have shared, do not suffer one of your old fellow-soldiers to mount the scaffold. Let a company of brave grenadiers shoot me. In dying I would have this last illusion: I died on the field of honor."

The man who wrote these lines was forty-six years old. He was born in 1769, the year in which Napoleon and Marshal Ney first saw the light. He was one of the bravest and most brilliant officers in the French army, and distinguished himself as aide-de-camp to General Bonaparte during the first Italian campaign and the expedition to Egypt. He was named Antoine-Marie Chamans, Count de Lavalette.

Some days before his departure for Egypt, in 1798, he married Emilie de Beauharnais, niece of the first husband of the woman who became the Empress Josephine.

Viscount and General Alexandre de Beauharnais, Josephine's first husband, was as marked a liberal as his brother, Marquis François de Beauharnais, was a reactionary. In the Constituent Assembly the latter was known as "faithful Beauharnais," because of his fidelity to the monarchy, or "Beauharnais sans amendement," because of his persistent opposition to all amendments the purpose of which was to restrict the royal prerogatives. The marquis married his cousin-german, the daughter of Count Claude de Beauharnais and the authoress Fanny

Mouchard. Of this union a daughter was born, who became Madame de Lavalette.

Marquis François de Beauharnais was much devoted to the royal cause, and emigrated in order to rejoin the brother of Louis XVI. at Coblentz, leaving his daughter at Paris in the care of domestics. The young woman was still there when General Bonaparte, whose niece she was by marriage, said to his aide-de-camp, some days before they set out for Egypt: "Lavalette, I can't make you chief of squadron, but I am going to marry you off. I want you to marry Emilie de Beauharnais; she is very handsome and well-bred. Do you know her?"

"I have seen her twice. But, general, I have no fortune; we are going to Africa, and I may easily be killed there. What would become of my poor widow? Besides, I have no taste for marriage."

"One has to marry to have children; that is the object of life," said Bonaparte. "You may possibly be killed, but in that case she will be the widow of one of my aides-de-camp, of a defender of his country; she will have a pension and be able to place herself advantageously. Now, nobody wants an *émigré's* daughter; my wife cannot bring her out. The poor child is worthy of a better fate. The business must be attended to promptly. Talk with Madame Bonaparte this evening. The mother has given her consent. Within a week the wedding, and I will give you fifteen days for the honeymoon. Then you will join me at Toulon."

"I will do anything you wish, general," was the reply. "But would the young woman accept me? I don't want to have any compulsion used."

"She is a child who is tired of the boarding-school. While you are away she will live with her grandfather at Fontainebleau. You will not be killed, and in two years you will be with her again. So! the affair is settled."

In the evening Madame Bonaparte said to her husband's aide-de-camp: "To-morrow we will go to Saint-Germain, and I will introduce you to my niece, who is a charming girl."

On the next day, General and Madame Bonaparte, Eugene de Beauharnais, and Lavalette, entered a carriage and drove to Madame Campan's school at Saint-Germain. It was a great event for the school. Presently four young people went down into the garden. Lavalette looked around anxiously for her who was to be his destiny. She was the prettiest. Her figure was erect, slender, and graceful; her face charming, her color fine, and there was about her a bashful embarrassment that made the captain smile.

It was decided to have breakfast on the lawn in the garden. Lavalette said to himself: "Will she accept me without repugnance?" The abruptness of the marriage and the suddenness of the departure disquieted him. After breakfast, he requested Eugene de Beauharnais, the girl's cousin-german, to take her to a lonely garden path, where he would join her. "I have," said he to her, "only my sword and the good will of the general, and I must leave you in fifteen days. Open your heart to me. I know I am disposed to love you with my whole soul; but this is not enough. If this marriage is not to your taste, let me know it; it will not be hard for me to find some pretext for breaking it off. My withdrawal will be accepted; you will not be worried. I shall keep your secret."

Emilie de Beauharnais lowered her eyes. Her only answer was a smile, and then she gave her bouquet to the aide-de-camp. They embraced. In a week they were married.

Lavalette had not the courage to bid his wife farewell. It would have been too painful to do so. Without speaking he set out for Egypt, whence he did not return for eighteen months. During the expedition Bonaparte had eight aides-de-camp. Four perished, — Julien and Sulkowski assassinated by Arabs, Croisier killed at the siege of Saint-Jean-d'Acre, and Guibert at the battle of Aboukir. Two others, Duroc and Eugene de Beauharnais, were seriously wounded. Merlin and Lavalette escaped. "Glory and fortune," said the latter, "cost a good deal with General Bonaparte."

Under the Empire, Lavalette, who had left military life, did great service as postmaster-general. Napoleon made him a count. As the cousin-german of Prince Eugene, of Queen Hortense, and the Grand Duchess Stephanie of Baden, who was the daughter of Count Claude de Beauharnais and a Mlle. de Lézay-Marnesin, the Countess of Lavalette had a splendid position at court, where she exercised the duties of lady of honor to her aunt, the Empress Josephine.

Lavalette remained faithful to the Emperor during the Restoration. He did not take the oath to Louis XVIII., and was not asked to do so. His conscience did not reproach him when, faithful to his old master, and after the flight of the King, he took possession, in the Emperor's name, of the post-office department on the morning of the 20th of March, 1815. He retained all the employees, without caring to inquire whether they were Bonapartists or royalists. One of his higher-grade employees officiously went to him with a list of suspects. Lavalette let him talk. When the man had finished his denunciations, Lavalette said: "Sir, have you ever looked an honest man in the face?" In his embarrassment the official managed to stammer out something. "Ah! well," said Lavalette, "learn to know me," and, taking the list, he threw it into the fire without reading it.

Lavalette was an amiable and intelligent man, kindly and modest, benevolent and ready to do a service, and he always had warm friends. Nevertheless, the reactionaries clamored loudly for his death at the outset of the Restoration. It was in vain that M. de Vitrolles told him that he would do well to look to his safety, and that Fouché himself, who was then making up the list of proscribed persons, gave him the same advice. He had the imprudence to stay at Paris, detained there by his wife's approaching confinement. He was arrested on the 18th of July, 1815, and incarcerated in the Conciergerie, where Marshal Ney already was. His cell was separated from the women's court only by a wall. "From eight in the morning till seven at night," said he, "there was a continual and deafening riot of the grossest, basest, and most depraved language that it is possible for tongue to utter. The jailors often had to run to re-establish order among these harpies. On this court the two windows of the Queen's prison opened, and while I was there the room, which I had to pass when I went into the yard, served as a parlor for such privileged prisoners as received visitors from outside. . . . The entrance was at the end of a dark corridor. The Queen had had only a bed, a table, and two chairs. A large curtain suspended in the middle of the room separated her from the gendarme and the jailor. . . . How many times have I walked in that prison when sadness and dejection came over me! There I found strength and courage again. I blushed at myself for complaining of the fate that might be in store for me, when I conjured up the dreadful destiny of the Queen of France. I am certainly the first who set on foot the movement to make a chapel of that cell. Shortly after my escape the order that this should be done was given and carried into effect."

In his solitude the prisoner heard music which came from an adjoining room. The musician was Marshal Ney. "He played the flute pretty well," says Lavalette in his touching Memoirs, "and in this way he was able to charm away his weariness for some days. But this resource was taken from him under the pretext that it was against the rules of the house. He liked to repeat a waltz which ran in my head a long time and which I used to hum. I never heard it anywhere else except once in Bavaria, at a rustic ball on the banks of Lake Starnberg. I was looking at young peasant girls thronging the fresh green turf. The melody was sweet and melancholy. The sound of the flute at once transported me back to the Conciergerie, and I went away in tears and pronouncing the marshal's name with bitterness. . . . In the daytime we used to walk in the little court without being permitted to be together, although the marshal was accompanied by a gendarme."

Lavalette gave orders that his wife, who was with child, was not to come to the prison, since so lamentable a sight might be disastrous to so sensitive and affectionate a woman. He wished to keep that frightful dungeon from the eyes of his daughter also. "Nevertheless," he says, "her mother sent her to me for my blessing on the eve of her first communion. Upon seeing my only child, apparelled in all the grace and freshness of youth, throw herself into my arms, bathed in tears, and presently falling at my feet in a deep swoon, my heart was torn with all the tenderness of paternal love. Then, for the first time, I felt all the depth of my misfortune. I could not control my sorrow; silent tears mingled with my groans, and I laid my hands on her head, unable to say a word."

Lavalette suffered cruelly. The well-known line: "'Tis crime that brings us shame, and not the scaffold," brought him no consolation. The thought of being guillotined, like a common criminal, in the Place de Grève, and of the anguish into which his wife and daughter would be plunged, haunted him like a nightmare. And yet he preserved his firmness except only when he gave his child his fatherly blessing.

What was it that consoled him? He himself shall tell us. "I did not seek moral strength in meditation or illusions that reality dispelled day by day. I found it in thinking of the Emperor. I suffered, but it was for him. My evil fate gathered lustre from the cause in which it had its birth. My name and destiny were allied with his imperishable fame; and then, were his sufferings not greater than my own? The perfidy of the English government had placed him on Saint Helena. What torments did not his exile at the world's end hold in store for him! I was ashamed to complain in view of such misfortunes. The revenge of the kings was heaped on us both, and I found consolation and glory in sharing it. The thought of this sustained me always and preserved me from every show of weakness."

Lavalette was produced at the assize court on the 16th of November, 1815. He heard his sentence calmly, and turning to his former subordinates in the post-office who had testified against him, he said: "Gentlemen of the postal service, I bid you farewell." On the night after he was sentenced he wrote to his old companion in arms, Marshal Clarke, Duke of Feltre: "See what you can do for me, and try at least to spare me the horrible agony of the scaffold. Have me shot by soldiers of the army, and death will seem almost a boon to me." The marshal replied in a letter containing these words: "All that is left for you is to commend your wife and child to the inexhaustible goodness of the King." When Louis XVIII. heard that the condemned man asked the favor of being shot, he answered drily: "No, he must be guillotined."

Marshal Marmont, Duke of Ragusa, who had been the friend of Lavalette's youthful days and his comrade in arms, then intervened in a way that does the greatest honor to his memory. Although the body-guard had received orders to prevent Madame de Lavalette from entering the Tuileries, he allowed her to go there on the 18th of December. The poor woman, weak and suffering, could not walk without pain, and had to be carried part of the way in a sedan chair, and this attracted considerable attention. Nevertheless, the marshal did not despair.

He decided that Madame de Lavalette and he should go to the guardroom together when the King should be at Mass. Should they arrive before that hour, Louis XVIII. would hear of their presence and not be present at Mass on that day rather than meet the suppliant. When the King had passed and was in the chapel, the marshal and Madame de Lavalette presented themselves at the foot of the grand stairway. The porter had received no instructions, and they went up without interference. But when they were on the threshold of the guardroom an officer cried out: "Marshal, you cannot enter with that lady on your arm." Marmont then appealed to the officer in charge.

He was a sub-lieutenant of the body-guard, Marquis of Bartillac, who married a Mademoiselle de Béthune, and a nephew of the Duke of Havré. The officer stepped forward, and the following dialogue ensued between him and Marmont: —

"It is Madame de Lavalette who accompanies you, marshal; she is forbidden here."

"I have just been told so; nevertheless, answer me frankly; you have orders to prevent her from entering, but have you orders to put her out?"

"No."

"Well, then; leave her alone. She is going to ask a pardon for her husband, and I hope she will secure it. What risk do you run? Has the nephew of the Duke of Havré anything to fear? The worst that can happen to you is a few days under arrest;

and, by submitting to this risk you run the chance of saving a man's life. It is a piece of good fortune; do not let it slip."

"Marshal, I will leave the responsibility with you. Madame de Lavalette may remain."

And then the marshal placed the petitioner near the door of the King's apartments and remained at her side till Mass was ended.

When the chapel-door opened, Baron de Glandève, major of the body-guard, went to the Duke of Ragusa and told him that the presence of Madame de Lavalette was contrary to orders.

"Yes," said the marshal; "but have you the King's orders to expel her?"

"No."

"Well, then, she shall stay."

Louis XVIII. appeared at the entrance. Madame de Lavalette cast herself at his feet and cried: "Pardon, Sire, pardon!"

The King replied: "Madame, I share in your justifiable grief, but I have duties laid on me, and I must do them." And he passed on.

"A symptom of the bitter spirit of the time," says Marshal Marmont in his Memoirs, "is that when the King had said these words the body-guards were fain to shout 'Long live the King!' which, in the circumstances, was a somewhat brutal and savage thing to do. Madame de Lavalette had another petition for the Duchess of Angoulême, and wished to present it. But the latter avoided it by a violent movement and a repulse, casting at her at the same time a furious look impossible to describe."

Louis XVIII. having re-entered his apartments, the marshal led the suppliant to her sedan chair and thence home. The poor woman was still deceived as to the King's intentions. But the marshal looked on the King's action in a clearer light; for, as he himself has said, the opportunity was too good and the surroundings too dramatic not to be used if the King wished to show mercy. However, the marshal determined to make another endeavor on the next day, the 19th of December, which was the Duchess of Angoulême's birthday, and the anniversary of her escape from the Temple twenty years previously; namely, on the 19th of December, 1795.

There was a community in misfortune between the two women which ought to have touched the daughter of Louis XVI. Madame de Lavalette's father was an *émigré* who had sacrificed himself for the royal cause. She might say to the Duchess of Angoulême: Madame, I kneel before you in the selfsame room at the Tuileries to which, on the 12th of August, 1792, my husband, mingling with the Swiss guards, came at the peril of his life to serve your family. . . . Madame, at this very moment my husband is in that frightful prison of the Conciergerie, in a dungeon next to that in which your mother was confined twenty years ago. . . . Madame, you know what the scaffold is, and surely you will never let my husband ascend it. . . . Madame, you who have suffered so much will take pity on my sufferings.

And the unhappy woman said to herself: "If I can speak with the Princess, if only for a minute, my husband is saved."

On the 19th of December Marshal Marmont found means to have her brought to the anteroom of the captain of the guards on duty. There she was to fall at the feet of the Duchess of Angoulême when the Princess mounted the stairs which were known as the King's stairs. But body-guards had been stationed everywhere, even on the upper floors, officials redoubled, and the doors watched to prevent surprises, and so the Duchess was enabled to go about in the interior of the Tuileries without danger of meeting the petitioner.

Notwithstanding all this, the poor wife was still the victim of illusions. "Marshal," she kept saying to the Duke of Ragusa, "they wish to delay the pardon of my husband till he is on the scaffold." Marmont replied: "Do not believe it. If he mounts it, he is a dead man. You say you want to find a way of escape for him. Now is the moment to find it, and I beg you not to defer it. Time passes." Madame de Lavalette acquiesced in the situation.

VIII

MADAME DE LAVALETTE

MADAME DE LAVALETTE had nothing now to expect from the mercy of the King. The anger of the salons was roused to the highest pitch. "Society rang with complaints," says Marshal Marmont in his Memoirs. "The little court ladies appeared to have lost their heads completely, and were inexorable. It was the fashion to be pitiless. The most atrocious language was used. They talked of nothing less than shooting me. 'How,' they said, 'are we to have an army, if a marshal of France is the first to forget the laws of discipline and to disobey orders? . . . Never, at any time, has Parisian society displayed passions more violent than then." More than one woman of the Faubourg Saint-Germain was furious against the condemned man, because, in his capacity as postmaster-general he had possibly come to know their secrets. They wished to have those secrets locked in his grave.

In the meantime Madame de Lavalette remembered what the marshal had told her. She was sick and overwhelmed with grief. During her husband's imprisonment she had given birth to a son whom she had just lost. The effects of confinement, the death of her child, and the sentence of her husband to capital punishment had so preyed on her health that she could no longer bear the jolting of a carriage, and was obliged to use a sedan chair when she made the slightest journey. But though her body was bowed down, nothing could touch her heroic soul. She secured permission to dine with her husband, and every evening she was carried to his prison. On the 19th of December, the day on which she had vainly tried to reach the Duchess of Angoulême, she went as usual to the Conciergerie, about six o'clock in the evening.

When she was alone with the condemned man, she said: "It is only too certain that we have nothing to hope for. We must do something, therefore, my dear, and this is what I propose. At eight o'clock to-morrow evening you will leave this place dressed in my clothes. You will go into my sedan chair, which will take you to the rue des Saints-Pères, where M. Baudus will be waiting with a cabriolet to take you to a hiding-place that he has found for you. There you will stay without danger till means are found to get you away from France."

Lavalette listened to his wife and looked at her in silence. She was perfectly calm and her voice was steady. He tried to say how mad this project seemed to him, but she exclaimed: "No objections! If you die, I shall die. Therefore do not reject my plan. I am profoundly determined. I feel that God sustains me."

In vain did he try to discourage her by speaking of the many jailors who surrounded him every night after she had left him; of the keeper who assisted her into the sedan chair; of the impossibility of being so well disguised as not to be detected, and, finally, of his invincible repugnance to leaving her in the hands of the jailors.

"What may not happen," cried the unhappy husband, "when my escape is discovered? Will not these brutes so far forget themselves as to maltreat you?"

He wished to speak further, but he saw by the pallor of her countenance and her impatient gestures, that he must relinquish all objections. "Give me your word to obey me, for it is our last resource." He took her hand. "I will do whatever you wish and in the way you wish it." This promise calmed her, and they separated.

Upon the departure of his wife, the prisoner said to himself: "The plan is impracticable. She is nearly half an inch taller than I. All the jailors are used to seeing me. Her figure is lithe and slender. It is true that suffering has made me remarkably thin, but the difference between us would be apparent to everybody. On the other hand, I am well prepared to die! Indeed, for two days I have been thinking of committing suicide with the weapon I have concealed. All this hangman's toilet and the slow procession on a cart from the Conciergerie to La Grêve has disturbed me, but my heart has remained firm. And now I must turn my eyes from death to enter on a foolhardy plan of flight! Burlesque is going to be mixed up with tragedy, for I shall be captured in woman's clothes, and perhaps they will have the barbarity to produce me in public in that ridiculous masquerade. But, on the other hand, how can I refuse what she asks? She seemed so happy in her project; so certain of its success! It would kill her if I did not keep my word."

It was the 20th of December, 1815. The petition for pardon had been definitely rejected in the council of ministers. The scaffold on which the condemned man was to be executed on the following day was in process of erection. At five o'clock in the afternoon Madame de Lavalette arrived at the Conciergerie, accompanied by her daughter, who was twelve years old. She wore a merino dress lined with fur, which she had been accustomed to use when returning from a ball, and in her bag was a black taffeta petticoat. "This is enough to disguise you perfectly," she said to her husband. Then she sent her daughter to the window and added in a low voice: "When the clock strikes seven, you must be dressed; everything is ready. As you go out, you must give your arm to Josephine and take care to walk very slowly, and when you pass the registrar's office you must cover your face with my handkerchief. I thought of bringing a veil, but unfortunately I am not in the habit of wearing one when I came here, and so it is not to be thought of. When going through the doors, which are very low, be careful not to get the bonnet feathers caught, for then all would be lost. I always find jailors in the office, and the warden is accustomed to give me his hand to assist me into the sedan chair which always stands near the exit-gate, though to-day it will be at the head of the great stairway. There you will meet M. Baudus, who will conduct you as far as the cabriolet and tell you where you are to be in hiding. And then — trust in God, my friend! . . . Do exactly as I say. Don't worry. Give me your hand; I want to feel your pulse. Good! . . . Now take mine; do you detect the least disturbance?" The poor woman did not see that she was in a high fever. "Above all," she added, "no displays of affection, or we are lost!"

Dinner is served. At this moment Madame Dutoit, little Josephine's aged nurse, enters the cell. Far from being useful, she will only be in the way, for she may lose her head when she sees the disguise. She begins to groan. Then Madame de Lavalette, in a subdued but steady voice, says to her: "No childishness! Remain at the table; do not eat or say a word, and smell at this perfume-bottle. Within less than fifteen minutes you will be in the open air."

It is a grim dinner. The condemned man thinks it

his last, and the food almost chokes him. None of the three speaks a word. At a quarter to seven Madame de Lavalette says to her husband: "Come; it is time to dress." Then she goes behind a screen with him, and arranges the woman's clothes he is to wear. The toilet is completed in three minutes. Young Josephine remains on the other side of the screen. Presently the condemned man reappears in his feminine costume. "How does your father look?" Madame de Lavalette asks her daughter. "Not badly," answers the poor child, with a bitter smile.

The decisive moment comes. He must go. M. de Lavalette says to his wife, who will take his place in the cell: "The keeper comes every night, when you have gone. Be careful to remain behind the screen, and make a little noise by moving the furniture. He will think that I am here, and then go away for a few minutes, which I must use in making my escape." Then husband and wife exchange a last look, without daring to embrace. The door opens. Lavalette goes first, his daughter following, while Madame Dutoit comes last. The wife remains alone in the cell, behind the screen. After crossing the corridor, the condemned man reaches the door of the office. He lowers his head so that the feathers in his hat may escape the top of the door-case. On raising his head, he sees five turnkeys lining the passage. As he puts his handkerchief to his eyes, they take him for his wife, and the jailor says, "You are going early, Countess." At last he arrives at the end of the room. But the hardest is yet to come. Will the turnkey who guards the iron gate open it? A new anxiety here. Lavalette puts his hand between the bars to attract attention. The turnkey hesitates for an instant, but turns the key. The prisoner walks out with his daughter and the servant. He is outside, to be sure, but that is not all. There is a flight of twelve steps to mount in order to reach the courtyard, and at its top is the police body-guard. The condemned man goes by them, slowly reaches the topmost step, and, with his daughter, gets into the sedan chair in the great court. The chair is borne on the road to the quai des Orfèvres, and stops opposite to the little street de Harlay. M. Baudus is there, opens the door of the chair, and says to Lavalette, "You know, Madame, that you have to visit the President." He leads the fugitive to a cabriolet, where a friend of his, M. de Chassenon, formerly Auditor to the Council of State, who is on the box with loaded pistols, is waiting. The cabriolet carries him to a very remote quarter on the Boulevard Neuf, where M. Baudus once more takes the lead. On the road, Lavalette has removed his feminine apparel, and replaced it with a jockey-coat and a laced hat. M. Baudus takes him on foot to the asylum prepared for him.

It is eight o'clock in the evening. The night is dark, and rain falls in torrents. The headlong paces of the horses of gendarmes who, doubtless, are carrying despatches relative to the escape of the prisoner, alone break the silence of the Faubourg Saint-Germain. After walking for nearly an hour, the rue de Grenelle is reached at the corner of the rue du Bac. M. Baudus says to Lavalette: "I am going into a house. While I am talking to the porter, you enter the court. On the left you will find a flight of stairs. Go up to the last landing, then into a dark corridor which you will find at the right. At the end of it there is a pile of wood; stay there and wait."

Lavalette thought he was dreaming. He seemed seized with vertigo. What house is it at whose door his guide is knocking? It is the hôtel of the Minister of Foreign Affairs, the residence of the president of the council, the Duke of Richelieu! Can there be treason? What can be the solution of the enigma? Meantime the door opens. M. Baudus enters. Lavalette follows. "Where is this man going?" asks the porter. "He is my servant." Lavalette goes up to the third floor and stops at the pile of wood indicated. A woman grasps him softly by the arm and pushes him into a dark room the door of which closes behind him. Placing his hands on a stove to warm them, he finds a candle and matches. He strikes a light and then examines his new domicile. It is a little garret-room with a very tidy bed, two chairs, and a chest of drawers. On the latter is a paper on which are written these words: "No noise. Open the window only at night; wear list slippers and wait patiently." Beside this paper are a bottle of excellent Bordeaux wine, some volumes of Molière and Rabelais, a pretty basket of sponges, perfumed soap, almond cream, and all the minor adjuncts of a careful toilet. Now more and more does the condemned man believe himself the sport of a dream.

A few minutes afterwards M. Baudus, who is publicist to the foreign bureau, enters the room, and seeing Lavalette filled with surprise, he says: " Calm your imagination; it is all true; on the day before yesterday Madame de Lavalette sent word that she would like to see me at her house, and when the servants had left the room and the doors were closed, she said: 'I wish to save my husband, since pardon cannot be secured; but I do not know where he can find asylum. Procure me the means of concealing him.' — 'Give me two hours,' I answered. 'I am on terms of the closest friendship with a family which has known misfortune, and whose courage and devotion are admirable.' 'Go quickly,' replied your wife; 'explain my position to them; they will give me life by concealing my husband.' I left her; I came here. . . . Listen! do not be impatient. You are now at the house of M. Bresson, chief of the exchequer department of the Minister of Foreign Affairs."

Lavalette was more perplexed than ever. "Let me proceed," said his interlocutor. "After the proscription of her husband, and profoundly grateful to the friends who concealed him, Madame Bresson vowed to save some unfortunate man who had been condemned on political grounds, if Providence would but kindly send one to her. I went to find her— 'Your prayer is answered,' said I; and then I told her your story and that of Madame de Lavalette. 'Would that he might come!' she replied with enthusiasm. 'My husband is absent, but there is no need of consulting him when doing a good deed; he shares my feelings. I will go and prepare a room where the unhappy man may be safe. Run and tell Madame de Lavalette. It is by a sort of miracle that you came to me.' Now, you know how important it is to our generous friends that no one should ever know that they gave you this asylum; the whole family would be ruined. M. Bresson needs his employment; he has a daughter and nephews to establish; a functionary and lodged in a house owned by the King, and who is honored with the confidence of his minister, he is under no illusion as to the irregularity of his action, but, on the other hand, he is convinced of your innocence, and what are all these considerations when weighed in the balance against a man's life? We intend to get you away from here, and see you across the frontier, and this will be no easy matter. But Providence will not permit us to fail."

M. Baudus withdrew, and Lavalette remained alone for two hours, hardly daring to breathe, and reflecting mournfully on the situation of his poor wife, left by him in his cell. About eleven o'clock in the evening, the door opened again. He saw an elegantly dressed woman enter, veiled and accompanied by a girl about fourteen years old. The lady threw herself into his arms. "In God's name, raise your veil, Madame, that I may at last know the angel to whom I owe my safety!" — "We are not acquainted with each other," said she, unveiling. "But I am happy to be associated in the heroic deed of Madame de Lavalette." She laid some food on the stove. "There is your dinner," she added. "You will have poor fare, but we had to steal from ourselves to nourish you. I will confide our secret to none of the domestics; all of them room in this corridor, and the next chamber is occupied by my nephew Stanislas. Therefore make no noise in the morning; make your bed and sweep your room yourself. As the chamber is supposed to be unoccupied, the least noise heard in it might ruin us all."

Magnanimous hospitality like this is honorable to human nature in a time of bloody reaction when a sort of White Terror recalled the detestable passions of the Red Terror. "I knew M. Bresson no better than his wife," says Count de Lavalette in his Memoirs. "I had seen him once, five years before, when I set out for Saxony, and perhaps once again when I returned, and when our business connections were ended, — since I did not remain in diplomatic life, — we never met again. M. Bresson was a man of very agreeable appearance, of delicate and cultivated intelligence, and an energy of character of which he had often given the most distinguished proofs. It was not his attachment to the Emperor that led him into so dangerous a situation in order to save me; for I doubt that he ever had much liking either for his person or his government. It was a profoundly humane feeling and a most courageous protest against political sentences, of one of which he himself had been the victim."

M. Bresson was born at Darney, in the Vosges, in 1760, and was one of the representatives of that department in the Convention. He voted against the death of Louis XVI. Outlawed after the 31st of May, he took refuge among the Vosges peasants, who sheltered him and saved his life at the risk of their own. After the 9th Thermidor, he had a seat in the Convention again, and subsequently he was a member of the Council during the Hundred Days. In 1799 he became head of the exchequer division of the Ministry of Foreign Affairs, and held that office till 1825. (After the Revolution he abandoned the "de" to which he was entitled. He opened up the diplomatic career to his nephew, who was ambassador to Madrid under the reign of Louis Philippe, and negotiated the famous Spanish Marriages.)

Let us now return to the hiding-place of the condemned man in the mansion of the Minister of Foreign Affairs, and describe what is taking place there on the evening of the 20th of December, 1815. Madame Bresson has just left Lavalette. M. Bresson enters. "I have just been at the salons of some of the high dignitaries," says he to his guest, with a laugh.

"You can have no conception of the dread and consternation by which everybody is overcome. No one at the Tuileries will go to bed; they are all convinced that some great plot is about to explode. They see you at the head of the army, and all Paris springing to arms. I shouldn't wonder if the foreign troops, who are setting out for home, were kept back. They talk of closing the gates. Imagine what the effect of that would be. The milkwomen couldn't come in to-morrow, and so there would be no more milk for the breakfasts of those good ladies! And just to think that it was I, I who have you under lock and key, who heard all these lamentations!"

Meantime, what is going on at the Conciergerie? What has become of Madame de Lavalette? The jailor enters the cell a few minutes after the prisoner has left it. On seeing the wife in place of the husband, he gives a cry of surprise. Madame de Lavalette throws herself upon him, trying to keep him in the room, but he breaks away from her by force. Then the jailors and policemen rush headlong in every direction, looking for traces of the sedan chair. They find the chair, but within it is only the prisoner's daughter.

The late Duke of Broglie says in his *Souvenirs:* "Nothing can convey any idea of the joy occasioned all over Paris by the condemned man's escape, — that is to say, all over Paris outside the court and the Faubourg Saint-Germain. A little more, and the city would have been illuminated. Early in the morning M. de Montrond came to my house and told me with a coolness that he alone could keep up in pleasantry: 'Dress yourself; get your weapons; a terrible crime has just been perpetrated; in defiance of all laws, human and divine, M. de Lavalette has escaped from jail in a sedan chair, and as soon as he heard the news the King jumped into another sedan chair. He is pursuing him in hot haste, but it is feared that he will not capture him. M. de Lavalette's carriers have the start, and he is not so pursy as the King.'"

The mystification of the proscribers caused genuine amusement. On the 26th of December, M. de Rémusat wrote to his mother: "Good-morning, mother. This letter will reach you on New Year's Day, and it grieves me much that now, for the first time, I cannot begin the year at your side. But I am hardly in trim to do so, seeing that for the last eight days I have almost died of laughter. Although our politics is going to the devil, yet the approach of the Carnival gives it such a little air of burlesque that I have determined to look on instead of going into black. In the first place, what do you think of M. de Lavalette's escape in a sedan chair? M. Anglès, the prefect of police, fainted dead away when he heard of it. M. Bellast, the procureur-general, was sent to interrogate Madame de Lavalette in prison, and she was so much disturbed and broken-down that she answered his questions only with bursts of nervous laughter, which were duly recorded in the report. Meantime, there is the Chamber, buzzing, muttering, and in a tumult. And there was that beautiful meeting on Saturday! M. de Bouville swears that being dressed like a woman, M. de Lavalette *must have betrayed his sex in his walk*, and all agree in the opinion that his escape is a sufficient reason for throwing the Amnesty Bill over. There is nothing to do but laugh at such talk, otherwise it would produce horror. . . . You should have seen a little lady in pink at M. de Marbois's house, purse her lips and say mincingly to the keeper of the seals: 'Sha'n't we go back to our old modes of punishment?'"

Madame de Lavalette was kept in seclusion at the Conciergerie, where she was confined in Marshal Ney's cell, which overlooked the woman's court. Annoyed by the loud cries and indecent language of these unfortunates, constantly assailed by a thousand terrors, in the blackness of darkness, when the keepers retired, and imagining at every minute that they were bringing her husband back to prison, she passed twenty-five days and nights without a moment's sleep. Her agitation and sufferings ended by driving her mad, and she did not recover her reason till twelve years afterwards.

M. and Mme. Bresson were finally obliged to take their domestics into the secret. None of them betrayed it. Lavalette remained hidden in Paris till the 7th of January, 1816, the day on which he was executed in effigy on the square of the Palais de Justice.

Everything was strange in this affair in which reality surpassed the fictions of the wildest romance, and not the least strange thing about it was that in the end he owed his deliverance to an English general, Sir Robert Wilson, who was formerly a bitter enemy of Napoleon, but who was indignant at the persecution of the Bonapartists. With the aid of two of his countrymen, Mr. Bruce and Mr. Hutchinson, General Wilson furnished Lavalette with a British uniform, and, with the greatest difficulty, succeeded in getting him out of France. He found refuge in Bavaria. Prince Eugene de Beauharnais, his wife's cousin-german, gave him a friendly reception. But the proscribed man was still in fear of a requisition from the French legation. He had to live in retirement and under a fictitious name in Bavaria; nor was it till 1822 that a pardon opened the gates of France to him again. On this subject M. Cuvillier-Fleury says, in an interesting note: "Lavalette thought to spend some happy days in France, but when he arrived at Paris, one voice was silent amid the congratulations with which his return was greeted. It was his wife's voice. From the decisive hour in which, with a supreme effort, she bade him flee, and remained as a hostage in his stead, she had not once seen him. She saw him reappear without emotion and without shedding a tear. Did she even recognize him? Poor unfortunate! She lost her reason that he might be saved. The last trial surpassed all the rest."

Lavalette, who died on the 15th of February, 1830,

passed his last years in tranquillity. His Memoirs end with this touching phrase: "Madame de Lavalette's health is at last so far restored that I can have her with me. At times she is plunged in a profound melancholy, but she remains sweet, lovable, and good. We live in retirement, and summer in the country pleases her greatly. I have retained my independence, — the chief of blessings, — without a pension, without distinction, and without indemnity, after a long career dedicated to the service of my country; but still offering prayers for liberty, which may, perhaps, never be granted, and living in the midst of memories of a great epoch and a great man."

To sum up all, few episodes in the history of the nineteenth century are so dramatic and touching as the captivity and escape of Count de Lavalette. Now that political passions have died away, one can hardly believe that such exaggerations, such injustice, and such cruelties could ever arise from party spirit. No matter what opinions he may hold, who is there to-day whose heart is not melted at the recital of the heroism of Madame de Lavalette, or who does not render all homage to her energy, suffer in her sufferings, and share in her woes? How can one help pitying that admirable woman and that little girl who was associated in such a touching way with her mother's devotion? Ah, well! can it be believed? Yet in 1815, in aristocratic salons at Paris there were shrieks of rage, — and curses directed not only against the mother, but against the little child,

— against a girl only twelve years of age! Her filial piety was treated as a crime! In his Memoirs M. Guizot describes this shameless prodigy of hate with mingled sorrow and surprise: "At that time," says he, "I heard a woman of fashion, who on ordinary occasions showed sense and goodness, say, apropos of the way in which Mademoiselle de Lavalette had assisted her mother to save her father: 'The little villain!' When such frenzied sentiments and language burst bounds around kings and their advisers, they are plain warnings of what is coming."

Lavalette himself thus tells the story of the persecution of his pleasant-mannered and innocent child: "My daughter entered the convent in such a transport of joy, and agitated with such powerful emotion, that she could not explain the way in which she had helped to save her father. But when all came to light on the next day, the lady superior, whose establishment had just come under the protection of the Duchess of Angoulême, was seized with fear. My daughter was ordered not to speak; the nuns, and even some of her fellow-pupils, held aloof from her, as if she had been tainted with the plague. Will it be credited? The relatives of several of the pupils told the lady superior that they would withdraw their children from the convent if Josephine Lavalette remained in it. And thus did fear, personal interest, and perhaps the vilest passions, make a sort of crime and a reason for persecution out of a laudable and generous action that should have served as an example to the young. Six weeks afterwards, when Madame de Lavalette was released, she at once withdrew her daughter from the convent."

The sentiment of justice, which is the crowning glory of human nature, always ends by asserting its rights when once political crises have ceased to exist. Lavalette, the man once condemned to death, the man who had been executed in effigy, died universally esteemed and honored. M. Cuvillier-Fleury was right in saying: "Spirits of men of all parties who are condemned for political reasons and stricken down in your strength by the thunderbolts of the storm, let the fate of Lavalette be your consolation! You are rehabilitated in the person of this man." Those who had proscribed him themselves honored and admired his great-hearted wife. Statesmen should reflect on this lesson when they are tempted to give themselves up to hatred or anger. The passions of the reaction of 1815 were futile, and the name of Madame de Lavalette will shine with immortal splendor in the constellation of heroines who did their duty, and of martyrs to devotion.

We recently had the honor of paying our respects to her daughter, Josephine de Lavalette, the widow of Baron de Forget, — to her who, seventy years ago, had aided in the miraculous escape from the Conciergerie. Of all living women, she is the only one who took part in the events of 1815. Loved and respected, the Baroness of Forget lives at Paris in the house in which her mother died, No. 19, in the rue de La Rochefoucauld. Her large parlors are a museum hung with portraits and souvenirs of her family. Under Horace Vernet's picture of the Conciergerie at the moment of the storied escape, is a sword of Murad Bey's which General Bonaparte gave to his aide-de-camp, Lavalette, on the very evening of the battle of the Pyramids. It was with deep veneration that we saluted the worthy daughter of the heroine of conjugal love and the noble woman who in her admirable old age still preserved all the quickness of intelligence, every charm of conversation, and every amiable quality of mind and heart.

These lines were written in October, 1886. Some days afterward the Baroness of Forget died at Paris.

IX

THE BEGINNING OF 1816

BEYOND contradiction, the year 1815 was one of the most terrible and dolorous in the history of France. On the 1st of January, 1816, the president of the Chamber said to the King: "Sire, your faithful subjects in the Chamber of Deputies wish you, and are preparing for you, a most happy new year." Little tact or cautiousness was shown in these laconic words, and the King thought that there was a certain air of patronage about them. The year 1816 opened in the midst of a complete reaction which Louis XVIII., more moderate than those by whom he was surrounded, sought in vain to suppress. There were no such ideas of pacification, conciliation, and clemency as had marked the beginning of the first Restoration. The second was as ruthless as the first had been benignant. The passions of the ultra-royalists knew no bounds. The aristocratic salons of Paris were notorious for their hate and bitterness. The escape of Lavalette had made them insane.

Debate on the amnesty bill was opened in the Chamber on the 2d of January. In spite of the King, the regicides who had taken any part whatsoever in the events of the Hundred Days, were added to the list of the proscribed. This measure was carried at the session of the 6th of January through the influence of General de Béthisy, a former officer in the army of Condé, who exclaimed: "Gentlemen, never permit yourselves to forget that the motto of our fathers was: Right, Honor, and the King. And if inflexible honor impels us for an instant to go beyond the King's wishes; and if, displeased at his faithful servants when he sees them oppose his royal and pious clemency, he for a moment shall turn aside from us that kindly regard, which is our highest reward, we will say with the people of the west and with the noble soldiers of the throne and altar whose love for the Bourbons nothing can change: 'Long live the King when he is himself!'"

The anniversary of the execution of Louis XVI., instead of recalling the words of pardon written in the martyred King's will, inspired the ultra-royalists with what they called a sacred wrath. Clemency was taxed with weakness and pusillanimity. The opinion that it was the King's first duty to reassure the good and make the wicked tremble was endlessly repeated. On the 9th of January, Chateaubriand recounted in the Chamber of Peers the events that had taken place since the 21st of January in the preceding year. "How sincere," said he, "then seemed the repentance of some men! How gladly did the King pardon them! But when their second treason drove us from our native soil, did they think that we should ever be here once more to celebrate the second expiatory rites? They hoped nevermore to hear of those dead men who now bear witness against them before the living God. It was in order to confound them, that God packed within the little space of a year events that could hardly be crowded into an age; men and things went headlong, rushing by like a torrent, and in France all has passed, so to say, between two funerals. Setting out from a tomb, we returned to a tomb and, of all the projects then in mind, not one has been carried into effect except that which Louis XVIII. formed in regard to the remains of the King, his brother."

In the following words the author of the *Génie du Christianisme* then recalled the pathetic disinterments of 1815: "In the opened grave, I saw, gentlemen, the bones of Louis XVI. together with the quicklime that had consumed the flesh, but which could not remove the traces of the crime. I saw the skeleton of Marie Antoinette intact under the shelter of a vault that had formed above her, as by miracle. The head alone was displaced and, in the form of that head (Great God!) could still be recognized the features which expressed at once the graciousness of a woman and the majesty of a queen. That, gentlemen, is what I saw; those are remembrances over which we can never shed enough of tears, and those are deeds which man can never expiate! Though you raise in memory of those great victims a monument like the tombs which defy the ages in the deserts of

Egypt, you will not even then have done enough, nor would even so great a mass of stones hide from view the traces of blood that can never be effaced. . . . Religion alone can make our marks of grief equal to the greatness of such adversities. For that it needs neither magnificent pomps nor splendid mausoleums; a few tears, a day of fast, an altar, a simple stone on which the name of the King is carved, will suffice him."

At the very time when the Restoration was becoming pitiless to the valiant soldiers of France, at a time when the blood of the bravest of the brave was yet smoking, and many proscribed men were going into exile, the *Moniteur* of the 16th of January, 1816, published the following article, the mildness of which contrasted strangely with the still recent vigorous proceedings: "Saturday, the 20th of January, will be a day of general mourning throughout France. A great expiation will take place. Madame and all the Princes will go to Saint-Denis. The will of the martyred King will be read in forty thousand churches. On this great and solemn occasion, may all hatreds, all ultra opinions, and all thoughts of ambition and vengeance cease! As the price of the blood that he shed on the scaffold, the best of kings demands from the abyss of the tomb, or rather from the height of heaven, the reconciliation of all his children and the peace and happiness of France. The sons of Saint Louis have entered into their heritage; be it ours to preserve it. They keep watch over us; let us keep watch over them. The whole great family of Frenchmen is held in the heart of the King. The King should be held in the hearts of that mighty family."

The final funeral solemnities of Louis XVI. and Marie Antoinette were celebrated on the 20th of January at the abbey church of Saint-Denis. Monsieur the King's brother, the Duke of Berry, the Prince of Condé, the Dowager Duchess of Orleans, and the Duchess of Bourbon were present. The Duchess of Angoulême was there also. The place she occupied was closed, and thus her sorrow was hidden from all eyes. It is easy to understand the emotions that swayed her soul when she listened to the solemn reading of her father's will. The ceremony made a strong impression upon her. No place of sepulture has a more mournful grandeur than the abbey church of Saint-Denis. The royal vault of the Bourbons is the most sombre place in the crypt. No light enters it save from the dark crypt itself; no eye can pierce into it except through a small grated window and by the use of a torch which casts only a doubtful and sinister light upon the interior. Those sepulchral shadows aroused most serious reflection in the minds of those who beheld them. Throughout the whole day the capital put on an appearance of exceptional gravity. In the evening all the theatres were closed.

The Chambers took advantage of the anniversary of the 21st of January to unite in an address to the

King, in which terms were employed expressive of their horror of regicide. The address ended as follows: "Sire, we have not fallen away from the loyalty of our ancestors. So long as your illustrious race exists, we will be faithful to it. We will ever recognize as our lawful kings only the princes of that race on whom the law of primogeniture impresses the characteristics of your race. Before God and man we swear that the French name shall be lost in oblivion rather than we be false to our oaths of honor!" This address was signed by all the peers and all the deputies without exception, and they expressed their desire that it should be carved on a bronze tablet, together with all the signatures, and be sealed in the expiatory monument which they were about to decree for a public square, that should be called the Place du Vingt-et-un Janvier. It might be curious to note how many of the signatories were faithless, less than fifteen years later, to an oath so solemn.

The emotion caused by the action of the two Chambers was still felt when an unexpected accident cast new lustre on the memory of Queen Marie Antoinette. A letter was discovered which the Queen had written to her sister-in-law, Madame Elisabeth, on the morning of the day on which she was executed. It began in this way: "My dear sister: I write to you for the last time; I have just been condemned, — not to a shameful death, for it is so only to criminals, — but to rejoin your brother. Innocent like him, I hope to display the same firmness that he showed in his last moments. I am calm, as one always is whose conscience does not upbraid him. I greatly regret leaving my poor children. You know that I exist alone for them and for you, my good and tender sister. In what a position I leave you who, through your friendship, have sacrificed everything to be with us! . . . Take my blessing to the two. I trust that some day when they are older they may be with you and enjoy to the full your tender care. . . . Let my daughter remember that, at her age, she should always aid her brother with the counsels her wider experience will give her and her affection may suggest! . . . Let both remember that in their condition they can be really happy only through being united! Let them follow our example! What consolation in our misfortunes did not our friendship yield! And happiness is doubly enjoyed when it is shared with a friend; and where can one find happiness more tender and more dear than in his own family? Let my son never forget the last words of his father, who said to him expressly: 'Never seek to avenge our death!'"

Nothing more touching and Christian-like can be imagined than the conclusion of the letter. The Queen wrote: "I sincerely crave God's pardon for all the faults I have committed since my birth. I hope that in His mercy He will hear my last prayers, and those which I have so long offered that He would receive my soul in His pity and goodness. I ask pardon of all whom I know, and particularly of you, my sister, for all the trouble that I have involuntarily given you. I pardon all my enemies the evil they have wrought. I bid adieu to my aunts and all my brothers and sisters. I have had friends, and the thought of being forever separated from them is one of my heaviest regrets in dying; let them be assured that I thought of them till my last moment."

When Marie Antoinette had ended this pathetic letter, she covered it with kisses and tears, and sent it to Bault, the keeper of the prison, begging him to transmit it to Madame Elisabeth. The keeper did not dare to comply with this request, and took the letter to Fouquier-Tinville, the public prosecutor, who, instead of sending it to its destination, confiscated and added it to the documents of the trial. After the 9th Thermidor, the Conventionist Courtois, who was intrusted with the examination of Robespierre's papers, found among them this memorable letter, of whose existence no one yet knew, and, in February, 1816, when M. Courtois's house was searched, it was discovered by the government agents. Louis XVIII. decided that on the 22d of February, it should be formally communicated to the Chamber of Deputies by Count Decazes, Minister of Police, and to the Chamber of Peers by the Duke of Richelieu, President of the Council. As soon as the reading of it was ended, M. de Chateaubriand arose and said: "Gentlemen, it is just a month since the day when you were summoned to Saint-Denis. There you listened to the Gospel of the day,— the will of Louis XVI. Four hours before her death Marie Antoinette wrote what you have but now heard. Did you notice in that letter any sign of weakness? Deep in her cell, Marie Antoinette wrote to Madame Elisabeth as calmly as she would have written had she been surrounded with adoration and pomp at Versailles. The chief crime committed by the Revolution was the King's death, but the most appalling crime was the death of the Queen. The King preserved at least something of royalty amid his hardships and even to the scaffold. The members of the tribunal of those pretended judges were many; the son of Saint Louis had a priest of his religion when he went to death, and he was not dragged there in the common cart of victims. But the daughter of Cæsars, clad in rags and reduced to patching her own garments, insulted before an infamous tribunal by a few assassins who called themselves judges, carried to execution on a tumbrel, and yet always a queen! ... Gentlemen, I would need the courage of that great writer herself to finish this recital."

In this address M. de Chateaubriand was wrong in saying things that were not in accord with the forgiving spirit so admirably shown by the martyred Queen. "Twenty-three years," said he, "have passed since that letter was written. Those who took part in the crimes of that period (those of them, at least, who have not rendered an account of their deeds before God) have been living in what is called prosperity; they have cultivated their fields without molestation, as if their hands were guiltless. The man who kept the letter of Marie Antoinette bought the estate of Montroisier. The very judge of Louis XVI. wrote a panegyric in French verse on M. de Malesherbes, and erected on his estate a monument to the defender of Louis XVI. Let us not admire him; rather let us weep for France. The inexhaustible impartiality which produces neither remorse nor expiation, the fact that crime may legally sit in judgment on virtue, shows that all is in disorder in the moral world, and that good and evil are confounded with each other. But let us give thanks to Providence, whose eyes are never withdrawn from the wicked; he thinks that he escapes through revolutions; he mounts to happiness and power. Generations pass; the years roll by and all seems forgotten. Suddenly the vengeance of God meets the criminal face to face, and says, as it opposes his way: 'I am here!' In vain does the will of Louis XVI. offer pardon to the guilty; they are bewildered; they themselves would have torn up that will; they did not desire that it should be preserved. The voice of the people speaks in the voice of the Chamber of Deputies; sentence is pronounced and, by a series of miracles, the first result of that sentence is the discovery of the will of the Queen."

Marie Antoinette's letter produced a profound

impression on both Chambers, and it was decreed that each year, on the 16th of October, which was the anniversary of the execution, it should be read from church pulpits, just as Louis XVI.'s will should be read on the 21st of January. Every deputy and peer received from Louis XVIII. a fac-simile of his sister-in-law's letter, and each of the Chambers sent a deputation to the Tuileries to thank the King. "I am much touched," said the sovereign, "with the sentiments you express. In communicating to you the most moving document I ever read, I desired that you should share in the grief and admiration that stirred my heart."

The deputations were then presented to the Duchess of Angoulême in her apartments. M. Lainé, speaking on behalf of the Chamber of Deputies, said: "Madame, the King has permitted us to express to Your Royal Highness the sentiments aroused within us by the letter of your august mother. Those noble words reawakened our grief. But that grief is assuaged at the sight of Your Royal Highness. We deemed that Marie Antoinette lived again in Maria Theresa: hers were the same virtues, the same courage; and in seeing how the religious feelings of both Princesses shine brightly forth in you, our hearts are at rest and open once more to hope and consolation." Chancellor Dambray spoke to the same purport, in the name of the Chamber of Peers: "In this memorable document," said he, "we reach once more the prolific source of the lofty virtues, the living image of which we are proud to possess. That sublime writing shows us also the principle of that touching unity that is to-day the good fortune of your august family. Madame, may that great Queen, who was preparing our destinies while so tenderly thinking of yours, receive in heaven the respectful and admiring homage which the Chamber of Peers loves to pay to her memory!"

The Duchess of Angoulême answered briefly. Her adulators essayed to pretend to be more affected than they really were, while she struggled to conceal her emotion. Austere and sincere, like her soul, her grief was never factitious or theatrical. It would have seemed profane to her, had she expatiated on it. There is modesty in tears.

X

THE ASHES OF LOUIS XVII

THE child, the king, the martyr, whom Victor Hugo has celebrated in an immortal ode, had no tomb; and while his successor ruled at the Tuileries, even the place where his own ashes reposed was unknown. Formal respect had been paid but now to the memory of his father and mother, but none in memory of him. Nevertheless, even in his hardships, he had been the Most Christian King, the King of France and Navarre, and, though he had never been anointed at Rheims, there was another sacrament — that of misfortune — which was his.

On the 9th of January, 1816, Chateaubriand spoke as follows in the Chamber of Peers: "Gentlemen, I think we have omitted something. Among so many causes of grief our tribute of tears has not been paid impartially. In all that we have undertaken to do and have done, the infant King, the young martyr who sang the praises of God in the fiery furnace, has hardly been mentioned. Should we forget him because he occupied so small a place in our history? But how slowly did his sufferings cause his days to pass, and how long was his reign because of his woes!

Did ever an aged king, weighed down by the burdens of a throne, bear so heavy a sceptre? Did ever the crown press with such weight on the brows of Louis XIV. on his way to the grave as did the diadem of innocence on the forehead of Louis XVII. on his way from the cradle? What has become of that royal pupil left to the tutelage of a jailor? of that orphan who might have said, like the heir of David: 'My father and mother have forsaken me'? Where is the brother of the orphan of the Temple and her comrade in adversity? Where shall one go to ask him that terrible and all too well-known question: 'Capet, dost thou sleep? Awake!' He wakes, gentlemen, in celestial glory, and he asks a tomb. Curses on the wretches who, this day, render so many reparations necessary! Withered be the parricidal hand that dared to lift itself against that son of Saint Louis; the King till now forgotten in our annals as he was forgotten in his prison!"

The Chambers voted that a monument in some style, and on some spot selected by the King, should be erected in the name and at the expense of the nation, in expiation of the crime of the 21st of January. At the same time, the following article was voted: "The King shall also be authorized to order, in the name and at the expense of the nation, the erection of a monument in memory of Louis XVII., Queen Marie Antoinette, and Madame Elisabeth." At the session of the 13th of January, the Chamber of Deputies added the subjoined words: "And of the

Duke of Enghien," which addition was adopted by the Chamber of Peers. By royal ordinance Louis XVIII. decreed that the monuments should stand in the Madeleine church, the completion of which he also ordered.

On the 1st of March, 1816, M. Decazes, Minister of Police, wrote to M. Anglês, Prefect of Police:—

"MY DEAR COUNT: By the ordinance of the 14th of February, His Majesty decreed the place where the pious monument to the memory of Louis XVII. is to be placed. It is now necessary — and I have already directed your attention to the subject — to discover the remains of that illustrious victim of the Revolution. It is known that on the 8th of June, 1795, the young King was interred in the cemetery of Sainte-Marguerite, in the Faubourg Saint-Antoine, in the presence of two civil commissioners and the commissioner of police for the Section of the Temple. The young King ought to be deposited in Saint-Denis. I request you to give me an account of the precise measures you have taken to this end, and what has been the result of them. If you have not already done so, it will be necessary to summon the commissioners and others who were present at the interment."

The search was long and minute, but resulted in nothing. A man of the name of Decouflet, who was beadle of the parish of Quinze-Vingts, said that in 1802 his friend, the gravedigger Bétrancourt, *alias* Valentin, while preparing a grave in the cemetery of

Sainte-Marguerite, pointed out to him a spot from which two feet of earth had been dug. The gravedigger uncovered a stone of the foundation-wall of the church, on which was a cross, and said that at some time there must have been a monument there, since the coffin of Louis XVII. was underneath. This gravedigger was no longer alive in 1816. The declarations of his widow and the witnesses of the inhumation were contradictory. According to some, a private burial-place had been chosen for the royal child, while others said that his corpse had been thrown into the common ditch. For the rest, it was claimed by some people that the funeral and interment of Louis XVII. in the cemetery of Sainte-Marguerite had been only simulated, and that his remains had been buried at the very foot of the tower of the Temple. (In his unpublished Memoirs General Count d'Andigné, who was imprisoned in the Temple in 1801, expresses this opinion.) Finally, several persons asserted that the young King's remains had been taken from the cemetery of Sainte-Marguerite to that of Clamart.

In a letter written on the 1st of June, 1816, the Prefect of Police gave M. Decazes an account of the outcome of the search. The letter ends as follows: "The commissioners who had charge of the inquest incline to believe that if the precious remains of the young King are lost among those of the other dead, they lie in the place designated by the widow of Bétrancourt, *alias* Valentin, and by Decouffet."

No excavations were made in the cemetery. The day was spent in explorations. The clergy of the church of Sainte-Marguerite, in alb and surplice, were waiting for the delegate of the Minister of Police, when, after some hours of delay, the curé received an official letter announcing that the search must be abandoned. In his book on Louis XVII., M. de Chantelauze thus explains this sudden change: " An opposition, as malevolent as it was implacable, had already taken it in hand to cast doubts on the authenticity of the remains of Louis XVI. and Marie Antoinette. And not only did this opposition try to cast ridicule on the royal exhumations by pretending that only false relics had been discovered, but it blamed Louis XVIII. in most violent terms for evoking, with odious ostentation, the bloody spectres of his family. This time the opposition struck a telling blow. It was the dread of imprudently reawakening the most cruel recollections of the Terror, rather than any of these undefined rumors, that prevented Louis XVIII., who was at once moderate, politic, and sagacious, from following up the search ordered for the discovery of the grave of his royal nephew."

The supposition of M. de Chantelauze does not seem to us quite admissible. However that may be, the people who asserted that Louis XVII. left the Temple alive, did not hesitate to say that if the excavations were not continued, it was because the son of Louis XVI. and Marie Antoinette was still living. Another circumstance seemed to give color to their belief in the tale of the various impersonators of Louis XVII. Though he gave up the excavations ordered by him for the discovery of the remains of Louis XVII., Louis XVIII. was desirous of having a formal service celebrated at the church of Saint-Denis in memory of the young King. Louis XVIII. then learned from the primate of the abbey of Saint-Denis that the ancient rules of the abbey permitted funeral services to be celebrated only for princes whose bodies reposed in its vaults. According to M. de Chantelauze, this was why he did not deem it proper to proceed.

We have already explained the reasons which lead us to believe that the child who died in the Temple was really Louis XVII., and on this point we agree with the conclusions drawn by MM. de Beauchesne and de Chantelauze, and several times confirmed by judicial decisions. We shall always hold that by forbidding the excavations it once had ordered, and in not having funeral services for the young King celebrated at Saint-Denis or elsewhere, the government of the Restoration increased the doubts that were entertained by certain people. It was asked why a government founded on the principle of heredity should concern itself so little about Louis XVIII.'s immediate predecessor.

M. de Beauchesne himself makes some melancholy reflections on this subject, in the place that was once the cemetery of Sainte-Marguerite, for the cemeteries crumble away like ruins, *etiam periere ruinæ*. He says: "Nothing saddens the heart more than the appearance of a forsaken cemetery. Alas! Scarcely in the midst of the tumults that surround us do we think of those who fall at our side. It is with stronger reason that we trample with indifference on those who have fallen before us. It is not fifty years since this cemetery was closed to the dead, and now the living do not know the road to it. Worldly pleasures cover regrets as sods cover graves. No longer is there any trace of human foot on this grass, no longer a little path leading to a beloved tomb. A few trees have remained because they were young, and because their owners would not have profited greatly by hewing them down. Down there in the corner generations after generations of corpses have succeeded each other, for in this narrow world one disputes possession even when life is over, and the dead is driven off to make room for the dead. How many times within this funereal enclosure, among crumbling tombs and neglected shrubbery, and long since covered with nettles and briers, have I asked that terrible and all too well known question: 'Capet, where art thou? Awake!'"

The young King's biographer adds with bitterness the following words: "It seems that in France there has been an unanimity of forgetfulness in regard to this cemetery. And yet it was here that the royalty of thirteen centuries, begun at Rheims, finished its career. 'Tis here that the youngest of your race returned to dust while your own dust was swept from out your tombs. But, vacant or occupied, your tombs still show the way you went, and one may read your actions in history or visit the simulacrum of your coffins in Saint-Denis. Nothing remains of that child, and dead, he has no stone." And in conclusion M. de Beauchesne expresses the regret that the sainted daughter of Louis XVI., as faithful to misfortune as misfortune was faithful to her, was unable to bring a prayer or a tear to the spot of earth that had consumed her brother, because there was no trustworthy information as to where he lay.

Who shall say that at times the Duchess of Angoulême was not tempted to exclaim: "But if I have been deceived? . . . If my brother be yet alive?" Beyond doubt, this thought did not remain fixed in the mind of the unhappy Princess, but who shall say that it never crossed it as a vague and cruel suspicion?

CONCLUSION

THE Restoration had now been in existence for two years, and the Duchess of Angoulême saw that under the gilded ceilings of palaces as in the dungeon of the Temple, she was condemned to a life of sorrow and disappointment. At the beginning of 1816 she was still looked up to and received the homage of all. At the fête given on the 5th of February by the royal guards to the national guard of Paris she shared with the King in the enthusiastic demonstrations of the assemblage. In the midst of applause she made the tour of the twelve tables that were decorated with escutcheons bearing the names of Saint Louis, Francis I., Henri IV., Louis XIV., Renaud, Roland, Duguesclin, Bayard, Sully, Crillon, Condé, and Turenne. A marshal of France or a lieutenant-general presided at each of the tables. Fifteen hundred persons attended the fête, five hundred of whom were elegantly dressed women, who added greatly to the splendor of the scene. A cantata was sung, the words of which were by Chevalier Ducis, a captain of hussars in the royal guards, and nephew of the celebrated poet; the music was composed by Cherubini.

At the fête given to the royal guards by the national guard of Paris in the hall of the Odéon, the pious Princess was equally the object of general enthusiasm. The box of the royal family, which was at the centre of the first tier in the gallery, was decorated with great magnificence. The play was an impromptu called *Chacun à son tour, ou l'echo de Paris*. In speaking of the verses, the *Moniteur* said: "It is impossible by quoting the couplets to give any idea of what took place; their happy turn, the choiceness of the melody, the chorus that accompanied them and was loudly repeated by the audience amid waving plumes, the King profoundly moved, his family rising in response to such touching applause, and to devotion so spontaneous, free, and unanimous, — one must have seen all this, for it cannot be expressed in words."

Whenever the Duchess of Angoulême appeared at the theatre, she was received with applause. On the 30th of January she attended a gala representation at the Opera. A cantata was sung, in which the following lines were enthusiastically cheered: —

"Daughter of kings, no longer fear;
See naught but happiness before thee;
The French will wipe away each tear
They caused to flow, and will watch o'er thee."

These fêtes and adulations had no fascination for the daughter of Louis XVI. The pomps that surrounded her gave her no pleasure. It was not after coming from the church of Saint-Denis, it was not on the morrow of the anniversary of the murder of her father, that she could find amusement in a theatrical representation or a reception at court. She knew too well the vicissitudes of fortune to be dazzled by artificial prestige or be deceived by wealth and human grandeur. After the calamities of her family she felt out of place at a ball or a play. Her appearance could evoke only memories and arouse reflections which were out of harmony with earthly joys. A château inhabited by her would have resembled a church rather than a palace. Even in moments of triumph everything contributed to her sadness. At the Tuileries, even on fête days, under brilliant chandeliers and amid music, she recalled the terrible scenes of the 20th of June and the 10th of August, which her uncle, Louis XVIII., had not witnessed, but at which she had been present. Sometimes she fancied she saw phantoms flitting through that fatal place. Nothing could distract her from her sombre thoughts and Christian meditations; the Tuileries could not make her forget the Temple, which had been destroyed from top to bottom and of which not one stone remained. She could have wished to shut herself up in the little room which had served her father as an oratory, and to revisit the chamber that had been occupied, first by her mother and next by her aunt. But no; nothing remained, — nothing but the dolorous and eternal memory of it.

The Duchess of Angoulême was not the dupe of

flatterers. They recalled the adulations given to her mother. She was vastly edified by the way in which the courtiers had gone from one party to the other. When officers vowed fidelity equal to every proof, she remembered the defection of the Bordeaux garrison during the Hundred Days. That brief but instructive period had made her reflect bitterly on the fickleness of the French character. She already saw afar off the coming of a new revolution. The conduct of the government did not satisfy her. Louis XVIII. had placed power in hands that she thought neither sure nor faithful. She saw that the policy of the ministry was one of expedients and not of principles, and, had she been allowed to speak, she would certainly have opposed both its tendencies and its acts. But she made no endeavor to cause her ideas to prevail and, living in a world of contemplation, she made a hermit's cell of her oratory. In 1816, though young in years, she was old in sorrow. One wondered that so many emotions and griefs had not yet whitened her hair.

A woman grave and austere, like the Duchess of Angoulême, must always inspire more veneration than sympathy in a society amiable, but frivolous, like that of Paris. While respecting and holding her in the highest honor, the world was only moderately concerned about the pious Princess. The curiosity that she aroused on her return to France was already dying away. A younger woman, gayer and more fond of pleasure, was desired, in order to bring relief to a court that was looked upon as too sombre and morose. That woman was the sprightly Princess who was to marry the Duke of Berry. She was said to be full of spirit and grace, and it was regarded as certain that her smile would illumine the Tuileries like a ray of light. The Duchess of Angoulême was about to be left in an obscurity which, for that matter, suited her modesty and piety. Henceforth, the Duchess of Berry would take the first place. Merchants and artists knew her as a patron of arts and commerce. Wonderful things were said about her disposition, half French and half Neapolitan. She would bring to Paris the impulsiveness and vivacity of lands where the sun shines. After the Terror, society had an inextinguishable thirst for distractions and amusements, and similarly, in 1816, people wished to forget the misfortunes of war and invasion, and to make merry, now that its distress had departed. The Duchess of Angoulême was but the setting sun. The rising sun was the Duchess of Berry, and already the eyes of all were turned towards her.

INDEX

Abrantès, Duchess of, her story of the *Émigrés* at Tortoni's, 75; on the character of Louis XVIII., 85; on the Duke of Berry, 104; quoted, 111, 112.

Adélaïde, Princess, described by the Baroness of Oberkirch, 149.

Alexander I. at Compiègne, 20; at Paris, 44; his sentiments for Louis XVIII., 46; takes leave of the King and quits Paris, 48; his partiality for Prince de Beauharnais, 46; conversation with him respecting the Bourbons, 49; causes religious service to be held in the Place de la Concorde, 50.

Angoulême, Duchess of, a woman of the Tuileries, 1; return of, to France, 2 *et seq.*; at Compiègne, 7; her appearance described, 13; entry of, with the King into Paris, 32 *et seq.*; her agitation, 37; appearance of, at the Tuileries, 47; called Madame during the reign of Louis XVIII., 108; change in her after the Restoration, 109; at the opera of *Œdipe à Colone*, 110; called the New Antigone, 110; her melancholy, 112; her dislike of Talleyrand, 115; the members of her household, 115 *et seq.*; her character and bearing described, 116 *et seq.*; the interest of the people in, 118; at Vichy, 119 *et seq.*; at Lyons, 121 *et seq.*; her virile character, 127; her visit to Versailles, 152; present at the fête of the Hôtel de Ville, 154; at the Théâtre Français, 180; at the hospitals, 182; at Bordeaux, 185; hears of the landing of Napoleon, 187; ordered by the King to remain at Bordeaux, 224; receives Baron de Vitrolles with the King's letter, 225; sends a letter to the French ambassador at Madrid, 227; letter of, to Count de La Châtre, 228 *et seq.*; likeness of her character to that of Maria Theresa, 231; calls a general counsel, 237; visits the troops in their barracks, 238; commands them to resist no longer, 242; leaves the city, 244; proclamation of, 245; embarks on the *Wanderer*, 246; is offered an asylum by the King of Spain, 246; enters London, 247; guest of the Count de La Châtre, 248; actively engaged in politics, 251; the objects of her mission to England, 252; joins the King in Ghent, 253 *et seq.*; returns to England, 260; her return to France, 275; without illusions, 276; goes with her husband to Bordeaux, 279; her journey a continuous ovation, 296; reception of, at Toulouse, 297; talks of Fouché's dismissal, 298; declines to receive Fouché, 303; comes to regret the execution of Ney, 337; furiously repulses Madame de Lavalette, 349; deputations from the Chambers presented to, 382.

Angoulême, Duke of, at the Restoration, 99 *et seq.*; not a success at court, 101; devoted to the

INDEX

King, 102; sent by the King to visit the West of France, 105; hears of the landing of Napoleon, and is ordered to go to Nîmes, 187; his first successes, 248; arrested by Grouchy, 249; set at liberty, proceeds to Madrid, 249; rumors concerning, 277.

"Antigone, the New," 110.

Artois, Count of, a man of the old régime, 93; an optimist and under illusions, 95; his household, 97; sent by the King to visit the East of France, 105; sent by the King to Lyons to arrest Napoleon's progress, 190; swears allegiance to the King, 205.

Augereau, Marshal, meets the Duchess of Angoulême at Lyons, 122, 125.

Aumale, Duke of, heir of the Duke of Bourbon, 146.

Baudus, M., conceals M. de Lavalette, 359.

Beauchesne, M. de, quoted, 390.

Beauharnais, Prince Eugene de, the Czar's partiality for, 46, 48.

Beauharnais, Emilie de, her family, 339; her first meeting with Lavalette, 341.

Bellart, M., address of, as public prosecutor of Marshal Ney, 320.

Bernadotte at Compiègne, 18.

Berry, Duke of, 99 *et seq.*; his character, 102 *et seq.*; sent by the King to visit the North of France, 105; his lack of tact, 106; his noble qualities and his death, 107; receives in the Tuileries, 180, 181.

Berthier, Marshal, meets Louis XVIII., 8; address of, to Louis XVIII., 13.

Beugnot, Count, quoted, 22, 209; his inscription on the statue of Henry IV., 25, 39; Memoirs of, quoted, 262; on the selection of Fouché as Louis XVIII.'s Minister of Police, 201.

Blacas, Count of, 24; letter of, to Prince of Castelcicala, 251.

Bordeaux, reception of the Duke and Duchess of Angoulême in, 186 *et seq.*, 279; defection of the troops at, 238.

Boulogne, Abbé de, sermon of, at the burial of Louis XVI. at Saint Denis, 174, 177.

Bourbon, Duke of, a representative of the old régime, 141; his career, 146.

Bourbon, Duchess of, her career, 146; receives a pension from Napoleon, 148.

Bourrienne, on the King's entry into Paris, 39.

Bourmont, Marshal, a witness against Marshal Ney, 315, 317 *et seq.*

Brayer, General, despatch of, concerning Napoleon's landing, 189.

Bresson, Madame, conceals Lavalette in her house, 359 *et seq.*

Bresson, M., 362.

Broglie, Duke of, on the state of things in Paris after the landing of Napoleon, 200, 201; on the departure of the King, 220; on Fouché and Talleyrand, 265; his vote for Marshal Ney's acquittal, 323; on the escape of Lavalette, 364.

Carnot, quoted, 61.

Castelcicala, Prince of, correspondence of, with the Count of Blacas, 251.

Cauchy, M., reads the death-warrant to Marshal Ney, 325.

Censeur, the, quoted, 159.

Chabrol, M. de, presents Louis XVIII. with the keys of Paris, 32; address of, at the fête of the Hôtel de Ville, 157.

Chantelauze, M. de, on the opposition to the royal exhumations, 388.

Chateaubriand, on the Duchess of Angoulême, 4; quoted, 5; describes Louis XVIII.'s arrival at Compiègne, 9, 11, 13; quoted, 28, 36; his admiration for Louis XVIII., 42, 44, 50; on society at the court of Louis XVIII., 54; on his character, 81, 86; his confidence in the royalist cause, 164; speech of, on the burial of Louis XVI. and Marie Antoinette at Saint Denis, 168, 171, 175; thinks Napoleon is to be "harried," 191; agrees with Marmont about barricading Paris, 209, 211; on the Duchess of Angoulême at Bordeaux, 254, 257, 258, 263, 264; on Fouché, 301 *et seq.*; recalls, in the Chamber of Peers, the events of 1815, 373; address of, upon the letter of Marie Antoinette, 380; tribute of, to Louis XVII., 384.

Clausel, General, approaches Bordeaux, 228, 235; carried away by the prestige of Napoleon, 234 *et seq.*; demands that the gates of Bordeaux be opened, 237; pays a tribute to the courage of the Duchess of Angoulême, 242.

Compiègne, the Château of, 7; Louis XVIII. at, 8 *et seq.*; the court reconstituted at, 18.

Condé, Prince of, a representative of the old régime, 141; his career, 142 *et seq.*; anecdotes of him, 144.

Constant, Benjamin, quoted, 31, 200; signed article of, in the *Débats*, 214.

Court of Louis XVIII., the, 51 *et seq.*; functionaries of, 55.

Crétineau-Joly, M., quoted, 105.

Cuvillier-Fleury, quoted, 367.

Davoust, Marshal, testifies concerning the amnesty accorded by the plenipotentiaries, 319.

Decaen, General, at Bordeaux, 226; his perplexities, 233; the crowd clamor for his life, 243.

Delpierre, Abbé, confesses Marshal Ney, 328; accompanies him to his execution, 330; letter describing his interview with Madame Ney after the execution, 332.

Descloseaux, preserves the memory of the burying-place of Louis XVI. and Marie Antoinette, 167.

Domon, General, 194.

Dupont, General, bestows military decorations, 59.

Elisabeth, Madame, her character reflected in that of the Duchess of Angoulême, 114.

Émigrés, their confidence in the restitution of their property, 183.

Enghien, Duke of, his birth and parentage, 146 *et seq.*; monument to, 386.

"Father Violet," nickname of Napoleon, 185.

Fiévée, M., quoted, 118.

Fouché, swears loyalty to Louis XVIII. at Saint Denis, 265; the King talks of his dismissal, 298; his selection as Minister of Police urged by the royalists, 300; his fall, 303; marries Mademoiselle de Castellane, 303; dismissed, 304; made French Minister at Dresden, 304; letter of, to Louis XVIII., 304; to the Duke of Richelieu, 305 *et seq.*; stricken down by the law against regicides, 308.

Francis II. takes leave of the King, 48.

Ghent, Louis XVIII. at, 255 *et seq.*

Gouvion, M., anecdote of, 324.

Guizot, on Louis XVIII., 88; on the court of Louis XVIII. at Ghent, 256; on the affair of Louis XVIII. and Fouché, 299; quoted, 310, 333 *et seq.*

Havré, Duke of, 54.
Hortense, Queen, receives from Louis XVIII. the title of the Duchess of Saint-Leu, 148; her salon the Bonapartist hotbed, 184.
Hôtel de Ville, fête of the, 154 *et seq.*; list of ladies at, 155.

Jacob, the bibliophile, on the Baroness de Krudener, 285.
Josephine, death of, 47.
Journal des Débats on the death of Josephine, 48; quoted, 151, 179, 192, 194, 198, 206, 212, 213; becomes *Journal de l'Empire*, 221; describes the entrance of Napoleon into Paris, 222; language of, at the Second Restoration, 271, 275; report in, of Marshal Ney's execution, 335.
Jouy, M. de, 70, 73.

Krudener, Baroness de, interests herself in General de Labédoyère, 284; her character and career, 284 *et seq.*; first meeting with Labédoyère, 285; letter of, to Madame de Labédoyère, 286; visits Labédoyère in prison, 288; her reflections on his death, 295.

Labédoyère, General de, the era of vengeance inaugurated by the execution of, 278, 281 *et seq.*; arrest of, 283; his family, 283; the Baroness de Krudener interests herself in, 284; before the council of war, 289; his defence, 290; condemnation of, 291; letter of, to his mother, 292; his will, 293.
Labédoyère, Madame de, intercedes for her husband, 286; is repulsed by the King, 294.
La Châtre, Count de, letter of the Duchess of Angoulême to, 228; Duchess of Angoulême the guest of, in London, 248, 250.

Lafayette, M. de, conversation of, with Alexander I., 49.
Lamartine on the personal appearance of Louis XVIII., 76; an enthusiastic royalist, 77, 95; on the Count of Artois, 98; on the attitude of the great ladies during Marshal Ney's trial, 321; describes Ney's guards, 327; censures the murder of Marshal Ney, 334.
Lavalette, Count de, 338 *et seq.*; his marriage to Emilie de Beauharnais, 339; his career under Napoleon, 342; arrest of, 344; sentenced, 347; plan of his escape, 353 *et seq.*; escape of, 357 *et seq.*; his hiding-place, 359; remains hidden with the Bressons, 366; escapes to Belgium, 367; quotation from his Memoirs, 368; his daughter, 369.
Lavalette, Madame de, importunes the King for her husband's pardon and is refused, 349; proposes to her husband to escape in her clothes, 353; loses her reason, 366, 368.
Lavalette, Josephine de, her trials at school, 369; death of, as the Baroness de Forget, 371.
Legitimists, jealousy of, the, 62.
Lettres du Cousin et de la Cousine, 70.
Louis XVI., body of, exhumed and buried at Saint Denis, 168 *et seq.*; monument erected to, 170; final funeral solemnities of, celebrated, 376.
Louis XVII., monument of, 385; search for his grave, 386.
Louis XVIII., return of, to France, 2 *et seq.*; his progress to Paris, 3 *et seq.*; remarks of, at Compiègne, 7 *et seq.*; his reply to Marshal Berthier, 14; his politeness to the officers of the army, 16; receives Talleyrand, 20; interview of, with Alexander I.,

20; entry of, into Paris, 32 *et seq.*; at Notre-Dame, 34; at the Tuileries, 38, 51; his court, 52; his household, 55; and the petitions of old royalists, 70; his part in *Lettres du Cousin et de la Cousine*, 70; his personal appearance as described by Lamartine and others, 76 *et seq.*; his character and intelligence, 80 *et seq.*; his belief in royalty, 87; founded the throne on moderate principles, 89; his life at the Tuileries, 91; his exercise, 92; at the fête of the Hôtel de Ville, 156 *et seq.*; attends the ceremony of the distribution of the flags, 161 *et seq.*; attends the opera and theatre, 179 *et seq.*; receives the news of Napoleon's landing, 189; sends the Count of Artois to Lyons, 190; cheered by the National Guard, 193; calls a session of the Chambers, and proclaims Bonaparte a rebel, 191; proclamation of, 197; his speech to the Chambers, 202 *et seq.*; declares his intention to remain at the Tuileries, 210; but refuses to turn it into a fortress, 211; reviews his military household, 215; leaves Paris, 219 *et seq.*; summons the Duke of Orleans to Ghent, 252; his residence and habits at Ghent, 255 *et seq.*; his phantom ministry there, 256; returns to France, 264; at Saint Denis, 265; enters Paris, 266; his escort, 267; ill at ease, 269, 272; his clemency, 273; refuses to pardon Labédoyère, 294; letter to, from Fouché, denouncing the Duke and Duchess of Angoulême, 304; refuses to pardon Lavalette, 349; address to, by the Chambers, Jan. 21, 1816, 377; sends to the Chambers the letter of Marie Antoinette, 379; deputations from the Chambers to, 382.

Louise, Marie, the Archduchess, at Aix-les-Bains, 126.

Maison, General, in command of French troops at Ghent, 258.

Malouet and the story of the old naval officer, 69.

Marie Antoinette, body of, exhumed and buried at Saint Denis, 168 *et seq.*, 376; monument erected to, 170, 386; discovery of a letter of, written on the day of her execution to Madame Elisabeth, 377.

Marmont, Marshal, meets Louis XVIII. at Compiègne, 10, 16; describes Louis XVIII.'s Bourbon pride, 42; criticises the military household of the King, 57; his description of Louis XVIII., 78, 84; compares the Dukes of Berry and Angoulême, 104; on the infirmities of Louis XVIII., 109; proposes to the King to put the Tuileries and the Louvre in a state of defence, 208; allows Madame de Lavalette to go to the Tuileries, 347, 351; Memoirs of, quoted, 349; on the violent passions of the court ladies, 352.

Martignac, M. de, sent from Bordeaux to confer with General Clausel, 236; asks for a further delay, 237.

Metternich, Prince, quoted, 88.

Moncey, Marshal, meets Louis XVIII. with congratulations, 5; refuses to take part in the council of war to try Marshal Ney, 312.

Monsieur, see Count of Artois.

Moniteur, the, describes the parade of the allied troops, 41; quoted, 100; on the Duchess of Angoulême at Vichy, 119 *et seq.*; quoted, 163; respecting the burial of Louis XVI. at Saint Denis, 175; gives first news of Napoleon's landing to the Parisians, 190;

quoted, 197, 205, 216; Sauvo, editor of, 268; on the movements of the allied sovereigns, 270.

Moreau, Madame, at Paris after the Restoration, 134.

Mortier, Marshal, cannot condemn Marshal Ney, 312.

Nain Jaune, the, 182; on Napoleon's return, 197.

Napoleon at Elba, 40.

Napoleon, lands at Elba, 40; on a free press, 88; calls the Duchess of Angoulême "the only man in her family," 127; pensions the mother of the Duke of Enghien, 148; first news of his landing, 185, 189; enters Paris, 221.

Napoleon's Marshals, sentiments of, under the Restoration, 60.

Nettement, M. Alfred, quoted, 176.

Ney, meets Louis XVIII. at Compiègne, 10; compares him with Napoleon, 11; expected to arrest the progress of Napoleon, 197; goes over to Napoleon, 207; should have been pardoned by the King, in M. Guizot's opinion, 310; withdraws from Paris, 311; arrest of, 311; ferocity of the great ladies against, 313; his fury of indignation against Marshal Bourmont, 316; counted on the protective nature of the capitulation, 320; conviction of, 322; receives his death-warrant, 325; bids farewell to his family, 326; his execution, 331; the expiation of his murder in 1848, 335.

Ney, Madame, at the Tuileries to beg for her husband's life, 329.

Oberkirch, Baroness of, quoted, 149.

Œdipe à Colone, opera of, the court at the, 110.

Orleanism, the birth of, 137.

Orleans, Duchess of, her return to Paris, 132, 133; her salon, 136; not at harmony with the Duchess of Angoulême in London, 252.

Orleans, the Dowager Duchess of, 134; receives a pension from Napoleon, 148.

Orleans, Duke of, at Palermo, 129; goes to Paris, 130, 131; his career, 135; disliked by the King and by the royalists, 137; his double character, 139 *et seq.*; the representative of the new ideas, 141; sent by the King to Lyons, 190; suspected of ambitious designs, 251; refuses to obey the King's summons to come to Ghent, 252.

Paris, aspects of, under the Restoration, 64 *et seq.*

Polastron, Countess of, her death, and the influence over the Count of Artois, 97.

Pozzo de Borgo urges the King to return to Paris quickly, 264, 265.

Prussia, King of, at Paris, 43.

Puymaigre, Count of, his description of Louis XVIII.'s court, 51; quoted, 65; on the Prince of Condé, 144; quoted, 184; on the sentiments of the army in Paris on the return of Napoleon, 193 *et seq.*; quoted, 215.

Récamier, Madame de, salon of, after the Restoration, 66.

Rémusat, Madame de, on the bloodthirsty speeches of the great ladies against Marshal Ney, 313.

Rémusat, M. de, on the escape of Lavalette, 365.

Restoration, the Second, 262 *et seq.*; the proscribed of, 277.

Richelieu, Duke of, letters to and from the, and Fouché, 305; the prosecutor of Marshal Ney, 314.

Saint-Ouen, Declaration of, 24.

Sauvo submits to Vitrolles articles

for the *Moniteur Officiel*, 218; reinstated as editor of the *Moniteur*, 268.

Savary, 40.

Schwarzenberg, Prince, fête of, 46.

Soult, Marshal, his pronounced royalist tendencies, 165 ; says he can rely on the army, 182 ; proclamation of, to the army on Napoleon's landing, 193.

Spanish troops asked for by the Duchess of Angoulême, 227.

Spectator, the story in, told by Louis XVIII., 7.

Staël, Madame de, her impressions on returning to France, 44 *et seq.*; on society after the Restoration, 52 *et seq.*, 61, 64 ; salon of, 66; quoted, 74, 153 ; on the obsequies of Louis XVI., 177 ; thanked by the King for a copy of Necker's defence of Louis XVI., 180; on the landing of Napoleon, 188, 190; pays her respects to the King after Napoleon's landing, 195 ; her comments on the return from Elba, 196.

Talleyrand meets Louis XVIII. at Compiègne, 19; and the Prince of Condé, anecdote of, 145; Fouché meets Louis XVIII. at Saint Denis, 264; appointed Grand Chamberlain, 304.

Talleyrand, Madame, sings hymns to the Bourbons, 29.

Thiers, M., on Louis XVIII.'s appearance, 79; on the Duke of Orleans and the Orleanists, 138.

Trognan, M., quoted, 132, 136.

Tuileries, Louis XVIII. and his court at, 51.

Vaulabelle, M. de, quoted, 117, 138.

Vichy, the Duchess of Angoulême at, 119 *et seq.*

Viel Castel, Baron, on Napoleon's companions-in-arms, 17 ; quoted, 116, 137, 250; on the proscriptions of the Second Restoration, 278; testifies to the ferocity against Marshal Ney, 313.

Villenoisy, Captain de, faithful to the King, 240.

Vitrolles, Baron de, quoted, 18, 20, 23, 27, 35, 39, 43, 58; his account of the petitioners for rank, 69, his *Lettres du Cousin et de la Cousine*, 70; his description of Louis XVIII., 79; sends Louis XVIII. a despatch containing the news of the landing of Napoleon, 189; quoted, 210, 216; sent by the King to Bordeaux, 217, 218; delivers the King's letter to the Duchess of Angoulême, 225; on the proposal as to the Spanish troops, 227 ; on the reception of the King in Paris, 268, 298, 300.

Wellington, the Duke of, at Ghent, 257.

Wilson, Sir Robert, aids Lavalette to escape, 367.

www.ingramcontent.com/pod-product-compliance
Lightning Source LLC
Chambersburg PA
CBHW030214170426
43201CB00006B/80